27

Print and cover design: Nora Pauwels

Cultural Critique

Cultural Critique (ISSN 0882-4371) is published three times a year by Oxford University Press, 2001 Evans Road, Cary, NC 27513, in association with the Society for Cultural Critique, a nonprofit, educational organization, with the support of National University, San Diego and Sacramento.

Manuscript submissions. Contributors should submit three copies of their manuscripts to Donna Przybylowicz, *Cultural Critique*, Department of Social, Cultural and Literary Studies, National University, 9320 Tech Center Drive West, Sacramento, CA 95826-2558. Manuscripts should conform to the recommendations of *The MLA Style Manual;* authors should use parenthetical documentation with a list of works cited. Contact the editorial office at the address above for further instructions on style. Manuscripts will be returned if accompanied by a stamped, self-addressed envelope. Please allow a minimum of four months for editorial consideration.

Subscriptions. Annual subscription rates are $27 for individuals and $50 for institutions. Outside the United States please add $12 for normal delivery and an additional $5 for air-expedited delivery. Subscription requests and checks (payable in U.S. funds) should be sent to Journals Customer Service, Oxford University Press, 2001 Evans Road, Cary, NC 27513.

Back issues. Single copies of back issues are $9.95 for individuals and $20 for institutions. Outside the United States the price is $15.50 for individuals and $25 for institutions. Copies may be obtained from the Journals Fulfillment Department, Oxford University Press, 2001 Evans Road, Cary NC 27513.

Advertising and permissions. Advertising inquiries and requests to reprint material from the journal should be directed to the Journals Department, Oxford University Press, 2001 Evans Road, Cary, NC 27513.

Indexing/abstracting. *Cultural Critique* is indexed/abstracted in *The Left Index, Alternative Press Index, Sociological Abstracts (SA), Social Welfare, Social Planning/Policy and Social Development (SOPODA), International Political Science Abstracts, MLA Directory of Periodicals,* and *MLA International Bibliography.*

Postmaster. Send address changes to Journals Customer Service, Oxford University Press, 2001 Evans Road, Cary, NC 27513. Postage paid at Cary, NC, and additional post offices.

Photocopies. The journal is registered with the Copyright Clearance Center, 21 Congress Street, Salem, MA 01970. Permission to photocopy items for the internal or personal use of specific clients is granted by Oxford University Press provided that the copier pay to the Center the $5.00 per copy fee stated in the code on the first page of each article. Special rates for classroom use are available through the CCC or by contacting the Journals Department, Oxford University Press, 2001 Evans Road, Cary, NC 27513. Requests for permission to photocopy for other purposes, such as for general distribution, resale, advertising, and promotional purposes or for creating new works, should also be directed to Oxford University Press at the same address.

Tiptree and Haraway: The Reinvention of Nature

Judith Genova

> I am not saying: if such-and-such facts of nature were different people would have different concepts (in the sense of a hypothesis). But: if anyone believes that certain concepts are absolutely the correct ones, and that having different ones would mean not realizing something that we realize—then let him imagine certain very general facts of nature to be different from what we are used to, and the formation of concepts different from the usual ones will become intelligible to him.
> —Ludwig Wittgenstein, *Philosophical Investigations*

What, if any, is nature's effect on thought? Indeed, the issue has special urgency for those who seek a nonsexist society: Does the invention of such a society require new facts of nature—a new physiology or mode of reproduction?[1] On the one hand, Wittgenstein will not risk a causal hypothesis about the relation between the two; on the other, he is sure that different facts will mean different concepts. Despite his informed reluctance to theorize about causality,[2] his commitment to a deep connection between the way things are and the concepts of a culture is manifest throughout his work:

© 1994 by *Cultural Critique*. Spring 1994. 0882-4371/94/$5.00.

> What if something *really unheard-of* happened?—If I, say, saw
> houses gradually turning into steam without any obvious
> cause, if the cattle in the fields stood on their heads and
> laughed and spoke comprehensible words; if trees gradually
> changed into men and men into trees. Now, was I right when
> I said before all these things happened "I know that that's a
> house" etc., or simply "that's a house" etc.? (Wittgenstein, *On
> Certainty* 513)

Wittgenstein's point is that in such widely different circumstances,
right and wrong no longer apply. While he does not believe that
thoughts are written on our genes as determinists argue, he cannot
abide the relativist solution that they are written nowhere. Happily, according to my lights, he does not opt for the traditional
synthesis: nature and culture mutually affect each other in dialectical or interactionist fashion. I have always found this tactic either
disappointingly wise or incoherent, a vague gesturing at an all
important, but never elaborated idea, et cetera. For him, new concepts, a systematically different culture, *depend in some sense* on different physical arrangements.

Donna Haraway, a postmodern feminist theoretician, agrees
with him. For her too, nature plays a role that cannot easily be
dismissed: "And yet, to lose authoritative biological accounts of sex
. . . seems to be to lose not just analytic power within a particular
Western tradition, but the body itself as anything but a blank page
for social inscriptions, including those of biological discourse"
("Situated Knowledges" 197). Distancing herself from typical postmodernisms, she refuses to abandon nature to the devices of human imagination: "In its scientific embodiments as well as in other
forms, nature is made, but not entirely by humans; it is a co-construction among humans and non-humans. This is a very different vision from the postmodernist observation that all the world
is denatured and reproduced in images or replicated in copies"
("The Promise of Monsters" 5). Like so many other feminist theoreticians, especially feminist scientists, Haraway cannot accept total
human control. Nature's voice needs to be liberated from the distortions of humanists as well as scientists.

Haraway's reservations are shared and brilliantly dramatized
by a new breed of thinkers, women writers of science fiction.[3] Perhaps the genre, blending as it does the discourse of the real with

that of the imaginary, allows more play across the borders. Whatever the reason, many have begun experimenting with new concepts of nature and culture. In her latest work of xenogenesis, a trilogy beginning with *Dawn*, Octavia Butler argues that the need for hierarchy is the fatal genetic flaw in human beings. To survive, she urges, we must evolve. Ursula K. Le Guin has also speculated in this area. Her novel *The Left Hand of Darkness* considers the different societal practices attendant upon other biologies and forms of sexualities. As Joanne Blum says, "Le Guin's question ... is, What happens to our conception of humanness and of human interaction, when gender is eliminated?" (62). While there are many others I could mention, one in particular, Alice Sheldon, better known as James Tiptree, Jr., is especially preoccupied with this problem. Her visions complement Haraway's theorizing perfectly.

In story after story, Tiptree explores the consequences of believing that biology locks us into certain behaviors and societal practices. While she rejects the biological determinism that her critics attribute to her, she does so not only with style, but without abandoning an independent and critical role for nature. Like Donna Haraway, she does not see nature as culture's silent dummy. Rather, both thinkers see themselves as rescuing nature from the clutches of determinist science. The task, as Haraway, who writes a kind of nonfictional science fiction, sees it, is to reinvent nature. Her latest book, *Simians, Cyborgs and Women: The Reinvention of Nature,* is dedicated to understanding nature's role in our cultural identities: "Above all, it is a book about the invention and reinvention of nature—perhaps the most central arena of hope, oppression, and contestation for inhabitants of the planet earth in our times" (1).[4] In addition to exposing the various sexist and racist constructions of nature by the life sciences, Haraway undertakes the task of imagining a new nature for a new world order. Just as Edward Said demanded that we stop orientalizing, i.e., creating a face for the other and then pretending that the face we created was always already that of the other, Haraway insists that we stop naturalizing, i.e., normalizing the conditions that science constructs. Indeed, her formulation of the problem makes a normative version of the question possible, Ought we to reinvent nature if that is what it takes to change society? Her brave answer, like Tiptree's, is, yes, of course.[5]

Alice Sheldon Is James Tiptree, Jr.

Most critics read Tiptree as a determinist. They claim that her dim view of the mechanics of human sexuality dooms society to sexism. For them, Tiptree offers no escape from a sexist society. Lillian Heldreth, in a much quoted passage, says, "Tiptree seems to see no hope for feminist equality, no release from the bondage of violent sex, and no hope for the human race" (30; also qtd. in Blum 72; Barr 22). In another passage, she says, "She [Tiptree] sees the plight of twentieth century women to be grave and frightening because the facts of human biology preclude real equality, not because women are inferior to men, but because sex is so tightly linked to violence for human males" (26). Despite my disagreement with this reading, I cannot fault it easily. Tiptree exerts herself to mislead her readers. In part, I think she wants to sweeten the victory; only if the case for determinism is made most plausible will its rejection be significant. Basically, however, she loves to tease and tempt her readers. A brief look at two of her most famous stories will show how Tiptree baits the trap.

In stories like "Houston, Houston, Do You Read?" or "The Screwfly Solution", one can easily see the plausibility of Heldreth's reading. In the first story, Tiptree's case against biology and men's physiology, in particular, seems airtight. Men's glands, she argues, make them either adolescent (as his name implies) fuckers (Bud), authoritarian Gods (Dave), or emasculated scholar/scientists (Doc/Lorimer) secretly envying alpha males: "'Gawd . . . ' Bud's hand clasps his drooping penis, jiggles it absently until it stiffens. 'Two million hot little cunts down there, waiting for old Buddy. Gawd. The last man on Earth . . . *You don't count, Doc.* And old Dave, he's full of crap'" (Tiptree, *Houston* 79; emphasis added). Bud, Dave, and Doc—the son, the father, and the holy ghost—are the three faces of the one Godhead. Their monosyllabic presence testifies to their monolithic self-sufficiency. As the story commences, these three strays from the most important male con games of Western culture—sex, religion, and science—have been found wandering in space by an all-female spaceship from Earth's future, the Gloria.

The boys ("men" seems too dignified for these characters), victims of too close an encounter with a sun erection (the big one), while flying a mission from the late twentieth century when Houston was a main space station, have been transported into the future. Their insistent calls to Houston—"Do you read?"—go unanswered until they are heard by the mommies of the future. Thrilled at the prospect of meeting real men (men have become extinct in the future world), the women rescue them. However, their brief stay on board convinces the women that men cannot live without dominating women. Bud tries to rape them all; Dave gives them religion; and Doc lives these assaults vicariously, while all the time denying he is like them. Rather than bring the men home and risk the peace, the women kill them. The moral of the story seems to be that there is no hope for nonviolence and equality with men around: "As I understand it, what you protected people from was largely other males, wasn't it? . . . We can hardly turn you loose on Earth, and we simply have no facilities for people with your emotional problems" (91).

No, Tiptree's title taunts, the men of Houston, the epitome of the male space program, do not and probably cannot read. Reading is a civilized act of animals who can escape the demands of their bodies. Men, unfortunately, and the culture that expresses their desires and needs, cannot overcome their ancient bodily drives. Perhaps her play on reading as an activity of higher evolutionary status and reading as understanding, getting the message, is directed especially at science fiction's typically all male audience. They just don't get it. Like Lorimer in the story, who continually compares women to chicks, ants, gibbons, or space bunnies, even plants, our culture tends to reduce women to lower animals. Women are anything but human for Lorimer and Western culture. Tiptree's revenge is that it is the women who hear them calling, understand them, and read.

In "The Screwfly Solution," her grimmest story, the women of the world are being killed by men in the act of making love. The story is told in a series of letters between a husband, Alan (Adam), and wife, Anne (Eve). This dramatic technique works nicely since their very separation delays the ending, their ending, thus making the telling of the story possible. As the ugly truth begins to dawn, the situation is coolly explained to Alan by the voice of science: "A potential difficulty for our species has always been implicit in the close linkage between the behavioral expression of aggression/predation and sexual reproduction in the male. . . . Males of many species bite, claw, bruise, tread, or otherwise assault receptive females during the act of intercourse; indeed, in some species the male attack is necessary for female ovulation to occur" (69). While the passage warns of the dangers of sex, "The sex was there, but it was driving some engine of death" (68), the assumption is that something has gone wrong with the mechanism switching off the predator response during sex. For the scientist, the problem is caused by a dysfunction; the normal situation has gone rogue. He suspects that a virus of some sort is responsible. Latitudes and longitudes tracking the progression of the phenomena are reported throughout the story to support this interpretation. Indeed, the opening line of the story sets the scene in the humid equatorial regions where presumably humans first appeared: "The young man sitting at 2° N, 75° W sent a casually venomous glance up at the nonfunctional shoofly *ventilador* [sic] and went on reading his letter" (53). The cleverness of the setting is matched only by the suggestion that the shoofly ventilator is dysfunctional which is exactly what is suspected of men's sexual urge. The casual intensity of Alan's anger at the ventilator, however, warns us that Mr. Everyday, someone still presumably untouched by the supposed virus, is already a screwfly needing shooing.[6] And indeed, Tiptree suggests that the situation is a normal, not an extraordinary one, "Whatever, it's our weak link, he thought. Our vulnerability. . . . The dreadful feeling of rightness he [Alan] had experienced when he found himself knife in hand . . ." (70). The normal situation is always already rogue for Tiptree. The violence inherent in male/female relations makes society itself impossible and not just a nonsexist society. The biological premise becomes so real in "Screwfly" that one finds oneself checking the latitude and longitude of one's own abode.

Like a good detective writer, Tiptree relentlessly leads readers to believe that nature is the culprit. And like good detective readers, we should have become suspicious. Other stories, "Love is the Plan, the Plan is Death" or "Out of the Everywhere," widen the scope of her charge against nature. Men's aggressive, competitive, hierarchical nature can do nothing but end their existence as well as women's. The rhythm of life, its random, casual alterations of births and deaths, the self-destructive nature of mother love, the lethal effects of children's curiosity, all lead inevitably to human misery. Her passive observation of Dr. Ain in "The Last Flight of Dr. Ain," who travels round the world disseminating a lethal virus to destroy the human species, is perhaps the strongest statement of her frustration at human folly. The only solution, it would appear, is to go off with the aliens as the women do in another of her stories, "The Women Men Don't See" or take the suicidal solution of Thelma and Louise in the recent movie *Thelma and Louise*.

Tiptree's novels, *Up the Walls of the World* and *Brightness Falls From the Air,* continue to hammer unmistakably at the innate brutality of the human species and its determination to destroy this planet and every other planet with which it comes into contact. Both books are about light, delicate, airy creatures whose contact with muscular, brute earthlings almost destroys them. Sarah Lefanu calls "the potential for cruelty, for inflicting pain . . . Tiptree's central concern" (108). Everything she writes contributes to the interpretation that there is no hope because human physical and behavioral repertoires make any kind of nonviolent-sexed society impossible, and sexism, for Tiptree, is lethal.

Biting hook, line, and sinker, Robert Silverberg, in a famous introduction to a collection of Tiptree stories, gives the ultimate determinist reading by arguing that a woman could not have produced this literature: "It has been suggested that Tiptree is female, a theory that I find absurd, for there is to me something ineluctably masculine about Tiptree's writing. I don't think the novels of Jane Austen could have been written by a man nor the stories of Ernest Hemingway by a woman, and in the same way I believe the author of the James Tiptree stories is male" (xii). (Tiptree guarded her identity closely; no one knew her identity until she was outed late in her career.) Everyone was fooled by her masquerade: "She fooled us good and proper. And we can only thank her for it," says Ursula K. Le Guin ("An Introduction" 182). Indeed, I believe she fooled us even more than Le Guin realizes. Not only is Tiptree no determinist, she isn't even the female that Le Guin confidently takes her to be. However, to see this is to begin to understand her new view of nature.

Alice Sheldon begins her reinvention of nature with herself; she becomes James Tiptree, Jr. As the equation with which I began this section says, Alice is James. Using the strict "is" of identity, I mean to claim that Alice became something new, a hybrid being,

Alice/James. Neither, nor both, male and female, she hoped to dash the categories altogether. Her full name, created by stringing together all her identities, Alice James Raccoona Tiptree Sheldon, Jr., warms the heart of any boundary-crosser: Alice is for woman; James is for man; Raccoona, for animal and Tiptree, for plant; as for Sheldon, it names the structures of culture, while Junior announces that culture is patriarchal. Freed by her exercise in physical change, her "sex change" as she referred to it, her imagination was able to produce something new. Just like the marvelous title to a collection of her stories, *Star Songs of an Old Primate*, she had become an old primate able to sing star songs.

Her metamorphosis was obviously produced by her rich imagination; however, this was possible only because of an equally rich and bountiful nature. Underlying her faith in fiction's worldmaking powers is an unusual and dynamic view of nature. Instead of the narrow and rigid view of nature's possibilities as it is so often portrayed by patriarchal science, Tiptree saw nature as a world of infinite plasticity and endless variation. Nature was not fixed, but more mutable than even culture or society. The best evidence for this claim comes from her most used pseudonym, James Tiptree, Jr. While she minimizes her choice as a matter of mere preference, claiming that the name appealed to her when she saw it on a jar of preserves in the market ("A Woman Writing" 51), the incongruous vision of a tipped tree tips her hand. Gardner Dozois (what's in this name?, I wonder) calls "tiptreeish" an impossible adjective. Trees are stalwart; they grow straight. Like rocks, they are there— the most immovable of living objects. Everyone in Western culture knows that. But, what, the name itself asks, if trees were not so straight, a little warped perhaps? And what if they were not so permanent? The answer should be obvious: trees, plain old regular natural trees, are for the most part more tipped than straight, more ephemeral than solid. How, Tiptree frets, did trees get so fixed, so impoverished in our cultural imaginations? Her work challenges the tendency of both science and art to flatten and reduce nature, making it far more predictable than it really is. The digs at science fiction, which punctuate her stories, suggest that not even the wild stories of science fiction can match nature's dreaming: "'How much of that is for real, Doc?' Bud rubs his curly head. 'They're giving us one of your science fiction stories'" (*Hous-*

ton 37). Nature, she shall insist, cannot be cast as straight woman to an artful and punning culture. As the more famous Alice knew, nature is too funny, too tipped for that.

The Tiptree twist to Silverberg's determinist view that writing is gendered and Le Guin's nongendered view is that her prose was gendered, but not either male, or female. Above all, it was not sexist. The creature she had become, Alice/James, could produce something new. Le Guin's belief that Tiptree's true identity as female proves that there is no such thing as male or female writing is too modern, too humanist for Tiptree's lights. As an experimental psychologist and ardent observer of nature, Tiptree would never underestimate nature's influence. I suspect Tiptree realized that there was such a thing as male or female writing, or that there could be such a thing, and therefore would not object to this idea. She was always saying things like, "Women can be over-obsessed by minutiae, by trivial concerns with no broad implications. This is only natural in a gender evolved to rear children" ("A Woman Writing" 48). Nature exists; that is, non–human-made physical conditions obtain which affect how we think and live. Accordingly, in order to change our thoughts and dreams, we must change the gender/sex roles. The irony for Tiptree is that this is possible. We must allow our imaginations to be as versatile as nature. Nature never said there were only two genders; culture did that. Our fictions must actualize other possibilities, both those that are already there and those that could be there. A second look at the two stories developed earlier shows how her new view of nature spares us determinism while preserving the importance of nature.

In *Houston,* while men are portrayed in the story as violent and responsible for the nuclear destruction of the world, they are curiously not responsible for their sex's demise. Instead, women, as Lorimer accuses, have "poisoned" men (90). Lorimer speaks for the patriarchy in mentioning Eve's biblical crime. Tiptree, however, has another kind of poison in mind: "Women are *natural* poisoners" (3; emphasis added). In the context of the story, she is referring to their genetic make-up. After the nuclear holocaust, a virus attacked the X gene. Since the disease was recessive, women could survive since they have two Xs, but men who have only one X chromosome could not. The additional fact that women carry all the eggs they will ever produce from birth clinched the extermination of the male sex. The women of the future reproduced by cloning the remaining genetic material. Through hormone treatment, they even created some male types to do the heavy work. Nature has its effects and takes its course. Yet, the twists abound.

First, despite all the male violence, it is the women who have unwittingly killed the men. Second, men die because they are part female. This irony is particularly merciless for Lorimer who has spent his whole life denying his femaleness. From the opening of the story and his life, when he mistakenly finds himself in the "girls' can," to his and the story's end in another "girls' can," the spaceship Gloria, he adamantly proclaims his virility. If only he could have gotten the point and realized how vulnerable virility is: "His fly open; his dick in his hand, he can still see the grey zipper edge of his jeans around his pale exposed pecker" (1). Third, at the end of the story, the women knowingly kill the men. Indeed, in the last exchange of the story, they seem as callous as the men when they were in control: Lorimer asks,"'What do you call yourselves? Women's World? Liberation? Amazonia?'" Lady Blue replies, "'Why, we call ourselves human beings. . . . Humanity, mankind.' She shrugs, 'The human race'" (92). Tiptree's point is not that women can be as violent as men, thereby unlinking behavior and physical conditions. All along, she has insisted on nature's strong voice in culture's affairs. Her point is that we are not determined to live under those conditions. We can live in a menless world. The story mocks determinism, not by denying a connection between nature and culture, but by denying that nature cannot be changed.

A different twist occurs in "Screwfly." The screwfly solution refers to the strategy of genetically manipulating a species so as to use the very behavioral repertoires that the species has used for survival to destroy it. For example, Alan is about to tamper genetically with caneflies who have taken to using humans as incubators for their young. His idea is to disrupt the reproductive pattern by having the males mate with sterilized females, thus eliminating "naturally" the population of caneflies. All the genetic engineer need do is adjust ever so slightly a potential in the system as it exists. Alan's experiments with caneflies is a drama within a drama. The larger one concerns human mating patterns which for some reason are leading to the destruction of the species, rather than its continuation. As I suggested earlier, the story makes it seem as if Catharine MacKinnon were right; sex is violence against women pure and simple. But then the Tiptree twist occurs, the *deus ex natura*.

At the end of the story just before Anne, the last woman on earth, commits suicide, we learn that it was aliens all along who were tampering with our sexuality. Anne sees an apparition, an alien "angel," and says with typical, wry Tiptree humor, "*I think I saw a real estate agent*" (75). Aliens were manipulating us just as Alan was manipulating the caneflies. They were colonizing the earth. Thus, power, greed, and the imperialistic motives of another species were responsible for the termination of "man," not the normal violence of men and sex. It is not natural after all, mocks Tiptree, that men should brutalize women and see it as part of the behavioral repertoire of sexual reproduction. They, we, are being manipulated by aliens. The vulnerable link in our behavioral chain is our susceptibility to the idea that we are determined to live in certain ways. Tiptree is never tired of sending this message.

Her complex attitude toward nature is made most directly in this story. Studying the notes of another scientist trying to understand what has happened, Alan reads: "'Man's religion and metaphysics are the voices of his glands. Schonweiser, 1878.'" In response, Alan thinks: "Who the devil Schonweiser was Alan didn't know, but he knew what Barney was conveying. This murderous crackpot religion of McWhosis [referring to Reverend McIllhenny who was circulating women-hating pamphlets] was a symptom, not a cause. Barney believed something was physically affecting the Peedsville men, generating psychosis, and a local religious demagogue had sprung up to 'explain it'" (61). While this simple determinism does not reflect Tiptree's position—here one most remember the end of the story where the territorial desires of another species become responsible for the disease affecting the men, not men's normal sex behavior—she has more sympathy for this position than believing it a matter of hatred, or misogyny. For Tiptree, it is as if hatred were too personal, too psychological a concept to account for men's sexist treatment of women. Nor does it explain the fact that young boys are also slaughtered by the ravenous men. Rather, either territorial expansion, from the point of view of the end of the story, or natural force, from the point of view of the middle of the story, is to blame; that is, forces larger than individual intention or will predominate.

Like Wittgenstein, Tiptree is saying that new ways of thinking require new bodies, but not in a causal or strictly necessary sense. In fact, Tiptree's new view of nature includes a different view of space and time. Nature cannot produce the other since there is no time lag, no gap, for causality to fill. Causality is a relation that connects things externally; nature and culture are related, on the other hand, internally. A few comments on her style will help make this point.

According to Robert Silverberg, one of the most prominent features of her writing is "his ability to create a sense of sustained and prolonged movement . . . a sense of *extended process,* that makes the scene literally unforgettable" (xvii). Silverberg is right; the attenuation of the scene for what seems like an eternity is palpable. The descriptions of the slow, ponderous progress of the huge being wandering space in *Up the Walls of the World* is a perfect example. The creature is vast but moves at a snail's pace; its voyage seems endless. Its voice is recorded only in capital letters, and its story is told piecemeal fashion, interspersed between the other narratives. The capitals not only distinguish the creature's voice and story from the others going on simultaneously, but slow one down as well. Sentences with all capitals are harder to comprehend, and the interweaving of the voice with others also prolongs the story's movement. One must stop to get one's bearings. The creature is not in space; we feel we are suspended in space itself, endless space.

Her other stylistic trait, also recognized by Silverberg, of jagged, staccato phrasing, "dialogue broken by bursts of stripped-down exposition" (xv), which one would think the opposite of the "slow music" of the sustained process, creates the same sense of an endless present.[7] Both styles, along with her penchant to tell stories backwards, or shuffle the time-frame, interrupt our passion for cause/effect narrative. Time/space cannot be easily divided into a past, present, future, a here, there, or up/down. Causality that depends on the separability of two distinct moments and spaces is frustrated in such a universe. Only duration seems to exist; the endless present in which things affect each other by becoming expressions of each other. While Tiptree has no new name for the interaction she sees between nature/culture, she seems to have a sense that causality is an insufficient relation.

Is it nature? Is it culture? For Tiptree, these questions are misconceived. To dramatize her position, she stacks all the cards toward making us believe that there is no hope but that we will be victims of our own biology. And then just as one accepts this message, she exonerates nature and blames such willful displays of culture as greed, avarice, ignorance. Has nature failed the human species for Tiptree or culture? The answer is neither. Her final irony is that only humans fail themselves by thinking cheap and small about both nature and culture. Just as Sheldon gave birth to herself, she ended her life, killing first her ailing husband and then herself. So much for nature's natural course.

Donna Haraway Is a Cyborg

"A Cyborg Manifesto," probably the most fictional piece of nonfiction in the feminist canon next to Hélène Cixous's "The Laugh of the Medusa," presents a nonfictional kind of science fiction. For Haraway, the category of science fiction challenges any easy distinction between fiction and nonfiction. For her both facts and fictions are made by human action. Why, then, can she not interweave both forms of discourse in her own metacritiques of science? In flaunting the normal truth-telling/seeking, measured style of the documentary essay, Haraway exemplifies her avowed goals of breaching boundaries, collapsing dualisms, inventing new categories of classification. With the joy of a whale at play, she breaks the still waters of philosophical and biological writing, displacing the normal and natural forever. Who, perhaps one should ask, what, is this fearless creature who would advance humanity to a new evolutionary level?

As she tells us in her avowedly personal tone, she is a cyborg, or rather aspires to be one: "I would rather be a cyborg than a goddess" ("Manifesto" 181). Appropriately, she prefers to think of her action as one of regeneration, rather than rebirth. The identity she invents for herself crosses the boundaries between machine, non-human organism, and human: "A cyborg exists when two kinds of boundaries are simultaneously problematic: 1) that be-

tween animals (or other organisms) and humans, and 2) that between self-controlled, self-governing machines (automatons) and
organisms, especially humans (models of autonomy). The cyborg
is the figure born of the interface of automaton and autonomy"
(*Primate Visions* 139). It is also a hybrid of fiction and reality, a new
being that is more and more becoming a social reality: "The cyborg
is a matter of fiction and lived experience that changes what counts
as women's experience in the late twentieth century" ("Manifesto"
149). To embrace a cyborg future is to relinquish the need for purity, origins, a self/other dualistic consciousness, and the fear of
our evolutionary other. The future for Haraway, like technology,
need not automatically be dreaded. Becoming a cyborg may not
be the great loss it seems to others. In fact, it is to be preferred if
it enables a better society.

As with Tiptree, Haraway begins by a reimagination of herself. She introjects the other and becomes other than herself. Haraway has become another kind of being; her classification is cyborg,
not human. Using the "is" of class inclusion this time, instead of
identity, she counts as a cyborg. Her imagination of a new identity
makes new narrative strategies possible for her and perhaps new
social relations, new politics, possible for all of us; that is, it transforms how we live and thus ultimately moves from the realm of
imagination to the realm of the real. Only split, non-whole selves
can do this: "The split and contradictory self is the one who can
interrogate positionings and be accountable, the one who can construct and join rational conversations and fantastic imaginings that
change history" ("Situated Knowledges" 193). Science fiction, I believe, is born from split and contradictory selves. The "natural-
technical object" has a different view of the world. As with all postmodern theories, Haraway's being and writing disrupt what we
take to be the normal: "This identity [U.S. women of color] marks
out a self-consciously constructed space that cannot affirm the capacity to act on the basis of natural identification, but only on the
basis of conscious coalition, of affinity, of political kinship" ("Manifesto" 156). The normal, the natural, deserve to be banished from
our conception of nature. Just as a state of affairs is not in itself
good or bad, no state is in itself natural. Alternatively, one might
put the point this way: since every state is potentially a natural one,
no state can be considered natural. The natural has been essen-

tially a term of appropriation, not description; it has normative, not descriptive force.

The importance of autobiography, of inventing oneself and locating subjects in their context, cannot be overestimated in Haraway's work. The self-referential gesture functions to situate knowledge and remind one of its embodiment. More importantly, one's thinking and being are so integrally related that adjustments in one affects states of the other. Once again boundaries are being transgressed, those between the I and the We, the informal and formal, the personal and the political, the real and the fictional. Ironically, Haraway's commitment to identity politics makes her an unwilling standpoint theorist. Yet, I doubt she would mind as long as one were allowed to multiply standpoints indefinitely and according to a very inventive and prudential scheme. What matters for her is not who you are, but what you might become.

The newness of Haraway's message is that perhaps the only way or maybe the most effective way of avoiding the dualisms of Western culture is literally to go beyond them by becoming something that simply eludes the categories the dualism describes—to go where no "man" has gone before. One does not breach the boundaries only in thought, but in reality. One uses one's mind to transform what one is. This is impossible to imagine only if one lives in the exclusion of nature/culture; then the comment that one can't change what one is by thinking about it finds a place. Then, lectures on Darwinian inheritance apply. However, once beyond the dualism, once the two domains are not exclusive and are not described in exclusive fashion, the effects of minds on bodies makes perfect sense. Haraway's view of meaning makes this point nicely: "Meanings are applications; how meanings are constituted is the essence of politics. No one can constitute meanings by wishing them into existence; discourse is a material practice" (*Primate Visions* 111). Echoing Wittgenstein's point that meaning is use, Haraway is suggesting that meanings and discourse are as material, as nonfictional as rocks. The meaning of "nature," for example, is a concrete practice, not an abstract exercise. Words are deeds. In this view, metaphysics and science are always already political acts, but just for that reason, not necessarily ideological ones.

In Haraway's hands postmodernism becomes something new.

It rejects dualisms, boundaries, etc., not by ignoring them, or pronouncing them bad and dead, but by literally inventing something that cannot be grasped with the old dualisms. Philosophy, the discourse invented by Plato, and the nonfictional forms of explanation derived from it and continued ad nauseam can wither away since we have evolved into beings for whom those discursive practices no longer make sense. Even her prose resists categorization, rather especially her prose. Since her prose is the act by which she regenerates herself, it becomes the womb of her new being and therefore the very life-line to the future.

Like science fiction, Haraway's prose creates an elsewhere from which to view our current situation: "I want readers to find an 'elsewhere' from which to envision a different and less hostile order of relationships among people, animals, technologies, and land" (*Primate Visions* 15).[8] Another passage from this same text provides a revealing gloss on her concept of "elsewhere": "Space and the tropics are both utopian topical figures in western imaginations, and their opposed properties dialectically signify origins and ends for the creature whose mundane life is outside both: civilized man. Space and the tropics are 'allotopic'; i.e., they are 'elsewhere,' the place to which the traveler goes to find something dangerous and sacred" (137). Accordingly, if her story is to provide an "elsewhere" for those of western imagination, it should capture this danger, trade in taboos, and wallow in estrangement. And it does. Jargons from widely different disciplines bang against each other, tucking layers of information in serpentine clauses (closets) that give an unending feel to many of her sentences. Moments like these are ponderous and daunting. Yet, they have their own logic. The density fits the thoughts being expressed. A clear, concise syllogism would be all wrong. Those who ask for clarity are clearly missing the point. The picture she paints is blurred all the way down; it cannot be brought into better focus by better writing.

Other aspects of her style are equally telling. Consider her description of Frederick Wiseman's documentary *Primate:*

> Leaving the portrait gallery, the camera takes the viewer up the drive into a complex of scientific buildings, to a hall of cages, where filmmakers (bearded) and scientists (bearded) discuss gorilla sex in front of a male-female pair of that ape

species. The sound track gives us a fragment of a discussion on data collection in ape sex research. The scientist explains the observation and caging system: 'We don't want them doing things when we can't see it.' In the scientist's office we see photographs of copulating gorillas and get a discussion of sexual behavior observed in the field by George Schaller. (*Primate Visions* 117)

This passage is typical of her travelogue or art history lecture style in *Primate Visions*. Perversely, she focuses on details usually missed by the scientists. She is expert at listening or looking in at the crucial moment when the scientists expose themselves. The scene of instruction, of knowledge production, for example, loses its credibility when reframed with her skeptical, ironic voice. For example, the juxtaposition of "complex of scientific buildings" with "hall of cages" humorously blurs the two. The beards breach the line between the hairy scientist, filmmaker, and gorilla. The movie, the photographs of copulating gorillas, the admission of voyeurism, the strange obsession with primate sex make those involved look foolish. What is this, Haraway asks, but bestial pornography under long, dry titles? Deftly, she deconstructs the scientists' accounts of their practice. Her goal is to recapture science, to make it new for a new being: "Feminists reappropriate science in order to discover and to define what is 'natural' for ourselves" ("The Past" 23).

High on her list of biology's sacred cows is the belief that species endlessly reproduce themselves. For Haraway this is wrong even from an evolutionary point of view. Elephants come from something which is not elephant—not nothing, nor some other, more fundamental or simple stuff, just some other complex stuff. The mechanism for the metamorphoses may be mutation; but since the causes of mutation are not clear, mutation may be a mixed bag of things. Cyborgs are not the product of classical mutation; yet, humans have already begun to look, feel, and think like them. Classical taxonomy imposed an order on nature that never really existed. It was a simplification, a reduction for the sake of theory and order. Plurality and alterity have always been the hated other of the one, the same, the only. Reappropriating science means letting the chaos of nature back in and refusing to tame it with the stultifying straight lines of abstraction.

Science has always constructed nature. As computers are making clear, reproduction involves production: to re-produce something, e.g., weather patterns, requires the creation of a coded process that produces those patterns in what might be an entirely different way from their original production. Indeed, the terms "simulation" and "original" are losing their distinctness. Haraway makes science's world-making capacities clearer than any other feminist critic today: "The form in science is that artefactual-social rhetoric of crafting the world into effective objects. This is a practice of world-changing persuasions that take the shape of amazing new objects—like microbes, quarks, and genes" ("Situated Knowledges" 185). Scientists are world-makers just like novelists. Creating a kind of nonfictional science fiction of her own, Haraway shows the world-making potential of criticism and commentary as well.

Despite the fact that women have suffered more than men from the political uses of "natural," they resist the call to become cyborgs. Most are put off by the thought of evolving into a monster, half machine/half human. After centuries of conditioning, humans hanker for the natural, the organic, the myth of oneness and wholeness, and fear the artificial, the concocted. While psychologically understandable, the reluctance is politically dangerous. We must move on, especially since whether we like it or not nature/culture is already in motion producing the future.

Science Is Fiction

Both Tiptree and Haraway owe much to the discourse and ethos of science fiction. In critical ways, it enabled their self-regenerations and their visions of a different relationship between nature and culture. As I have suggested at different points in this essay, the genre builds the problem of nature/culture or the relation between fact and fiction into its very definition. Perhaps it is fitting to conclude with some comments on the genre.

Both the concept and practice of science fiction have been changing even as debate rages about what constitutes a work in science fiction. While everyone has their own definition, some seem more fruitful than others. A recent definition from feminist writers focuses on dealing with the other: "There was a time when a sound definition of the term was 'stories in which some scientific idea was extrapolated, and was integral to the action and plot'. This has not been the case for a long time. It would seem that anything with a streak of 'otherliness' fits the bill, alongside the usual hard core of spaceships and robots" (Saxton 205). Sarah Lefanu echoes this idea: "And they [horror and ghost stories] share with science fiction that sense of 'otherness': a concern with the effects of the strange, or the alien, or the unconscious, on the familiar and the commonplace, and an abiding interest in how the strange and the familiar can inhabit the same terrain" (184). The other may be cast in terms of other beings, or it can also be other times and spaces. Robert Scholes' notion that other times or places are as critical to science fiction as other persons can be incorporated under this idea of otherliness.

In some works by women, the problem is dealing with the self as other. Octavia Butler problematizes this idea in *Dawn*. Speaking of the Oankali, the people of the novel, Haraway says: "Their nature is always to be midwife to themselves as other. Their bodies themselves are genetic technologies, driven to exchange, replication, dangerous intimacy across the boundaries of self and other, and the power of images. Not unlike us" (*Primate Visions* 379). For Haraway, the Oankali are us, only we refuse to admit it. Humans too transform themselves and depend on such transformations for their survival. Yet, there is so much resistance to change. Butler's novel examines human resistance to change, to the strange, to the future.

The work of Tiptree and Haraway also makes extensive use of the self as other. Each has to operate on themselves first to make possible a different vision for nature. However, the primary thing that got otherized in their work is science itself. Seeing the discourse of science as fictional is critical to both their projects. For me, this is the enabling insight of science fiction as a fictional praxis: science is fiction.

The "is" in this sentence, "Science is fiction," introduces the last major use of "is," namely, the "is" of predication. Unlike the "is" of identity or the "is" of class inclusion, the "is" of predication attributes predicates to subjects, e.g., "Alice/James and Donna/Cyborg are happy." So my claim, science is fiction, says that science works by constructing stories about nature; it is a fictional discourse. However, this is not to say that it is counterfactual, or contrary to truth. Once again, as Haraway argues, fictions are not the antithesis of facts. Using the license granted to them by the label, "fiction" writers of science fiction have always known science's power to construct the real. More than any other group of writers of either fiction or nonfiction, they have noticed and furthered science's constructions of nature. While the genre's constructions are fictional in that they go beyond the known, they connect to the facts of science and reveal a commonality between them.

Perhaps myth is a concept that best captures science fiction's blending of fact and fiction. Rather than being fantastical, or individual, science fiction's constructions often aim at mythological status. Many commentators on science fiction have noticed its connection to myth. Wendy O'Flaherty, for example, says: "Science fiction provides a body of literature in which great mythological classics take refuge in a demythologized age. It is one of the few places in which we continue to create superheroes, the last survivals in a kitsch mythology of atheism" (31). She also notices the social thrust of the genre, the way in which it develops secular ritual communities, e.g., Trekkies. I feel the pull of these communities every time I buy a text; for some strange reason, since I usually avoid used books, I find myself wanting only used science fiction texts. I get a perverse pleasure reading about the new through the old. Joanna Russ's minimalist and materialist definition of myth as "material which has passed through other hands, that is not raw-brand-new," (10) is obviously far more accurate than one would initially think. The used books emphasize not only a community of readers but a community of ideas that transcend the individual. Michel Butor goes so far as to see science fiction as a collective myth: "The SF narratives derive their power from a great collective dream we are having, but for the moment are incapable of giving it unified form. It is a mythology in tatters, impotent, unable to orient our action in any precise way" (164). While I disagree that the stories are impotent, I find his attempt to see science fiction in some unexplained but Jungian way as a function of a collective or social conscious, rather than an individual one, aiming in the right direction. Science fiction has been able to have its unsettling, political edge precisely because of its social, mythological dimension.

Science fiction finally allows women to go where most men have not gone before. The imagination of other peoples, other places, or times brings perspective. We can see changes needed either in the way the world is or the way we think about the world. The critical point that I have argued in this paper is that the two are related: Changes in how we think and act require changes in what we are and vice versa. New thoughts may not require new ontologies, but the latter certainly facilitate the former.

Notes

Thanks to Julia Epstein, Elaine Hansen, Sandra Harding, and Ann Matter for their comments on an earlier version of this essay.

1. While most feminists today would dismiss this supposition outright, there is good reason to consider the possibility that new cultures require new facts. Certainly, the claim is more plausible if one believes that all societies known to recorded history have been sexist. Michelle Zimbalist Rosaldo is among those who argue this position. Since it is not my purpose to debate that issue, let it suffice to say that I am not denying the incredible number of different cultures and societies that a set of physical conditions can tolerate. I am only making a minimal claim: altered biological conditions is one way—one interesting and if not sure, at least likely way—to transform women's place and status.

2. Even if one could prove the necessity of certain facts, one could never show their sufficiency since it is always possible to imagine a totally different physical world in conjunction with our same concepts. Accordingly, to the extent that causality depends on sufficiency, it cannot describe the relations between nature and thought, or more broadly, culture.

3. Ursula K. Le Guin's fame in popular culture is only the tip of the iceberg. For the past 20 years, women have been turning to science fiction in record numbers. The open possibilities of the genre, no doubt, attracted attention. To mention only a few more names: Joanna Russ, Vonda McIntyre, Pamela Sargent, Suzy Charnas, Marge Piercy, and Suzette Elgin.

4. Shulamith Firestone was among the first feminist critics to argue that we must evolve into a new species in order to fully overcome sexism. Her position, however, is very different from Haraway's in that, for Firestone, we are trapped by our biology. For Haraway, our imaginations of our bodies imprison us, not the facts of biology.

5. The correspondence between Haraway's feminist theory and the themes of women's science fiction is no accident. Haraway is an avid reader of these authors and acknowledges their influence on her work. Her enthusiasm for science fiction has been contagious; I caught the passion from her.

6. Adam Frisch gives a spectacular analysis of another series of Tiptree sentences from "The Women Men Don't See": "We emerged dry-mouthed into a vast windy salmon sunrise. A diamond chip of sun breaks out of the sea and promptly submerges in cloud" (56–57). He sees this in terms of an internal polarization of

imagery: opposites are contrasted whenever possible, e.g., emerging/submerging, vague boundaries/detailed ones.

7. "Slow Music" is the title of one of her stories.

8. Haraway's view from elsewhere contrasts nicely with the standard philosophical view that Thomas Nagel has dubbed "the view from nowhere." Elsewhere, unlike nowhere, is embodied even if by other, alien bodies.

Works Cited

Barr, Marleen S. *Alien to Femininity: Speculative Fiction and Feminist Theory.* New York: Greenwood, 1987.

Blum, Joanne. *Transcending Gender: The Male/Female Double in Women's Fiction.* Ann Arbor: UMI Research P, 1988.

Butler, Octavia. *Dawn: Xenogenesis.* New York: Warner, 1987.

Butor, Michel. "Science Fiction: The Crisis of Its Growth." *SF: The Other Side of Realism: Essays on Modern Fantasy and Science Fiction.* Ed. Thomas Clareson. Bowling Green: Bowling Green U Popular P, 1971. 157–66.

Cixous, Hélène. "The Laugh of the Medusa." *Signs Reader: Women, Gender, and Scholarship.* Ed. Elizabeth Abel and Emily K. Abel. Chicago: U of Chicago P, 1983. 279–97.

Dozois, Gardner. *The Fiction of James Tiptree, Jr.* New York: Algol, 1977.

Firestone, Shulamith. *The Dialectic of Sex: The Case for Feminist Revolution.* New York: Morrow, 1970.

Frisch, Adam. "Toward New Sexual Identities: James Tiptree, Jr." *The Feminine Eye: Science Fiction and the Women Who Write It.* Ed. Tom Staicar. New York: Frederick Ungar, 1982. 48–59.

Haraway, Donna. "Manifesto for Cyborgs." *Simians, Cyborgs, and Women: The Reinvention of Nature.* New York: Routledge, 1991. 149–83.

———. "The Past Is the Contested Zone: Human Nature and Theories of Production and Reproduction in Primate Behaviour Studies." *Simians, Cyborgs, and Women.* New York: Routledge, 1991. 21–42.

———. *Primate Visions: Gender, Race, and Nature in the World of Modern Science.* New York: Routledge, 1989.

———. "The Promise of Monsters: A Regenerative Politics for Inappropriate/d Others." Unpublished essay, 1990.

———. "Situated Knowledges: The Science Question in Feminism as a Site of Discourse on the Privilege of Partial Perspective." *Simians, Cyborgs, and Women.* New York: Routledge, 1991. 183–201.

Heldreth, Lillian. "Love is the Plan, the Plan is Death: The Feminism and Fatalism of James Tiptree, Jr." *Extrapolation* 3 (1982): 22–30.

Lefanu, Sarah. *Feminism and Science Fiction.* Bloomington: Indiana UP, 1989.

Le Guin, Ursula K. "An Introduction to *Star Songs of an Old Primate.*" *The Language of the Night: Essays on Fantasy and Science Fiction.* Ed. Susan Wood. New York: Putnam, 1979. 179–84.

———. *The Left Hand of Darkness.* New York: Ace, 1969.

MacKinnon, Catharine A. *Feminism Unmodified: Discourses on Life and Law.* Cambridge: Harvard UP, 1987.

Nagel, Thomas. *The View From Nowhere.* New York: Oxford UP, 1986.

O'Flaherty, Wendy Doniger. "The Survival of Myth in Science Fiction," *Mindscapes: The Geographies of Imagined Worlds*. Ed. George E. Slusser and Eric S. Rabkin. Carbondale: Southern Illinois UP, 1989. 21–35.

Rosaldo, Michelle Zimbalist, and Louise Lamphere, eds. *Women, Culture and Society*. Stanford: Stanford UP, 1974.

Russ, Joanna. "What Can A Heroine Do? or Why Women Can't Write." *Images of Women in Fiction: Feminist Perspectives*. Comp. Susan Koppelman Cornillon. Bowling Green: Bowling Green U Popular P, 1972. 3–19.

Said, Edward W. *Orientalism*. New York: Vintage Books, 1979.

Saxton, Josephine. "Goodbye to all that. . . ." *Where No Man Has Gone Before: Women and Science Fiction*. Ed. Lucie Armitt. New York: Routledge, 1991. 205–18.

Scholes, Robert E. *Structural Fabulation: An Essay on Fiction of the Future*. Notre Dame: U of Notre Dame P, 1975.

Silverberg, Robert. Introduction. *Warm Worlds and Otherwise*. By James Tiptree, Jr. New York: Ballantine, 1975. i–xxv.

Tiptree, James, Jr. *Brightness Falls From the Air*. New York: Tom Doherty, 1985.

———. *Houston, Houston, Do You Read?* New York: Tom Doherty, 1989.

———. "The Last Flight of Dr. Ain." *Warm Worlds and Otherwise*. New York: Ballantine, 1975. 61–69.

———. "Love is the Plan, the Plan is Death." *Warm Worlds and Otherwise*. New York: Ballantine, 1975. 173–94.

———. "Out of the Everywhere." *Out of the Everywhere and Other Extraordinary Visions*. New York: Ballantine, 1981. 174–214.

———. "The Screwfly Solution." *Out of the Everywhere and Other Extraordinary Visions*. New York: Ballantine, 1981. 53–76.

———. "Slow Music." *Out of the Everywhere and Other Extraordinary Visions*. New York: Ballantine, 1981. 116–65.

———. *Star Songs of an Old Primate*. New York: Ballantine, 1978.

———. *Up the Walls of the World*. New York: Berkeley, 1978.

———. "A Woman Writing Science Fiction and Fantasy." *Women of Vision*. Ed. Denise DuPont. New York: St. Martin's, 1988. 43–59.

———. "The Women Men Don't See." *Warm Worlds and Otherwise*. New York: Ballantine, 1975. 131–65.

Wittgenstein, Ludwig. *On Certainty*. 1961. Ed. G. E. M. Anscombe and G. H. von Wright. Trans. Denis Paul and G. E. M. Anscombe. New York: Harper, 1969.

———. *Philosophical Investigations*. 1953. Ed. G. E. M. Anscombe, R. Rhees, and G. H. von Wright. Trans. G. E. M. Anscombe. New York: MacMillan, 1953.

Double Exposure, Double Erasure: On the Frontline with Anita Hill

L. A. Grindstaff

The television debut of *Clarence Thomas and Anita Hill: Public Hearings, Private Pain* marked the one-year anniversary of the Thomas/Hill hearings. The one-hour PBS documentary was produced for *Frontline* by Ofra Bikel, who confides in the first minutes of the program, "[T]he fact that the man and woman testifying were black seemed not to matter. This was beyond race—or so I thought. That was before I spoke with African-Americans I knew." A white woman, Bikel reportedly spent nine months interviewing dozens of black men and women "to comprehend the painful impact of the hearings" on members of the black community (S. King 4) and to prove to the wider American public that for these people the big issue at stake in the Thomas/Hill affair was race, not sex.

In an interview with the *Los Angeles TV Times,* Bikel says she set out to make a documentary on the battle of the sexes angle of the controversy, but scrapped her plans 10 days into production after talking with a middle-aged black woman who informed her that race mattered very much indeed. "By chance," Bikel interviewed more African-Americans and was "stunned" to learn they

© 1994 by *Cultural Critique*. Spring 1994. 0882-4371/94/$5.00.

felt the same way; "everything they said was a surprise to me," she confessed (S. King 4). *Public Hearings, Private Pain* thus turns on the discovery that the Thomas/Hill hearings were "about race" after all and explores the source of strong black support for the appointment of Thomas to the Supreme Court despite his conservative politics and lackluster career, and despite allegations of sexual misconduct leveled by law professor Hill.

Bikel's surprising discovery notwithstanding, the documentary does not so much provide new information or expose hidden insights as to image the discourses already in circulation in the black and mainstream presses at the time of the hearings. In particular, it gives voice to many African-Americans who saw Hill's behavior as treasonous for compromising the upward mobility of a fellow black, folks who were not necessarily "for" Thomas but who were disturbed by Hill's apparent willingness to break ranks and air "dirty linen" under a fascinated prime-time gaze. As Paula Giddings explains to Bikel, the issue in the black community was not whether Hill lied or not, but whether she should have come forward: "should she have challenged a black man who was on his way to the Supreme Court and made it an issue about male-female relationships, about sexual harassment, which is often not seen as a very important issue compared to the ascendancy of a black man to the Supreme Court?" Most African-Americans interviewed thought not. On the other hand, white people in general and white feminist women in particular who spoke about sexual harassment in the media generally failed to discuss race at all. *Public Hearings, Private Pain* thus offers a response to that silence.

The documentary opens with a "false start," a series of clips from Thomas's and Hill's testimony juxtaposed in a kind of shot/ reverse shot structure overlaid with dramatic music, and intermingled with brief excerpts from the "ordinary people" interviewed. A disembodied male voice-over introduces the video as "the untold story of what this event meant to millions of Americans." The false start concludes with a split-image freeze frame, Thomas one side, Hill on the other. We then get a long slow zoom-in on the Capitol Building followed by the start of the documentary proper with more shots of Thomas versus Hill. Not an unusual opening sequence, in fact not dissimilar to the beginning of the Drew Associates' *Crisis Behind a Presidential Commitment,* a documentary film aired on ABC dramatizing the showdown between President John Kennedy and Alabama Governor George Wallace over the entry of two black students to an all-white university in 1963. In each text, the initial juxtaposition of protagonist and antagonist already tells a tale of racialized political conflict. Unlike *Crisis,* however, in which the competing images signify two powerful men each with strong political backing, the "balanced" opposition of Thomas and Hill with the Capitol Building as neutral backdrop falsely equalizes the political terrain and masks *his* exclusive and gendered connection to white state power. The first minute of *Public Hearings, Private Pain* thus functions as synecdoche both for the video in its entirety and for media representations of the hearings more generally, in that it frames the controversy as an individual clash of wills between two equally credible people and therefore "disappears" Thomas's power and privilege over Hill.[1]

The rest of *Public Hearings, Private Pain* is divided, as the title implies, into two parts. The first documents both the nomination process and the ambivalence many African-Americans felt in response, as well as Thomas's quasi-mythical journey from Pin Point poverty to Supreme Court hopeful (a rags-to-riches story somehow more "real" to people than his conservative political record). The second part addresses Hill's allegations of sexual harassment. Ironically, Hill's appearance seemed to solidify rather than fracture black support for the Supreme Court nominee, for although she was characterized as a heroine by a few young women interviewed, the majority of the respondents felt her testimony had unduly victimized Thomas and irreparably damaged the black community. The documentary ends with a parallel set of images: shots of women applauding Hill on college campuses and at political rallies followed by Thomas's inauguration to the U.S. Supreme Court. Like the opening, this closure turns on the narrative juxtaposition of inequivalences: Hill gives a law school commencement speech, while Thomas takes a seat for life on the highest court in the land.

Clarence Thomas Goes to Washington

Public Hearings, Private Pain illustrates very well some of the complex racial dynamics at work in the Thomas hearings, highlighting the current tension between political representation *by* blacks and political representation *for* blacks—the difference, as Ronald Walters explains it, between merely having black skin and being "politically black" by working to end the racial oppression of African-Americans as a class, as a collective, and as a colonized people (217). Since he repeatedly attacked the entire civil rights agenda, denounced welfare and other liberal reforms, and even criticized the 1954 Supreme Court decision *Brown vs. Board of Education,* Thomas is not "politically black" in the view of many black scholars and activists.[2] Even newspaper reporters covering the nomination noted that the fact Thomas was black and staunchly supported by the likes of segregationists Strom Thurmond, Jesse Helms, and David Duke, who was President Bush's "big racial joke" (Morse; see also Mandel). Ultimately, it was for these reasons that, after much conflicted deliberation, the NAACP finally opposed Thomas's nomination. So did the Congressional Black Caucus Foundation (CBCF), whose leaders warned African-Americans against romanticizing Thomas's black skin and Horatio Alger past, concluding "Clarence Thomas is not our champion. He is the President's gesture" (CBCF 235). Yet as Robert Chrisman observes, a substantial proportion of African-Americans partially concur with the conservative critique of liberal social reforms, and believe a fresh approach to black empowerment may succeed where several generations of liberalism have failed (xxviii). According to some, Thomas may not be the best qualified candidate ever chosen, but he is also not the worst, and having him on the high Court is better than having no black representation at all; others supported Thomas while at the same time expressing hope that he would soften his conservative views once tenured.[3]

The tension between a politics of identity and a politics of position—what Cornel West calls "racial reasoning" versus "moral reasoning"—is one that members of the Bush administration knew how to manipulate with consummate skill, and it is a tension Bikel takes pains to highlight. A series of shots details the press conference where Thurgood Marshall announces his resignation from the Court. A reporter asks Marshall whether the President has any obligation to name a minority justice in his place, and Marshall replies, "[T]here's no difference between a white snake and a black snake, they'll both bite." At a second press conference, Bush announces the nomination of Thomas, anticipating reporters' questions by adding, "[T]he fact that he is black, and a minority, has nothing to with this in the sense that he is the best qualified at this time. . . ." Bikel herself states in voice-over, "[T]he nominee was known to be against government help, against affirmative action, and against welfare—but he was black. The President said Thomas's race didn't matter. He must have known it would matter to them." She then cuts to a medium close-up of Ella MacDonald, a woman who runs a foster-care agency in Harlem.

> *MacDonald:* Let me tell you what a tall black kid said about Thomas' appointment. He said, "mommy, mommy, he appointed a black man; mommy, mommy he appointed a black man." And when I repeat that I can almost regenerate the kind of emotion that came through this 5'10" 145-lb. sneaker-wearing black kid who belonged to me, and he said "mommy, mommy," and he was so excited. . . .

Bikel makes it clear Thomas's race was the most significant factor underwriting his support. She also suggests that the Democrats on the committee were unwilling to challenge Thomas on his professional qualifications and past record because they didn't know how to oppose a black man without appearing racist. Thomas's close personal friend, Lester Johnson, admits as much to Bikel, saying Thomas knew he was getting "an easy ride because he was black."

The "Democrat dilemma" was confounded by class distinctions as well. In his testimony before the judiciary committee, replayed in the documentary, Thomas makes much of his hard-scrabble climb out of rural poverty in Pin Point, Georgia, where he grew up under the watchful eye of his maternal grandfather, Meyers Anderson. Thomas tells of his grandparents, who "lived their lives in an era of blatant segregation and overt discrimination," and whose "sense of fairness was molded in the crucible of unfairness." Nevertheless, he says, "I've always carried in my heart, the world, the life, the people, and values of my youth." It is a compelling narrative of naked bootstrap individualism that captured the hearts and minds of millions of Americans watching. Yet Bikel manages to undermine the story by intercutting shots of Thomas at the hearings with those of his grandfather's closest friend, Sam Williams, who, in an interview with Bikel, offers an alternative, less sentimental, version of Thomas's relationship to his grandfather and to Pin Point poverty.

> *Thomas:* I watched, as my grandfather [clears throat, long pause] was called boy [clears throat]. I watched as my grandmother suffered the indignity of being denied the use of a bathroom. But through it all, they remained fair, decent, good people.
> *Bikel* (offscreen): Thomas cried when he talked about his grandfather.
> *S. Williams:* Yes, I know he did. But uh, I really didn't buy that.
> *Bikel:* You didn't?
> *S. Williams:* No, I didn't. Because his grandfather was disappointed. . . . I don't know whether he changed or not, but uh, the only thing did he have was a black skin. Clarence. Everything else was white as a sheet [laughs].

The view of Thomas as a self-interested careerist who abandoned his own people for political gain is not the only reading of the text, however. Immediately after Sam Williams speaks, Bikel offers another perspective on Thomas which suggests that his black skin and Pin Point past did more than cover a white interior: they made him a more complex person than his detractors were willing to acknowledge. Referring to his childhood poverty, Valerie Williams, a New York stock broker, says Thomas "suffered a lot" because he not only came from the wrong side of the tracks ("all black people in terms of white Americans come from the wrong side of the tracks"), he came from the wrong side of the *black* tracks. According to Valerie Williams, "[P]eople don't understand the anger that entails. When you're at the tail end of the tail end— there's a different kind of resonance there." Likewise, media consultant Emily Tines speculates that early experiences helped shape both Thomas's political views and his feelings toward African-

Americans. Because of the painful racial teasing Thomas endured as a child, Tines wonders whether he has "an internal tug of war going on about how he feels about us, his own people." She concludes, "Clarence Thomas both loves and hates black folks."

Anita Hill Speaks Out

Just as Thomas's nomination seemed fairly certain, a bomb drops: allegations of sexual harassment. Thus begins part two of *Public Hearings, Private Pain,* which includes a sanitized replay of Hill's charges and Thomas's categorical denial, accompanied by the horrified reactions of African-Americans—the "private pain" half of the story caused by the appearance of Hill. Rather than complicating the tensions surrounding his confirmation, Hill's charges helped to secure it. Indeed, polls published at the time of the hearings indicate support for Thomas among African-Americans increased from 57% to the mid-70s just after Hill testified.[4] Partly this had to do with the extreme publicness of Hill's disclosure. As Bikel states, "[W]hen Anita Hill, a 35-year-old law professor from Oklahoma, began to testify on October 11, it became one of the most watched public events in the history of television." Even those opposed to Thomas expressed displeasure, distaste, and frustration at what they saw as the dissemblage of a serious investigation into a national soap opera, a tawdry sex scandal/peep show that functioned primarily to titillate white Americans at the expense of African-American dignity. The reactions of Roger Wilkins, a scholar at George Mason University, and Sam Fulwood, a reporter for the *Los Angeles Times,* are representative:

> *Wilkins:* What did I think? Um, I thought—yuck. I had no inkling of it prior to that time, and I thought, I don't want this guy on the Court, but I don't want him defeated for this reason, I don't want to see a black person go through this.
> *Fulwood:* There's a widespread belief, and I happen to share it, that had Thomas been white and had the charges been leveled at him, it never would have been, you know, daylight to dusk, gavel to gavel, coverage on television, all three networks. That wouldn't have happened if he'd been white.[5]

But perhaps the larger reason behind the sudden upsurge of black support for Thomas after Hill testified had to do with the reluctance of many African-Americans to condone what they saw as the perpetuation of negative myths and stereotypes about black male sexuality. When Hill accused Thomas of discussing pornography and his own sexual capabilities and attributes in the workplace, and of repeatedly pressuring her for dates, many saw this as another chapter in an all too familiar story about black men as rapacious sexual predators. White Americans perhaps do not recognize that racial and sexual ideologies in the United States are inextricably intertwined, that racial differences are invariably infused with sexual desires and prohibitions. But African-Americans know this well, as Paula Giddings tells Bikel:

> *Giddings:* Racism has been based on sexual difference in many ways, and in many cases. It's not just race difference, not just color difference, but black people were defined by their being sexually different from whites in this society. So anything that smacks, that seems to confirm that view, especially when it's revealed in public, gives us a lot of ambivalence, makes us very nervous.

In *Black Skin, White Masks,* Frantz Fanon describes the white fear of blackness as a phobia of sexual anxiety that turns on the "imago" of the oversexed black male who is envisaged as having an enormous penis. The sexual potency of the black man in the collective unconscious of white society eclipses all other facets of his being: "one is no longer aware of the Negro but only of a penis; the Negro is eclipsed. He is turned into a penis. He *is* a penis" (170). As Mary Ann Doane observes in her reading of Fanon, "[W]hiteness hence relegates blackness to a certain corporeal schema, or, more accurately, to corporeality itself. . . . The collapsing together of the concrete, the corporeal, and sexuality indicates that the fate of the black is that of a body locked into its own non-generalizability" (225). The legacy of this imago clearly marks the discourses of Ella MacDonald, the Harlem foster-care mother quoted earlier, and Sabrina Brown, a young Washington, D.C., resident, which Bikel intercuts with shots of Hill's testimony as she is questioned by Senator Joseph Biden:

Brown: Why would they do something like that? I mean, I'm not *for* Clarence Thomas, at all, but why would they do something to say . . . we have another black, that we can put on the Supreme Court, but—he has a sex problem. I mean, that's what they're saying to us! . . . Why couldn't they bring up something he had done with, maybe his credentials or something were not in order, why did it have to be sex?

Sen. Biden: Did he just say, I have great physical capabilities and attributes, or was he more graphic . . . ?

Hill: He was much more graphic.

Biden: Can you tell us what he said?

Hill: Well, I can tell you that he compared his penis size, he measured his penis in terms of length. . . .

MacDonald: I said, oh my God, here we go again. I say here we go again. I mean here they gonna put his penis all over the TV. You know? I say, here we go again. Here we go again. . . .

From D. W. Griffith's *Birth of a Nation* to the Bush administration's representation of Willie Horton during the election campaign of 1988, white Americans have long exhibited a salacious appetite for what Stuart Clark calls "images of black men misbehaving" (40). As Clark observes, prior to Thomas's nomination, *the* black body most immediately associated with the Bush administration was Willie Horton, and from the beginning Thomas stood as a crucial corrective to the Willie Horton image, his "good" behaviors compensating for Horton's "bad" ones. It seems Hill's testimony in the Senate, however, threatened to re-cast Thomas in the role of sexual deviant, implying that underneath it all Thomas was just another Willie Horton in drag. Thus, when Hill entered the picture it was far from clear to those watching the hearings who played the hero and who the heavy.

The High-Tech Lynching

The perception of black men as sexually different has made black men especially vulnerable to accusations of sexual assault[6] and may also be responsible for the disproportionate number of black men in prison on rape convictions.[7] It certainly provided a compelling backdrop to Thomas's angry denunciation of the hearings as "a high-tech lynching for uppity blacks." In a stunning speech that ended three long, tense days of testimony, Thomas declared his interrogation before the Senate Judiciary Committee constituted a clear message "that unless you kowtow to an old order, this is what will happen to you. You will be lynched, destroyed, caricatured by a committee of the U.S. Senate rather than hung from a tree."

With these words, Thomas suddenly—and with great success—reinvented himself as a victim of racial discrimination, the beleaguered black man under attack from the white establishment. It was a gesture that generated an overwhelmingly favorable response among the general public and apparently among those interviewed in *Public Hearings, Private Pain* as well (only reporter Sam Fulwood and Bishop John Adams comment on the hypocrisy of the move, noting that Thomas played the "race card" because he was in danger of losing the nomination and he knew it would work). According to Bishop Adams, the lynching metaphor worked in part because it exacerbated the guilt of the white senators on the Judiciary Committee, and in part because it evoked strong feelings of sympathy from African-Americans. Thomas came to signify single-handedly not only racial oppression and victimization, but the notion of the black man as sacrificial scapegoat for white fear, anger, and hatred. Indeed, Rev. Benjamin Lett of Macon, Georgia, goes so far as to compare Thomas to Jesus Christ, suggesting the hearings were a kind of death by crucifixion from which Thomas suffered and was then reborn:

> *Rev. Lett:* There was a possibility of redemption now that he had been crucified, if you want to say he was crucified, he was then dead, then buried, if you want to use those terms, yes. . . . He found himself dead in the midst of his tracks, and there was a point of resurrection that meant a whole lot, he got to the point that he was exonerated, his honor was now with him, we say yes we gonna stand behind you, we gonna be with you, we know that you suffered. . . .

Most of the pro-Thomas sentiment expressed in the documentary, however, emerges as part of a more secular discourse emphasizing the need for blacks to "close ranks" in the face of an organized white conspiracy. Because of the history and legacy of racism in the United States and the perceived conspiracy against the black man, black women are expected to subordinate their femaleness to their blackness in the interests of racial solidarity. Bobbie Crook, a hairdresser in Macon, says "Anita should have just left everything alone, and just told him she was glad he had been appointed . . . let the dirt stay behind closed doors," while Leroy Thomas (taxi driver and former head of the Macon chapter of the NAACP) echoes the refrain:

> *L. Thomas:* I'm against what she did for harmony's sake, for racial peace and pride. She could have let that sleeping dog lie. I don't think that, uh, a person that was really looking out for the race would've done what Anita Hill did. . . . And as far as the thing of sexual impropriety, womanizing has never been as important in the black community as it has been in other communities, and I don't think it's that important in other communities.

If black women do not support black men unconditionally, they too get positioned as part of the white conspiracy. This discourse is perhaps best illustrated in the documentary by Rev. Wiley Jackson and Rev. Lett, both of whom position Hill as the unwitting pawn of white Americans, who, throughout history, have attempted to "divide and conquer" the black community by pitting the black woman against the black man. According to Rev. Lett, "[T]hey've pushed our women up, highlighted our women. If anyone was to get a job in the black community it was going to be the black woman over the black male. If anyone was going to get promotions, it was going to be the black woman over the black male." Rev. Jackson puts it to his Atlanta congregation this way: "they know, the devil know, the best way to get to a black man is to use a black Sister."

Another reason the lynching metaphor worked, according to Bikel, has to do with what media scholars call "cultural resonance" (Gamson and Modigliani 5). In any public controversy at any point in history, the dominant ideology limits which narratives are persuasive; those framings with cultural resonance have a natural advantage because they ring true with larger cultural themes, myths, and beliefs.[8] The Thomas/Hill conflict is no exception. Thomas was able to substitute lynching for sexual harassment—and hence his own victimization for Hill's—as constituting the real primal scene of the hearings, because as a symbol of racial oppression, lynching carries greater weight than the sexual abuse of black women. It is UCLA law professor Kimberle Crenshaw who makes this point in *Public Hearings, Private Pain:*

> *Crenshaw:* Lynching is very familiar to us. We've all heard stories about what happened to our men when accusations like this are made. It wasn't as clear, uh, that the black community had stories, had ways of understanding, what happens to black women when they are sexually harassed. . . . So it was going to be harder for her to appeal to people in the black community and it was going to be easy for him to do so.

Double Jeopardy

It was difficult for Hill to garner sympathy from fellow blacks not only because the past and present story of black women's sexual abuse has been marginalized in our culture and in our collective memory, but also because the very abuse of which Hill complained—sexual harassment—is largely perceived as a white woman's issue. Hill was caught in a no-win situation: as a woman she could not compete with Thomas in the contest over "racial authenticity" because the discourse of race is coded as male; as an African-American she was unable to lay moral claim as a victim of sexual harassment because the discourse of gender is coded as white. This is the "double jeopardy" experienced by black women and other women of color, a "betwixt and between status" Crenshaw elsewhere calls the dilemma of intersectionality ("Demarginalizing the Intersection"). It is a dilemma several women interviewed in *Public Hearings, Private Pain* say they can relate to. One is law professor Patricia King, and another is Abysinnia Washington, a young student from Spelman College in Atlanta, where Hill was invited to speak shortly after the Senate hearings:

> *King:* It's been drummed into us I must say, um, since birth that you don't betray black men, that the relationships between black men and black women—we've just sort of never fully explored. . . . And I think that many people saw her as a

traitor. She was a traitor to him, and she was a traitor to the community because she washed all that dirty linen in public. I'm glad she did.

Washington: In everything that we do the priorities that are placed upon us have to do with race, and how we can advance our struggle as a race, but not how we can address our needs as young black women—and black women are really left hurting in a lot of ways.

Although several press accounts published in October and November of 1991 name race as the key issue[9] and others explicitly discuss the intersectional dilemma of black women and other women of color,[10] most coverage—and television coverage in particular—tended to reproduce a deracinated he said/she said "battle of the sexes" construction of the controversy, a point Bikel drives home by juxtaposing shots of male and female reporters framing the issue as "the war between men and women." Nor do the three white feminist women shown discussing sexual harassment on prime time talk about the racial implications of the hearings, at least not in the clips Bikel uses. Consequently, white feminists generally and white feminist spokeswomen in the media especially come under fire from both Bikel and the women she interviews for failing to understand or discuss the racial dynamics and tensions involved. The statement made by New York stock broker Valerie Williams is illustrative:

V. Williams: American feminists cannot deal with race. . . . [T]hey never remembered that they were liberated from their kitchens because my grandmother cleaned them. And then one day 20 years later they look at me and say Valerie, why aren't we marching side by side, I don't understand, and I say my grandmother is still making five dollars a day and you're on Wall Street. OK, they're guilty. So when they can get something where the racial issue is marginalized or minimalized or doesn't count—you see, Thomas was black, Anita was black, sshhhwt, race goes out the window.

Herself one of those white feminists who thought race was irrelevant because both Thomas and Hill were black, Bikel then cuts to news footage of a crowd of mostly white women protesting outside the Senate chambers ("Stop Thomas now! Stop Thomas now!"), followed by an interview with media consultant Emily Tines, who points out that political cooperation between black and white feminists has historically been fraught with racial tension and distrust. "The very fact that a white woman . . . may have been the spokesperson speaking out on behalf of Anita Hill probably raised a lot of eyebrows among black women," Tines explains. "What is her motive for doing this? They don't care, those white feminists don't care about us."[11]

In the end it was Thomas, his conservative supporters, and white, liberal feminist women who seem to have benefited most immediately from the public exposure of Hill, according to Bikel. She illustrates this at the end of the video with a shot of senatorial candidate Barbara Boxer giving a speech to wild applause at a campaign rally, as Bikel herself notes in voice-over, "the hearings have changed the political landscape, energized women's groups, brought new faces to public prominence, and sexual harassment to the headlines." Then as Thomas is shown descending the steps of the Capitol Building with his wife and President Bush amid cheers and applause, Bikel adds, "[T]he President, too, got what he wanted. And few remembered, if they ever knew, the heavy price a whole community had paid." Finally we get a medium close-up of Thomas who says with emotion, "I, Clarence Thomas, do solemnly swear that I will support and defend the Constitution of the United States against all enemies."

What's Wrong With This Picture

Clarence Thomas and Anita Hill: Public Hearings, Private Pain is a tightly knit and carefully crafted documentary that attempts to decode the inscription of race in the Thomas/Hill hearings and explore its impact on selected African-Americans. Bikel gives voice to men and women who supported Thomas, to those who opposed him but nonetheless were sympathetic because they felt he had been victimized by the confirmation process, and to a few women who supported Hill while at the same time acknowledging the painful and problematic nature of her testimony. In so doing, Bikel has framed the text as her own personal "coming of age story" wherein she "discovers," presumably for the first time, that her own racialized subjectivity as a white woman positioned her to read the hearings differently from the African-Americans she interviewed. The video is thus at some level a rebuke to other white feminists for not recognizing the racial complexities, for not dealing with the conflicted emotions and attitudes Bikel herself had not at first understood. "I thought it was ludicrous what the white feminists did," Bikel says in an interview with the *Los Angeles TV Times*. "It was crazy. Night after night, those white faces explaining Anita Hill. I really understand why [blacks] were mad. Many said, Hill made money. She made a career out of it, which, you know, she did in a way. She's a celebrity" (S. King 4).

Aside from the fact that all her examples of white feminist behavior come from either herself or other media spokeswomen, aside from the fact that media representations of feminism in general are notoriously stereotyped and shallow, and aside from the fact that some white feminists knew very well that race "mattered" in the hearings, Bikel's representation of racial politics in the Thomas/Hill conflict is problematic primarily because she tends to reproduce the discourse that conflates "race" with "male" and thus perpetuates black women's disempowerment even as she tries to articulate its specificity. Consequently there is much speculation as to whether Hill should or should not have testified against a brother, yet no one accuses Thomas of "betraying his race" by harassing a sister in the first place. What we get is a documentary much like the hearings themselves: a story about the importance of "race" and therefore Thomas's inevitable victory since "race" is always already masculinized.

By setting out to "explain" African-American support for Thomas to a white audience presumed to be ignorant of the racial implications of the hearings, Bikel masks the extent to which Hill's "intersectional dilemma" is as much about sexual oppression and the trivialization of gender issues within the black community as it is about the inability of white feminists to deal with race. Veiled in the language of lynching, blackness as a mobilizing rhetoric worked to advantage Thomas and disadvantage Hill precisely because the discourse of race operates within a patriarchal cultural context. As Homi K. Bhabha observes, the principal function of the lynching metaphor was not to make those white senators feel guilty but to solicit their complicity in a masculinist attempt to contain the articulations of sexual difference—to disallow the gendering of racial identity and silence the feminist discourse on sexual harassment. Only through such disavowal could Hill, herself a victim of racism, be symbolically reconstituted as the dupe of a high-tech lynch mob. Only through such disavowal could Thomas and his backers conveniently fail to recall that lynching was a terrorist strategy aimed at those who challenged white hegemony, not at the president's handpicked men (McKay 285), that no black man was ever lynched on the word of an aggrieved black woman (Thomas 370),[12] and that historically women of African descent were the chief organizers *against* lynching and other forms of sexual terror (Giddings, "Last Taboo" 443). And only through such disavowal could Thomas use his blackness to deflect attention from what was really at stake in the hearings: his fitness to serve on the Court. Hill as a *raced* victim of sexual harassment in all of this was, as Lubiano notes, "both hypervisible and invisible at the same time" (348) and, in my opinion, now twice overexposed and twice erased—first on the Senate floor, and again in the *Frontline* documentary.

At issue here is not so much what the documentary allows, but what it disavows—those issues and concerns that lie outside the frame. There is nothing in the documentary, for example, that resembles the articulate outrage of black feminist scholars published in the wake of the hearings.[13] Nor is there anything to suggest that in November of 1991, one month after the hearings ended, more than 1,600 African-American women placed a full-page ad in the *New York Times* as well as in several smaller regional newspapers denouncing the racist and sexist treatment of Hill. The untold story behind the hearings was not that a majority of African-Americans supported Thomas's nomination (polls consistently showed as much), nor was it that many black women are reluctant to speak of sexual abuse because of community pressure to minimize intraracial conflict and avoid feeding painful historical stereotypes about black male sexuality. Both of these discourses were circulating in the mainstream press. For an Emmy Award–winning producer to "discover" 10 days into production that the hearings were "about race" after all—and to do so as the principal representative in the film of white feminism—is more than a little disingenuous. The hidden story here is not why so many African-Americans supported Thomas, but why more didn't support Hill. This is a story not only about race, but about the sexism within both white communities and communities of color that transformed Hill from a serious, articulate, Republican lawyer into a liar, a manipulator, a pawn of white liberal interest groups, a woman scorned, a lesbian, and even a delusional psychotic unable to distinguish fantasy from reality. It is a story about how the confirmation hearings of a Supreme Court nominee became an old-fashioned witch trial, and how a "high-tech lynching" came to mean—as Patricia Williams puts it—"a broad with a bullhorn" (37).

Bray points out that these skillful manipulations of Hill's character were effective because they are familiar, manageable images of African-American womanhood (94). In other words, the vilification of Hill had just as much "cultural resonance" as the victimization of Thomas. The unspeakable truth about the Thomas/Hill hearings is that America has never taken the sexual abuse of black women seriously, largely because black women have also been victims of sexual stereotypes. According to Giddings ("Last Taboo" 442–47), the perception of black men as oversexed and rapacious is built upon historical notions of black female lasciviousness: at a time when women were considered the foundation of a group's morality, it was widely believed that black men raped because their mothers, wives, sisters, and daughters were sexually promiscuous and morally "loose." Thus, at the core of the historical discourse on racial difference is the projection of the dark side of sexuality onto the black female body, which not only shapes the kinds of harassment black women experience but influences whether or not they are likely to be believed. As many contemporary African-American feminists have pointed out, the legacy of this discourse in legal proceedings and elsewhere is the common assumption that black women cannot be raped or sexually abused, and that sexual aggression directed against black women is less objectionable than when directed against white women; hence when black women do seek justice for mistreatment or abuse, their complaints are dismissed or trivialized. Not surprisingly, some studies of sexual assault suggest that the race of the *victim* (not the defendant) is the most salient factor determining the disposition of men convicted of rape (Crenshaw, "Whose Story Is It Anyway?" 419).

But the trope that Hill fit best was the stereotype of the black lady overachiever described by Wahneema Lubiano in "Black Ladies, Welfare Queens, and State Minstrels." If the welfare queen stands as synecdoche for the "pathology" of poor, urban, black culture, an all-purpose scapegoat for the failures of our political-economic structure, the black lady overachiever "is the flip side of the pathology coin, the welfare queen's more articulate sister" (340). In the "culture of poverty" discourse on the black family (best typified by the infamous Moynihan Report), the disproportionate overachievement of the black lady ensures the disproportionate underachievement of working class black males because such overachievement exists in a social context that presumes, as Moynihan himself points out, male leadership in public and private affairs. "There we have it," writes Lubiano, "whether by virtue of *not achieving* and thus passing on bad culture as welfare mothers, or by virtue of *managing to achieve* middle-class success . . . black women are responsible for the disadvantaged status of African Americans" (335).

In this narrative context, Hill's allegations surface as yet another example of black women's willing efforts to destroy the upward mobility of black men, precisely the discourse of treason and betrayal articulated by many of Bikel's interview subjects in *Public Hearings, Private Pain*. Given the stereotype of the emasculating black lady overachiever, Lubiano (347) wonders exactly who was the "uppity black" being punished in the Senate hearings? To whom did Thomas pose a threat that he was in danger of being lynched? Certainly not the white male Senate. Ironically it was Hill herself who was made to play the outlaw. In fact, according to Lubiano, Hill's timely appearance as outlaw was just what Thomas's confirmation process needed in order for Thomas "the Hero" to emerge (337). Never mind that it was Hill who was most vulnerable to the disciplinary effects of the symbolic lynching described by Thomas during the proceedings, in that she was subject to the degradation routinely experienced by sexual assault victims who dare speak publicly of their abuse or harassment from a position of relative powerlessness. As Amy Richlin observes, what happened to

Hill is entirely commonplace in the political economy of the rape trial: the very content of her speech provided the means by which to discredit her. Hill was "dirtied" by the very words she spoke, for "whereas the words she repeated were only alleged to be *his* words, millions of people had heard her say them again and again; what kind of woman would speak like that? His lips remained unsullied" (Richlin 1331).

Thus, the predominant stereotypes influencing the outcome of the hearings in Thomas's favor were as much about black women as black men. The difference was that people recognized Thomas as a legitimate representative of racial difference and a legitimate victim of racial oppression. It was precisely people's unwillingness to perpetuate negative stereotypes of black male sexuality that enabled Thomas to forge a false historical connection to lynching and obscure his true present connection to white state power. Stereotypes of black men in effect saved Thomas's nomination and ensured his confirmation. On the other hand, stereotypes of black women were also informing the Senate proceedings, stereotypes that affected Hill negatively but went largely unacknowledged and uncontested both in the hearings themselves and in the *Frontline* documentary.

At no point does Bikel suggest in *Public Hearings, Private Pain* that racial and ethnic identity were used in the confirmation proceedings to perpetuate negative myths and stereotypes about black women, to silence the feminist discourse on sexual harassment, or to mask Thomas's own privileged relationship to white state power. She does focus on the double jeopardy faced by black women in a culture where the emblematic woman is white and the emblematic black is male, and the pressures on black women to preserve racial solidarity by minimizing intraracial gender conflict. Yet because the documentary emphasizes the reactions of African-Americans who at some level sympathize with Thomas regardless of—or despite—his politics, it frames the issue of "race" as a question of loyalty that Hill is solely responsible for maintaining (should she have done it?) rather than problematizing the very nature of race loyalty itself by asking why this burden should be disproportionately hers. By accusing Thomas of sexual harassment, Hill transgressed a racial taboo, an inviolable code of silence that states a black woman does not challenge a black man in front of a white one, even if it means tremendous personal sacrifice. Interestingly, there is no such corollary sacrifice required of black men (see McKay 282), who seem capable of violating the codes of race loyalty only with regard to other men. Consequently, as West observes, the idea of black people "closing ranks" against hostile white Americans reinforces black male power exercised over black women (392).

In summary, if the Thomas/Hill hearings were a "cover story" for white state power (as Lubiano suggests), then the documentary is in some ways a cover story for black male power. For despite the rhetoric in the video of male weakness/female strength, of society having "raised black women up," of whites having driven a wedge between black men and women, it is men, not women, who control the sociosexual and professional relations in African-American communities (Giddings, "The Last Taboo" 463), a fact conveniently overlooked by Bikel. Thomas was nominated to the Supreme Court, not Hill, and according to Giddings it is men like Thomas who, since the 1970s, have emerged as powerful gatekeepers for the upward mobility of all blacks in the newly accessible corporate, political, and cultural spheres of influence (463). As a result, Thomas's unabashed espousal of bootstrap individualism masquerades as racial solidarity, while Hill's attempts to speak her reality emerge as its principal threat. Thomas's public refutation of civil rights reforms is interpreted by black neoconservatives as "diversity" within the black community, while Hill's decision to table charges against him signals her cooptation by white feminists and their liberal allies. Thomas's current alliances with the nation's most powerful men is buried by his rags to riches past, while Hill's own similar background is buried by her professional status in the present. Thus it is that black men, in the culture at large and in *Public Hearings, Private Pain,* come to occupy the position of "the race," while black women occupy no particular position at all save that of traitor to black men or mediator between black men and white women.

Many black feminist women and their supporters are concerned about the sexism as well as the racism that black women suffer. "In the last few years," writes Barbara Smith, "misogyny has become a growth industry in the African American community" (187). Of course, the same can be said of white communities. The point is, misogyny takes many forms, and one of them is sexual harassment of the sort experienced by Hill. Yet Hill garnered little sympathy from fellow African-Americans, both because her actions "betrayed" a black man, and because they aligned her with white feminism. If Thomas was "blackened" by the discourse of lynching, Hill was "whitened" simply by championing what is often considered a white woman's issue. Hence, as Margaret Burnham (311) observes, the hostile views of many blacks about white feminists kicked in to shape their feelings about Hill and Thomas, and much of the antagonism Hill felt was in fact directed against mainstream feminism. Television coverage of the hearings fed the misperception of Hill as the dupe of white feminists by interviewing white women experts on sexual harassment almost exclusively, despite the fact that, according to Crenshaw, black women are disproportionately represented as plaintiffs in sexual harassment cases ("Whose Story Is It Anyway?" 412).

Given Thomas's overt alliances to white (male) power, it is remarkable that people managed to perceive Hill as somehow "whiter" than he. Certainly much of the responsibility for this perception must be shouldered by mainstream feminism, which, as Bikel does not fail to point out, is often insensitive to issues of race. According to Kum Kum Bhavnani, "[I]n suggesting that claims of sexism are a means of perpetuating racism against black men, a suggestion that is powerful precisely because it has validity, Clarence Thomas fired his arrow at the Achilles' heel of one important manifestation of contemporary feminism in the United States, namely its silence on racism" (502). White feminist politicians and activists must act concretely to make "women's issues" such as sexual harassment relevant to black women and other women of color, as well as to working class and poor women; they can accomplish this only by addressing race and class as integral aspects of gender oppression rather than its additional burdens, and by participating in political organizing that directly challenges the multiple oppressions that women of color and poor women face. At the same time, it is important to recognize the coercive dimensions of race loyalty, specifically how notions of racial solidarity work to reinforce male privilege. For it is simply not true that any black woman who complains of gender discrimination is acting at the behest, and in the interests, of white feminist women, rather than in the interests of black women and African-Americans generally. As Crenshaw points out, this view incorrectly assumes a black woman cannot conclude on her own that rape, battery, and harassment are damaging to her as a *black woman* ("Race, Gender, and Sexual Harassment" 1473).

Identity Politics

The lessons of the Thomas/Hill hearings are varied and complex, as are those of the PBS documentary, which has packaged and framed the hearings to make some of those lessons more readily available than others. As we have seen, feminism as popularly conceived has yet to gain acceptance among the African-American mainstream, both because it is perceived as white (a fact Bikel emphasizes) and because of the patriarchal bias the black community shares with the larger culture (a fact much less noticed in *Public Hearings, Private Pain*). The hearings also illustrate the enormous power of "race" to mobilize strong black support for Thomas where there had been little before, and the power of the political right to make this sign work to the advantage of a conservative and racist administration with a long history of race baiting. This "reversal of fortune" (Bhabha 233) can only be understood within the current historical context largely ignored by Bikel in her framing of the debate, an era marked by cultural retrenchment and a growing politics of resentment against social welfare, the poor, feminism, women, and racial minorities. Barbara Ransby puts it this way: before the hearings began there was already "a national consensus which made Hill an acceptable target for the rage of racist white men and the vulgar distortion of race politics by an opportunistic and woman-hating black Conservative" ("Outrage" 20).

Both the hearings and the documentary illustrate the ways in which the signs of ethnic and racial identity can be used by conservatives to police other boundaries of difference—in this case, class and gender. And all over the country, universities, schools, small businesses, and corporations are "managing diversity" in the same way the Bush administration managed Thomas's nomination to the Supreme Court. Indeed, the sexual and racial politics of

Thomas versus Hill crystallized in a highly visible and dramatic fashion not only the politics of the right but the so-called "progressive" politics of multiculturalism, which also tend to marginalize issues of gender, sexuality, and class. We must question not only how a conservative black man in the White House comes to represent African-American oppression, but how it is that "multicultural" has become synonymous with multiracial and multiethnic. Why, for example, do feminism, Marxism, and queer theory not constitute central elements of this discourse?

Perhaps it is not the place for white feminists to point out sexism within the black community. Certainly we are well advised to clean the racism out of our own houses before knocking on others' doors. But it seems white feminists are better able to protest along with black feminists and other feminists of color the derogatory treatment of Hill by Thomas and the Senate Judiciary Committee than we are to serve as spokespersons for the personal views and "private pain" of the entire African-American community. Cashing in on her own privilege as high-tech voyeur, Bikel took it upon herself to be such a spokesperson. The result is a high-tech view of identity politics, where notions of blackness rely on problematic appeals to "racial authenticity," which in turn conceal and distort the political and ethical dimensions of ethnic identity. It may be that many African-Americans were sympathetic to Thomas because he is black, and that Thomas's past (and present) experiences with racism have informed his political alliances. But as Toni Morrison and others point out, the time for undiscriminating black unity is past, for in the case of Thomas such unity masks not only sexism and homophobia but a conservative free-market individualism that has never worked, and is not now likely to work, to the benefit of African-Americans, other people of color, white women, or the poor. Thus, instead of provoking discussions about moral justice, coalition politics, and black cultural democracy, the documentary that purports to reveal the untold story behind the Thomas/Hill affair tells quite a familiar tale after all.

Yet Bikel is not solely responsible for this articulation; although she framed their contours and authorized their meanings, the discourses in *Public Hearings, Private Pain* are culled from the culture at large. The subtext of the documentary is thus a kind of warning or challenge: we on the "left" have work to do if we are to present a compelling political alternative to the "racial reasoning" of identity politics. White feminists in particular have an investment in this project. As Christine Stansell observes, "[T]he shell game of identity politics . . . may protect white feminists from the uncomfortable business of learning and thinking aloud about male privilege in black politics. But unless we grow more skillful in our thinking and in our tactics, as we learned, we have little to counter the conservatives' sleight-of-hand" (267). Black and white feminists did come together on this issue, but it shouldn't take Anita Hill (a conservative Republican, after all) to make us recognize the urgency of rethinking and retheorizing the complex interconnections of race, class, and gender in the 1990s.

Conclusion: Melodrama and the Politics of Representation

Much has been made of the coincidence between the Thomas/Hill conflict and melodrama, mostly to illustrate the debased (i.e., sexual) content of the hearings and the scopophilic nature of their appeal. The analogy is always derogatory, in no small part because the discourse of melodrama/soaps is traditionally a feminine one; as Tania Modleski has remarked, there is no surer way to damn a text or an event than to invoke a comparison to soap opera (86). Not surprisingly, such comparisons are routinely applied to public sex scandals (the Thomas/Hill hearings, the Mike Tyson trial, the William Kennedy Smith trial), as if the public articulation of sexual difference and gender conflict renders the entire discourse of gender and sexuality inherently female, overblown, unreliable, and unbelievable. The shift and slide in the Thomas confirmation hearings from a masculine narrative to a feminine one, from a serious political investigation to a tawdry televisual melodrama, hinges on the appearance of Hill. Bikel says it quite plainly in her introductory voice-over at the beginning of *Public Hearings, Private Pain:* "It was a year ago that what began as a political battle became a national soap opera." In other words, it was a year ago that Hill leveled charges of sexual harassment against Thomas, turning a respectable process into a circus side-show. And even though most of the senators claimed to take sexual harassment "very seriously" (see Bhavnani 498), the manner in which they proceeded to investigate the charges, and the manner in which the news media then characterized the proceedings, seemed anything but serious.

By very definition, documentary is not melodrama, and in fact Bikel is careful to position her work within the more masculinist tradition of "serious journalism" by following the conventions of mainstream television documentary, using talking-head interviews, existing news footage, voice-over narration, continuity editing, bright, even illumination, and music to punctuate significant or dramatic moments and thematic transitions. And yet the general distinction between documentary as objective "truth" and melodrama as subjective fantasy is problematic. As film scholars Thomas and Vivian Sobchack point out, the documentary form often uses dramatic structures (such as suspense) and devices (such as music, parallel editing, and the manipulation of time) to vitalize its content; sometimes the drama is inherent in the event being filmed and requires minimal editorial intervention (336–73). *Public Hearings, Private Pain* exhibits all of these characteristics, as does television news. Perhaps the biggest difference between news and entertainment, documentary and melodrama, is that news and documentary embody what David MacDougall calls "the fallacy of omniscient observation" (281), where a few images create a world and we ignore the ones that could have been, but were not. Consequently, viewers may be caught up in a process of accepting highly discriminatory processes as factual givens, apprehending the reality presented by the documentary "as the only one actually there for the filmmaker to show" (Allen 38). In *Public Hearings, Private Pain,* for example, Bikel uses journalistic codes and conventions to frame and make sense of the images selected for presentation, which include interview segments, footage of the hearings, and news coverage of this footage (itself already packaged and framed by the networks). Consequently, her own narrative voice emerges as the guarantor of the "real," and the PBS *Frontline* documentary (bastion of respectable journalism) provides a kind of uncontested metadiscourse on the Thomas/Hill conflict and the public response to it.

I want to salvage melodrama as a critical tool of analysis by suggesting that the seemingly trivial, so-called women's discourse of melodrama can offer important and serious insights into the "crisis of representation" that marked Thomas's confirmation.

Melodrama in the cinema represents social anxieties or conflicts as sexual and familial ones, thereby inverting the more typical masculinist structure of narrative film where questions of sexual difference lurk beneath the social and the political. In other words, melodrama makes public the "private" discourses of sexuality and the family. The challenge is then to articulate the public discourses that discussions of sexuality displace. As we have seen in the Thomas/Hill hearings, charges of sexual harassment prompted charges of racism, which in turn managed to deflect critical inquiry into the social, political, and ethical implications of Thomas's appointment.

Melodrama shares more with the hearings than an interest in sexual conflict and confession; both melodrama and public spectacles like the Thomas/Hill affair turn most crucially on questions of visibility, representability, pretense, and masquerade. Visibility and representation are enormously problematic for oppressed groups. To the extent that white men appropriate the definition of "normal" for themselves, women and men of color are left in the paradoxical situation of appearing invisible and hypervisible simultaneously—invisible in structures of power and as authors of social discourse, yet hypervisible as representatives of "difference." In the politics of race, to be "colored" is to be always already marked and particularized, whereas whiteness is characterized by its very lack of specificity (Dyer 45). This everything and nothing quality of whiteness, according to Dyer, secures white privilege by making it difficult, especially for white people, to "see" whiteness (46). The power of whiteness here is thus the power of the voyeur: to see without being seen. On the other hand, blackness is a form of constant visibility and perpetual overdetermination, what Frantz Fanon calls "a racial epidermal schema" (110). In this schema, consciousness of the body is solely a negating activity.

Thomas's efforts to be colorless and invisible within the white male power structure—to be just another Supreme Court Justice—were thwarted when Hill stepped forward and fixed the nation's gaze upon him. His sudden visibility as a sexual harasser left him one alternative: the emergency exit marked "race." The hypervisibility of this new sign not only erased (and de-raced) the harassment allegations, it masked Thomas's conservative and careerist political record: his rejection of affirmative action and other social welfare reforms, his connection to lobbyists for South Africa, and his poor performance as head of the EEOC—in other words, the extent of Thomas's identification with whites in their exploitative relation to people of color and the poor. Indeed, as Doane reminds us, *this* is what most concerned Fanon in his analysis of the effects of racism on the black psyche: the troubling phenomenon of black identification with the oppressive attitudes and policies of whites toward the Other—especially when the black man is forced to realize he *is* the Other (227).

In film melodrama, crises of representation and identity function to break families apart, then bring them together again at the story's end employing one of a number of formulas: the hero defeats the villain, the "villain within" is reformed, or the villain turns out to have been the hero all along. More often than not, the villain is a woman's ambitions, which she must renounce as wicked and perverse because they undermine her capacity to be a good wife and mother and therefore threaten the stability of her family. Hill was not a good wife and mother to her community. She did not bite her tongue and swallow her pain. She refused to play the martyr, and she refused to sacrifice herself in the name of family solidarity. She was, therefore, an easy villain for Thomas to put away, and he did so in no less dramatic a fashion than a shoot-out at high noon. In these terms, a masculine discourse replaced the feminine one as the melodrama became a Western. Despite all the dust and confusion raised by this deft generic switch, however, it was not difficult to see that it was Thomas, produced and directed by the Bush administration, who was riding the white horse/White House and packing a gun.

Notes

1. Wahneema Lubiano has noted the same "balanced" representation of the Thomas/Hill conflict in newspaper photographs, writing
    [t]he side-by-side visual equality of representation obscures the dramatic disparity of power hidden by the juxtaposition: Thomas, head of the EEOC, judge, and friend of powerful men, chosen for his position and admired by our head of state, beneficiary of the apparatuses of state power—and a man who would be among the most powerful if confirmed by the Senate, next to a woman professor of law, holding a faculty position at a state university, and whose photograph was reproduced in the newspa-

per because of Thomas' alleged transgressions. This insistence on fore-grounding the *individual* nature of accusation and response—regardless of where one lays the blame—was characteristic of much of the media's discussion of these proceedings. (326)

Indeed, parallel images of Thomas and Hill also appear side-by-side in the *Los Angeles TV Times* article that advertises the premier of *Public Hearings, Private Pain*. There is a variation, however: immediately below Thomas and Hill is a photograph of Bikel herself, the white woman behind the camera who exposes the hidden meanings of the conflict.

2. For example, see the critiques of Thomas in the Toni Morrison edited volume *Race-ing Justice, En-gendering Power*, especially those by Higginbotham, Marable, Thelwell, and West. See also the following essays in The Black Scholar (ed.), *Court of Appeal:* Bell, Bond, Boyd, Boyd and Rojas, Davis, George, Henry, Hooks, Horne, Sales, Taylor, and Wright.

3. See in particular the essays by Angelou, Jackson, Jacob, Lowery, and Sudarkasa.

4. Poll data appeared in the *New York Times* 15 Oct. 1991; the *San Francisco Examiner* 14 Oct. 1991; *USA Today* 14 and 16 Oct. 1991; and the *Washington Times*, 16 and 20 Oct. 1991.

5. The view expressed by Fulwood is quite common among African-Americans writing about the Thomas confirmation hearings. Although both Stephen Carter ("Two Good People") and Orlando Patterson ("Race, Gender, and Liberal Fallacies") writing in *The New York Times* applauded the hearings for providing white America with the unique opportunity to witness "honest disagreement" between two intelligent, articulate, professional, and successful African-Americans, neither of whom conformed to existing media stereotypes of blacks, many others felt the only real winners in this grand daytime drama were white male politicians. Indeed, most seem to agree that the Thomas/Hill affair was "a spectacle of mutual degradation," one more chapter in a long saga of the manipulation of "sacrificial black surrogates" by a white ruling elite (Karenga 129, 131). As David Smith (192) puts it, "[I]t was primarily an exchange between two lily-white enclaves, the White House and the Senate, who cynically used Anita Hill and Clarence Thomas to stage rhetorical gestures toward the public." Lewis (140) suggests the hearings reinforced a general sense that race and African-Americans remain a commodity bought and sold for the pleasure of others. In this same context, Dent (66) likens the hearings to a boxing match ("Hill and Thomas entertained America by slugging it out"), while Karenga (132) says she is reminded of the "buck fights" and "nigger fights" whites staged for their own perverse enjoyment during slavery. Estelle Freedman notes another spectacular historical parallel—that of lynching, though not as a strictly disciplinary action in the sense used by Thomas during the hearings but as a form of "folk pornography." According to Freedman, just as Southern whites spread lurid tales of unprintable sexual crimes and gathered in crowds to gawk at black bodies dangling from trees, "so the modern American public seemed to find irresistible the chance to watch and hear the 'obscene' enter legitimate political discourse" (362). But perhaps the most common metaphor used to describe the hearings is that of the melodrama—or its televisual equivalent, the soap opera. At the beginning of *Public Hearings, Private Pain*, Bikel herself compares the hearings to soap opera ("it was a year ago that what began as a political battle became a national soap opera . . .") as do a number of scholars, journalists, and activists. According to Maulana Karenga, "[H]ere was soap opera itself—with all its dread and drama, suspense and sordid tales of sexual fantasies, inflated genital size claims, and declarations

of profound sexual need—and all with the added advantage of being *in living color*" (131, emphasis in the original).

6. See Freedman; Crenshaw "Whose Story Is It Anyway?"; and Giddings.

7. See Angela Davis *Women, Culture & Politics.*

8. Fisher uses the term "narrative fidelity" to describe the same phenomenon, while Snow and Benford use "frame resonance."

9. See Applebom; also Fulwood "Thomas Seen Shifting."

10. See the press articles by Becklund, Bray, Fulwood, P. King, Romero, and White.

11. A *Los Angeles Times* article published on the 9th of October states Emily Tines organized a group of about 200 women to protest Thomas's confirmation on the day of the Senate vote (see Becklund), but it is not clear whether this is the same demonstration shown in the documentary. If so, it is ironic that the very group of mostly white women organized by Tines, a black woman, is offered as visual "proof" that black and white women are rarely political allies.

12. June Jordan and Estelle Freedman make this point as well.

13. See especially the essays by Bray, Boyd, Crenshaw, Freedman, Giddings, Gillespie, Hull, Jordan, Lacour, Lubiano, Malveaux, McKay, Norton, Painter, Ransby, B. Smith, Stansell, Walker, and Williams.

Works Cited

Allen, Jeanne. "Self-Reflexivity in Documentary." *Cine-Tracts* 2 (1983): 37–43.

Angelou, Maya. "I Dare to Hope." *New York Times* 25 Aug. 1991, sec. IV: 15.

Applebom, Peter. "Despite Talk of Sexual Harassment, Thomas Hearings Turned on Race Issue." *New York Times* 19 Oct. 1991: A7.

Becklund, Laurie. "Women Angered by Inaction on Thomas Charge." *Los Angeles Times* 9 Oct. 1991: A1.

Bell, Derrick. "A Radical Double Agent." The Black Scholar 36–37.

Bhabha, Homi K. "A Good Judge of Character: Men, Metaphors, and the Common Culture." Morrison, *Race-ing Justice* 232–50.

Bhavnani, Kum Kum, with Dana Collins. "Racism and Feminism: An Analysis of the Anita Hill and Clarence Thomas Hearings." *New Community* 19.3 (1993): 493–505.

Bikel, Ofra, prod. *Clarence Thomas and Anita Hill: Public Hearings, Private Pain.* Frontline. PBS. 15 Oct. 1992.

The Black Scholar, ed. *Court of Appeal: The Black Community Speaks Out on the Racial and Sexual Politics of Thomas vs. Hill.* New York: Ballantine, 1992.

Bond, Julian. "The NAACP Judged Thomas by His Character, Not by the Color of His Skin." The Black Scholar 278–80.

Boyd, Herb, and Don Rojas. "Clarence Thomas and the Apartheid Connection." The Black Scholar 38–42.

Boyd, Melba. "Collard Greens, Clarence Thomas, and the High-Tech Rape of Anita Hill." The Black Scholar 43–46.

Bray, Rosemary. "Taking Sides Against Ourselves." *New York Times Magazine* 17 Nov. 1991: 56, 94–95, 101.

Burnham, Margaret. "The Supreme Court Appointment Process and the Politics of Race and Sex." Morrison, *Race-ing Justice* 290–322.

Carter, Stephen. "Two Good People." *New York Times* 13 Oct. 1991, sec. IV: 15.

Chrisman, Robert. Introduction. The Black Scholar xi–xliii.

Clark, Stuart Alan. "Fear of a Black Planet: Race, Identity Politics, and Common Sense." *Socialist Review* 21.3/4 (1991): 37–59.

Congressional Black Caucus Foundation (CBCF). "In Opposition to Clarence Thomas: Where We Must Stand and Why." The Black Scholar 231–54.

Crenshaw, Kimberle. "Demarginalizing the Intersection of Race and Sex: A Black Feminist Critique of Antidiscrimination Doctrine, Feminist Theory, and Antiracist Politics." *Feminist Legal Theory.* Ed. Katherine Bartlett and Rosanne Kennedy. Boulder: Westview Press, 1991. 57–80.

———. "Race, Gender, and Sexual Harassment." *Southern California Law Review* 65 (1992): 1467–76.

———. "Whose Story Is It Anyway? Feminist and Antiracist Appropriations of Anita Hill." Morrison, *Race-ing Justice* 402–36.

Davis, Angela. *Women, Culture & Politics.* New York: Random, 1989.

Davis, Henry Vance. "The High-Tech Lynching and the High-Tech Overseer: Thoughts from the Anita Hill/Clarence Thomas Affair." The Black Scholar 59–62.

Dent, David. "The Clarence Thomas Hearings and the Entertaining of America." The Black Scholar 63–66.

Doane, Mary Ann. *Femmes Fatales: Feminism, Film Theory, Psychoanalysis.* New York: Routledge, 1991.

Dyer, Richard. "White." *Screen* 29.4 (1988): 44–64.

Fanon, Frantz. *Black Skin, White Masks.* Trans. Charles Lam Markmann. New York: Grove Weidenfeld, 1967.

Fisher, Walter. "Narration as a Human Communication Paradigm: The Case of Public Moral Argument." *Communication Monographs* 51 (1984): 1–23.

Freedman, Estelle. "The Manipulation of History at the Clarence Thomas Hearings." *Southern California Law Review* 65 (1992): 1361–65.

Fulwood, Sam III. "Black Women Seen as Reluctant to Claim Harassment." *Los Angeles Times* 10 Oct. 1991: A8.

———. "Many Blacks See Pain and Harm in Controversy." *Los Angeles Times* 12 Oct. 1991: A1.

———. "Thomas Seen Shifting Focus to Race Issue." *Los Angeles Times* 13 Oct. 1991: A1.

Gamson, William, and Andre Modigliani. "Media Discourse and Public Opinion on Nuclear Power: A Constructionist Approach." *American Journal of Sociology* 95.1 (1989): 1–37.

George, Hermon, Jr. "Clarence Thomas: Loyal Foot Soldier to Reaganism." The Black Scholar 67–72.

Giddings, Paula. "The Last Taboo." Morrison, *Race-ing Justice* 441–65.

———. *When and Where I Enter: The Impact of Black Women on Race and Sex in America.* New York: William Morrow, 1984.

Gillespie, Marcia Ann. "We Speak in Tongues . . ." *Ms.* Jan.-Feb. 1992: 41–43.

Henry, Charles. "Clarence Thomas and the National Black Identity." The Black Scholar 83–85.

Higginbotham, A. Leon, Jr. "An Open Letter to Clarence Thomas from a Federal Judicial Colleague." Morrison, *Race-ing Justice* 3–39.

Hooks, Benjamin. "In the Matter of Clarence Thomas." The Black Scholar 272–74.

Horne, Gerald. "The Thomas Hearings and the Nexus of Race, Gender, and Nationalism." The Black Scholar 92–95.

Hull, Gloria. "Girls Will Be Girls, and Boys Will . . . Flex Their Muscles." The Black Scholar 96–98.

Jackson, Jacqueline Johnson. "'Them Against Us': Anita Hill v. Clarence Thomas." The Black Scholar 99–105.

Jacob, John. "Clarence Thomas: Affirmative Action and Merit." Keynote Address. National Urban League Annual Conference. Atlanta, 21 July 1991.

Jordan, June. "Can I Get a Witness?" *Progressive* Dec. 1991: 12–13.

Karenga, Maulana. "Under the Camouflage of Color and Gender: The Dread and Drama of Thomas–Hill." The Black Scholar 125–35.

King, Patricia. "Shackled to a Shadow of a Doubt." *Los Angeles Times* 8 Oct. 1991: B7.

King, Susan. "The Issue Was Race." *Los Angeles TV Times* 11–17 Oct. 1992: 4.

Lacour, Claudia Brodsky. "Doing Things With Words: 'Racism' as Speech Act and the Undoing of Justice." Morrison, *Race-ing Justice* 127–58.

Lewis, Earl. "Race as Commodity: Hill and Thomas as Consumer Products." The Black Scholar 139–42.

Lowery, Rev. Joseph. "The SCLC Position: Confirm Clarence Thomas." The Black Scholar 283–85.

Lubiano, Wahneema. "Black Ladies, Welfare Queens, and State Minstrels: Ideological War by Narrative Means." Morrison, *Race-ing Justice* 323–63.

MacDougall, David. "Beyond Observational Cinema." *Movies and Methods*. Vol. II. Ed. Bill Nichols. Berkeley: U of California P, 1985. 274–87.

Malveaux, Julianne. "No Peace in a Sisterly Space." The Black Scholar 143–47.

Mandel, Bill. "Thomas Stars in America's Nightmare." *San Francisco Examiner* 14 Oct. 1991: A3.

Marable, Manning. "Clarence Thomas and the Crisis of Black Political Culture." Morrison, *Race-ing Justice* 61–85.

McKay, Nellie. "Remembering Anita Hill and Clarence Thomas: What Really Happened When One Black Woman Spoke Out." Morrison, *Race-ing Justice* 269–89.

Modleski, Tania. "The Search For Tomorrow in Today's Soap Operas." *Loving with a Vengeance: Massed Produced Fantasies for Women*. New York: Routledge, 1982. 85–109.

Morrison, Toni. Introduction. "Friday on the Potomac." Morrison, *Race-ing Justice* vii–xxx.

———. *Race-ing Justice, En-gendering Power: Essays on Anita Hill, Clarence Thomas, and the Construction of Social Reality*. New York: Pantheon, 1992.

Morse, Rob. "The Thomas Clown Affair." *San Francisco Examiner* 15 Oct. 1991: A3.

Norton, Eleanor Holmes. ". . . And the Language is Race," *Ms.* Jan.-Feb. 1992: 43–45.

Painter, Nell Irvin. "Hill, Thomas, the Use of Racial Stereotype." Morrison, *Race-ing Justice* 200–14.

———. "Who Was Lynched?" *Nation* 11 Dec. 1991: 577.

Patterson, Orlando. "Race, Gender, and Liberal Fallacies." *New York Times* 20 Oct. 1991, sec. IV: 15.

Ransby, Barbara. "The Gang Rape of Anita Hill and the Assault Upon All Women of African Descent." The Black Scholar 169–75.

———. "Outrage Fueled by Racism, Sexism." *New Directions for Women* March-April 1991: 4, 20.

Richlin, Amy. "Roman Oratory, Pornography, and the Silencing of Anita Hill." *Southern California Law Review* 65 (1992): 1321–32.

Romero, Gloria. "What the Senators Failed to Understand." *Los Angeles Times* 16 Oct. 1991: B7.

Sales, William, Jr. "Comments on the Controversy Surrounding the Nomination and Confirmation of Judge Thomas to the Supreme Court." The Black Scholar 176–84.

Smith, Barbara. "Ain't Gonna Let Nobody Turn Me Around." The Black Scholar 185–89.

Smith, David Lionel. "The Thomas Spectacle: Power, Impotence, and Melodrama." The Black Scholar 190–93.

Snow, David, and Robert Benford. "Ideology, Frame Resonance, and Participant Mobilization." *International Social Movement Research. Volume 1*. Eds. Bert Klandermans, Hanspeter Kriesi, and Sidney Tarrow. Greenwich: Jai Press, 1988. 197–217.

Sobchack, Thomas, and Vivian Sobchack. *An Introduction to Film*. 2nd ed. Boston: Little, 1987.

Stansell, Christine. "White Feminists and Black Realities: The Politics of Authenticity." Morrison, *Race-ing Justice* 251–68.

Sudarkasa, Niara. "Don't Write Off Thomas." The Black Scholar 201–03.

Taylor, Clyde. "Clarence Thomas and the Question of Fitness." The Black Scholar 207–10.

Thelwell, Michael. "False, Fleeting, Perjured Clarence: Yale's Brightest and Blackest Go to Washington." Morrison, *Race-ing Justice* 86–126.

Thomas, Kendall. "Strange Fruit." Morrison, *Race-ing Justice* 364–89.

Walker, Rebecca. "Becoming the Third Wave." *Ms.* Jan.-Feb. 1992: 39–41.

Walters, Ronald. "Clarence Thomas and the Meaning of Blackness." The Black Scholar 215–18.

West, Cornel. "Black Leadership and the Pitfalls of Racial Reasoning." Morrison, *Race-ing Justice* 390–401.

White, Jack. "The Stereotypes of Race." *Time* 21 Oct. 1991: 66.

Williams, Patricia J. "The Bread and Circus Literacy Test." *Ms.* Jan.-Feb. 1992: 35–37.

Wright, Sarah. "The Anti-Black Agenda." The Black Scholar 225–28.

The Rodney King Verdict, the *New York Times*, and the "Normalization" of the Los Angeles Riots; or, What Antifoundationalism Can't Do

Michael Bernard-Donals

With the publication of Richard Rorty's *Philosophy and the Mirror of Nature,* antifoundationalist thinkers could legitimately claim that, with the overthrow of epistemology, hermeneutic analysis could give us the best and most useful information about "the world." Our understanding of the world is created—linguistically inscribed in a process of "redescription"—rather than "discovered" scientifically. So, the antifoundational object of analysis is the *vocabulary* used by people trying to describe their surroundings. It is useless trying to analyze the surroundings themselves, because you can never escape their mediated nature: they're always *descriptions,* and as such all we have to go on are the linguistic schemes that the various interlocutors have at their disposal. What this thesis fails to account for, though, is the object of knowledge, the object of all the descriptions that antifoundationalists like Rorty see as so important. We may be able to reconcile competing normal

© 1994 by *Cultural Critique.* Spring 1994. 0882-4371/94/$5.00.

descriptions (that is, abnormal discourse) by finding a "third vo-cabulary" with which to make descriptions, but the fact remains that there is something being described (and one would think at least in part) that is responsible for the difference of opinion. Moreover, redescribing something is not necessarily going to change it.

The rioting that occurred in Los Angeles during the last days of April and the first days of May 1992 after the verdict in the Rodney King police beating case appears to me to be a perfect example of an event (or, if you prefer, object of knowledge) that cries out for "redescription." My point in this paper will be that the riots cannot be adequately accounted for (or described) con-ventionally or normally and that any reconciliation of competing normal discourses (which could be called, in Rorty's paradigm, an abnormal conversation) that does not account for the event's com-plex overdetermined nature will create a "description" useless for setting an agenda for social praxis. We may be able, in looking at the mainstream print media's descriptions of the event, to see "other human beings as 'one of us,' rather than as 'them,'" through redescription, and in so doing see either "the details about the kinds of suffering being endured by people to whom we had pre-viously not attended," or "the details about what sorts of cruelty we ourselves are capable of" (Rorty, *Contingency* xvi). But these same descriptions have in most cases obfuscated the complex material forces at work in the riots and, rather than allow "moral change and progress," have worked to the contrary for moral complacency and social retrogression.

The first task of this paper, after a brief recapitulation of Rorty's version of antifoundationalism and some of its attendant problems, is to summarize the mainstream print media's accounts of the riots that followed the King verdict on April 29, 1992. For the purposes of this paper, my main source for these descriptions is the *New York Times*'s (and, as backdrop, the three major networks') coverage of the events immediately following the verdict. (My choice is in many ways arbitrary: the analysis of any medium would yield the same kinds of evidence. I chose the *New York* rather than the *Los Angeles Times* for practical reasons as well: it was the only national newspaper available to me at the time I wrote this article.) In elucidating the descriptions from the media, I will suggest that because of the nature of the events they were covering, they could do nothing but "normalize" what was a thoroughly abnormal series of events, and that they sought to "make commensurable" their accounts of material events that were difficult, if not impossible, to understand linguistically. I want to show how the normalization of these events has served, on the one hand, to disseminate information about the riots and conditions in South-Central L.A., but, on the other hand, has seemed to ignore the difficult and complex material conditions that preceded and fueled the events, thereby in effect stalling, not promoting, the social change that Rorty wishes he could encourage. Finally, I want to suggest an alternative analysis—derived from Roy Bhaskar's realist/materialist philosophy of science—that could be used to understand the riots in L.A., one that accounts for its "descriptions" while not discounting the material conditions it purports to describe.

Richard Rorty argues in *Philosophy and the Mirror of Nature* (*PMN*) for the obsolescence of epistemology because it has failed, since Plato and the sophists, to theorize adequately the relation between human cognition and objects of knowledge. He sees language theory as a way to reestablish some of that lost ground by giving philosophy and/or theory a way to consider how language works, but does not presume to understand the way the world works outside considerations of language. Rorty's champion in this enterprise is Donald Davidson, whose "pure" philosophy of language rests on the idea that correspondence is a relation "which has no ontological preferences—it can tie any sort of word to any sort of thing" (300).

> In giving up dependence on the concept of an uninterpreted reality, something outside all schemes and science, we do not relinquish the notion of objective truth—quite the contrary. Given the dogma of a dualism of scheme and reality, we get conceptual relativity, and truth relative to a scheme. Without the dogma, this kind of relativity goes by the board. Of course truth of sentences remains relative to language, but this is as objective as can be. In giving up the dualism of scheme and world, we do not give up the world, but reestablish unmediated touch with the familiar objects whose antics make our sentences and opinions true or false. (qtd. in Rorty, *PMN* 310)

Pure language theory is, as Rorty puts it, a way of "coping" with the world.

Rorty claims that philosophy's recourse to a "world without mirrors" (that is, a world without an overarching epistemology) is to establish hermeneutics, or "an expression of hope that the cultural space left by the demise of epistemology will not be filled— that our culture should become one in which the demand for constraint and confrontation is no longer felt" (*PMN* 315). As opposed to epistemology, which proceeds from the assumption that all contributions to a given discourse are commensurable, hermeneutics begins from the assumption that the set of rules under which such a discussion could be settled on every point where statements seem to conflict is not always possible and is never finally determinable. Hermeneutics is based on a model of discourse in which interlocutors "play back and forth between guesses about how to characterize particular statements or other events, and guesses about the point of the whole equation, until gradually we feel at ease with what was hitherto strange" (319). "What was hitherto strange" is "abnormal discourse," discourse of whatever kind—including scientific discourse—that is conducted within an agreed-upon set of conventions about what counts as a relevant contribution. "Abnormal discourse is what happens when someone joins in the discourse who is ignorant of these conventions or who sets them aside" (320).

Rorty suggests that we operate scientifically when the conversation is taking place in normal discourse, and operate hermeneutically when the conversation takes place abnormally. Citing Gadamer, Rorty notes that when there is no common ground on which to enter into a normal discourse, then —hermeneutically— "all we can do is to show how the other side looks from our own point of view. That is, all we can do is be hermeneutic about the opposition—trying to show how the odd or paradoxical or offensive things they say hang together with the rest of what they want to say, and how what they say looks when put in our own alternative idiom" (*PMN* 364–65). But restating things "in our own language" doesn't change the ground—impossible in Rorty's view— on which we stand to do the talking. In Rorty's view, then, freedom becomes, "through our capacity to *redescribe* [the] world (or relevant bits of it), something which is both positive and humanistically more recognizable—namely the capacity to create, and choose between, different vocabularies—that is, to speak or write 'abnormally'" (Bhaskar 170). By making a new, incommensurable description of herself stick, she makes it true, according to Bhaskar. Thus she creates herself, "which is to say 'overcomes' her previous or past self" (171).

For our purposes, one here needs to ask whether Rorty's distinction between normal and abnormal discourse obviates the existence of what Bhaskar calls "intransitive" objects of knowledge, those objects *about which* we form descriptions and which exist independently of our constructing those descriptions. That is, if, on the one hand, one conducts (scientific) investigation against a background of agreed-upon principles of observation, or, on the other, one introduces a new paradigm with which to produce observations, neither case suggests that there is nothing upon which to agree, but, on the contrary, both suggest a need for a way to describe and observe *something* that exists ontologically. Moreover, Rorty suggests that there is no way to discern whether what Kuhn has called revolutionary science is in fact progressive, since there is nothing objective (extraideological or extralinguistic) to which one can appeal in order to make such a judgment. But in response to this, Bhaskar notes that, though human explanations and interpretations of extra-ideological material must be constructed and therefore contingent, those explanations may be called progressive—by dint of their broader explanatory capacity—since the observations may be repeated and the results reproduced. In a sense, there's no need to suggest that simply because explanation of material objects and phenomena must be contingent, then the objects of that knowledge must also be called contingent.

At issue here is how (or whether) an act of redescription affects the material world in whose midsts a subject stands.

> [T]here is more to coping with social reality than coping with other people. There is coping with a whole host of social entities, including institutions, traditions, networks of relations and the like—which are irreducible to people. In particular, it would be a mistake to think that we had overcome a social structure, like the economy, state or family, if we were success-

ful in imposing our description of it on the community. (Bhaskar 175)

If there's going to be some change beyond simply changing the description of one's relationship to material (that is, extra-ideological) entities—given that these exist, though for Rorty it's hard, if not impossible, to theorize them—then we need a way not just to understand how subjects are formed through discourse but also how they are affected by material constraints—hunger, disease, wealth or poverty, leisure or work, various economic conditions, and so on—that also enter into the way humans engage with one another and construct their subjectivities. We are not necessarily completely determined by such material constraints, but they *are* imposed and we do need to account for them. Real freedom involves understanding how one's ideological surroundings are constructed in the best way one knows how and involves the ability to transform—by actively transforming the ways in which those ideological surroundings work—the ways in which the material conditions affect the subject.

At this point, I want to look at how the mainstream print media—one of the channels through which a large portion of the American public understands its relation to the events in Los Angeles in the spring of 1992—"inscribed" the aftermath of the King verdict. Within a few days of the first violence, the *New York Times*'s writers had largely framed the discussion of the riots in terms of race (not class) and in terms of presidential politics (not community-level social relations), and made Los Angeles out to be a kind of racial "war zone"—terms quite familiar to readers of the *Times,* many of whom are urban and Anglo—without considering the lived life of Angelenos living in South Central. You can begin to see how this happened in a front-page article by Mydans in the *Times* on April 30. A three-column headline, "Los Angeles Policemen Acquitted in Taped Beating," sits over a photograph of officers Wind and Powell embracing while officer Koon looks on, with the hint of a smile on his face. The text of the article reads, in part,

Four Los Angeles police officers were acquitted of assault today in the videotaped beating of a black motorist that stunned the nation. The verdicts immediately touched off a storm of anger and scattered violence in the city.

As residents set scores of fires, looted stores and beat passing motorists in the downtown area and pockets of predominantly black south-central Los Angeles, Mayor Tom Bradley declared a state of emergency, and Gov. Pete Wilson said he would send in the National Guard. . . .

Immediately after the verdict, an unusually impassioned Mayor Bradley appeared on television to appeal for calm in a city where the videotape has come to symbolize complaints about police brutality, racism and street violence.

"Today the system failed us," the Mayor said.

Immediately apparent in this excerpt are the conflicting depictions of what is occurring in Los Angeles and why. Though there is a causal connection established in the two sentences that begin the article between the announcement of the verdicts and the "storm of anger and scattered violence," the following paragraph reinforces the notion that it is the violence that is quickly becoming the "story," not the acquittal itself. Also notable in the connection between the violence and the verdicts is the confusion established by the article's author, Mydans, in Mayor Bradley's television appeal after the verdict. On the one hand, he appeals for calm in an "unusually impassioned" plea; on the other, he notes that "the system failed us." The clearest part of Bradley's statement is that the "system failed us," referring almost certainly to the acquittal of the four officers who, by way of the videotape that captured them beating King, became part and parcel of the "complaints about police brutality, racism, and street violence." His statement, though, is much like the one made by Benjamin Hooks the night the verdict was announced. Hooks, in speaking to the local chapter of the NAACP at Mississippi State University, stated: "[T]his is a joke, a tragedy." That is, coming from a mayor who—along with the governor—is in charge of "keeping the peace," a visceral reaction to the verdicts like the one reported in the *Times* by the mayor is incommensurable with his plea for calm, and expresses an anger and bewilderment that cannot, apparently, be made sense of in his public capacity as mayor. Likewise, the connection between the rioting and the announcement of the verdicts, while understandable (the rioting was, presumably, a pre- or extraverbal expression of anger over the verdict), refuses the linguistic link.

Mydans, in this article, is depicting—in Rorty's terms—a phenomenon or set of phenomena (namely, the violent incidents that occurred in areas of Los Angeles immediately following the King verdict) that are thus far (that is, on April 30, 1992) outside of a conceptual scheme. Mayor Bradley, and Benjamin Hooks, and Seth Mydans and the video newscasters were trying to understand—in Rorty's terms, "cope" with—those phenomena with various "languages" that are incommensurable because the events (the rioting) so far have not been sufficiently placed within a "scheme" or context so they can be discussed. (I remember myself watching television speechlessly, not knowing what to think, as helicopter newscasters filming the beating of motorists and the torching of storefronts were themselves unable to find the words with which to describe what they were filming; they just let the cameras roll.) Rorty suggests that it will be impossible to reconcile the phenomena and their descriptions to some state of affairs upon which everyone can agree. I think it is true that there was on the face of things nothing—no philosophical structure, no apparatus with which to verify the objective "truth" of the cause of the riots or their understandability—outside of our descriptions of the violence in L.A. with which to make sense of it. Rorty, though, goes a step further and says that it *is* possible to reconcile competing *descriptions* of events or phenomena in order to make them available for discussion and understanding. To do so, says Rorty, we "play back and forth between guesses about how to characterize particular statements or other events, and guesses about the point of the whole situation, until gradually we feel at ease with what was hitherto strange" (*PMN* 319). And this is what the *New York Times* reporters already had begun to do as they reported the L.A. riots, and what they continued to do more and more successfully as they began more satisfactorily to "cope" with the riots by inscribing them in "normal" language.

In the same edition of the *Times,* Mydans wrote another article, "Verdicts Set Off a Wave of Shock and Anger," that characterizes the violence spreading through certain parts of the city in much different terms than his front-page article. In section D of

the national edition of the paper, after noting the riots' similarity
to those in 1965 in Watts, he writes,

> Mobs of young men rampaged through the streets [of south-
> central L.A.] overturning and burning vehicles, smashing win-
> dows and spraying graffiti. Police officers, firefighters and
> news helicopters reported being shot at. . . .
>
> [The violence] began moments after the reading of the
> verdicts, in which a suburban jury with no black members ac-
> quitted Sgt. Stacey C. Koon and Officers Laurence M. Powell,
> Timothy E. Wind and Theodore J. Briseno of assault
> charges. . . .
>
> Helicopter and news cameramen showed gripping
> scenes of vicious beatings of motorists by groups of thugs, star-
> tling evocations of the videotaped footage of the beating of
> Mr. King.

This time the language has been more "normalized." This isn't the
language of surprise; this is the language of recognition. The biggest difference between this article and Mydans's first is the addition of an important fact in the sentence describing the verdict: it
was "a suburban jury with no black members" that acquitted the
four police officers of "beating and kicking a black motorist." This
article begins in a way that the section-one article did not, framing
the incident as racial. This is hardly surprising: for the year between the beating and the trial, newspapers and television news
had cast the beatings as racially motivated, citing a rumor that one
of the officers had made a remark about King "looking like an
ape," a rumor that itself nearly caused violence in April and May
of 1991.

Equally troubling is that not only are the riots connected to
what appeared to be a racially motivated beating and an equally
racially motivated acquittal, but the rioters are characterized as
"mobs" of "thugs." This kind of characterization became even
more prevalent in the next day's edition, particularly after the
April 30 beating of truck driver Reginald Denny, a beating that
was different in at least one respect from the beating of Rodney
King: it was televised live. A page 1 article by Jane Gross entitled
"Smell of Fear in Los Angeles" (placed directly below a photograph

of nearly two dozen African-Americans lying face-down in the street with their hands cuffed behind their backs while helmeted police guard them against a background of a graffiti-sprayed wall) includes the following:

> Throughout the sprawling metropolis, even in neighborhoods far from the epicenter of the violence, Angelenos sensed that the next car that passed might carry hooligans waving crowbars and axes, that the next store to burn down could be the one on their corner. This was not a disturbance with a clear perimeter, they came to understand, and while some street corners were safer than others, there was really no place to hide.
>
> The roadways were emptier than usual, but chaotic as a bumper-car ride as nervous motorists navigated a shifting maze of barricades and craned their heads skyward to track the newest plume of smoke rising in the heavy haze. The drivers' eyes darted from side to side, taking the measure of the stranger in the car beside them, plotting new routes as streets and highways closed and reopened, and gazing in horror at the ravaged and smoldering stores that dotted the city.

It is precisely "fear" that is the organizing principle—the "conceptual scheme" in Rorty's terms—of Gross's article, but a fear that is somehow familiar to readers of the paper. This is no longer the language of reportage, of pastiche. Rather, Gross here seems to be drawing a picture, setting the parameters of the discussion, by drawing on a language that makes readers think of, say, Soweto or Kuwait City, where there are "plumes of smoke" and "barricades," where "hooligans wav[e] crowbars and axes." What is true of South Africa and of Kuwait—that there are clearly good guys and bad guys, that in general terms the violence that exists can be portrayed in dichotomous pairs (blacks versus the white government, bad-guy Saddam versus innocent Kuwaitis)—seems to be true here. It is troubling that a discourse, which newspaper reporters have been using in South Africa and during the Gulf War, not to mention Sarajevo and Peru, can be used to "normalize" the situation in Los Angeles. But it is more interesting that, in connecting racial division to the rioting on the same ground that division has been "inscribed" on racial and religious grounds in "other," foreign situations, Gross and Mydans and writers at the *Times* have begun to use the problems of race as a way to make sense of what was going on in Los Angeles, as the "explanation which satisfies our need to tell a coherent causal story about our interactions with the world" (Rorty, *PMN* 341).

Probably one of the most cynical "redescriptions" of the riots and their causes reported by the *Times* was the one put forward by the presidential candidates (notably, George Bush and Bill Clinton) in the heat of the primary election season. As was the case with Mydans's and Gross's articles on the violence, the candidates went from trying to "cope with" a complex phenomenon and its various inscriptions, both in the visual media as well as in the press, to making these various inscriptions "commensurable"—and glossing over the dissonance that resulted from its material complexity—by casting it in political language. The president is reported to have used "words that reflected Americans' reactions to both the verdict and the rioting that followed it" when he noted that "[y]esterdays's verdict in the Los Angeles police case has left us all with a deep sense of personal frustration and anguish. Yet it is important that we respect the law and the legal processes that have been brought to bear in this case" (Mydans "23 Dead"). One can begin to see here an attempt to normalize the riots and their refusal to be inscribed. By the time these words had been uttered, Reginald Denny had already been pulled from his truck in a South-Central street and beaten nearly to death, and the images of that event, as well as others, had been broadcast live to much of the nation. Presumably, this latter beating had been an expression of "personal frustration and anguish" by those who stopped and beat Denny. Asked why he thought Denny had been beaten so severely, Bobby Green—who had helped drive Denny to the hospital after having seen the beating on television—said, "Because he is white" (Stevenson). To the men who beat Denny, it may have been the case that, because he was white and so unaffected by what was going on in L.A. as to be driving though South-Central, he gave the appearance of being out of place, something or someone unrecognizable: something "other." In the same way that the beating of Rodney King was indescribable to the point of having to let the videotape "speak for itself" in the trial, and in the same way that television anchors had to struggle to find words or else simply let

videotape roll on the screen while they sat wordlessly, the appearance of Denny in his truck on that street was abnormal, and so
the young men who beat him were attempting to "cope with" the
phenomenon with an equally abnormal—and nonverbal—action.
That Mr. Bush could be said to speak in words that "reflected"
the reactions seems incongruous at best and just wrong-headed at
worst. It is simply the case—though in Rorty's terms, scientifically
based epistemological explanations might be quite difficult to
come up with for the King verdict and for the riots that followed—
that the attempt to normalize the riots in terms that Americans
could understand does not begin to explain (let alone "reflect")
what was going on out on the street. To then follow this "reflection"
with the statement that we ought nevertheless to "respect the law
and legal processes that have been brought to bear in this case" is
a tremendous contradiction, one that hermeneutics—in which the
"hope of agreement [among possible conversations, or, at least, ex-
citing and fruitful disagreement] is never lost so long as the conversation lasts" (Rorty, *PMN* 318)—cannot easily accommodate.

The political normalization of the aftermath of the King verdict took, as Michael Wines put it in an article in the May 1 edition
of the *Times*, a "partisan turn" (see also Wines, "White House Links
Riots to Welfare;" Apple, "Bush Says Largess Won't Help Cities").

> [T]he President moved further from his initial expres-
> sion of "frustration" about the King verdict and began con-
> demning the rioters. . . . "We must condemn the violence and
> we must make no apology for the rule of law or the need to
> live by it," he said.
> [Clinton later said in a speech to an integrated crowd in
> Birmingham:] "No nation would permit what's going on in
> Los Angeles tonight, where the automatic and semi-automatic
> weapons in the hands of lawless vandals who are using this
> King verdict as a simple excuse to go wreak violence and shoot
> people are running unchecked in the streets. And it is wrong."

In Seth Mydans's banner-headlined May 1 article, he notes that
"the verdict itself seemed mostly forgotten in the energy of the
vandalism and looting that continued throughout the day and into
the night" of April 30. It appears, similarly, that for both Clinton
and Bush, the verdict—or, at least whatever it was that "caused"
the rioting—was forgotten amidst the discourse that tries desper-

ately to move the force of the events that are taking place away
from the largely unverbalizable, uninscribable and toward a rhetoric that valorizes the law which, in the words of Ronald Dworkin
(an antagonist of Rorty and Fish), inscribes "innumerable decisions, structures, conventions, and practices [which] are [its] history" (159). Although it could be argued—and Dworkin does—
that it may *not* be the case that there is a beginning to the "chain"
of decisions that produce the law's history, the language of the law
(and here Fish and Dworkin agree) still "articulates consistency"
(qtd. in Fish 385). And it is this consistency that is particularly
problematic, since it was the "rule of law" that could, in the eyes of
many, be seen as directly responsible not only for the "failure" of
the jury to convict the four police officers who beat Rodney King,
but for the beating itself. The convenience of terms like "lawless
vandals" or, in another article, "thugs," does reconcile two irrecon-
cilable phenomena—the apparent lawlessness of the verdict and
the equal disregard of the law that establishes public tranquility—
but to use it on the same day that the president asks the residents
to obey and respect the "rule of law" empties it of all its power to
signify, to normalize, the context of the discussion taking place in
the *Times*.

As I've tried to show, redescription in antifoundational terms
does work to reconcile incommensurable descriptions of "the
world," like the riots in Los Angeles in the spring of 1992. But
those descriptions—*because* they attempt to discursively bridge the
gap between complex understandings of the world—make it difficult to understand the *objects* of those descriptions, namely, the
material conditions of existence in Los Angeles and the rest of the
country after the acquittal of the officers accused of beating King.
Neither Bhaskar nor I will dispute the Rortyan/Kuhnian thesis
that scientific (or any systematic) accounting for phenomena is
contingent, or that those accounts are inextricably bound with the
socially constructed linguistic accounts of the same phenomena.
Bhaskar's project, though, does dispute what on Rorty's account
of things turns out to be a subsumption of scientific investigation
to hermeneutic constraint. Rather than suggest that science operates hermeneutically, Bhaskar proposes realism as an alternative
to hermeneutics, which entails a theory of "the nature of the being
... of the objects investigated by science—roughly to the effect
that they exist and act *independently* of human activity, and hence

of both sense-experience and thought" (13; emphasis added). While it is a worthwhile project to understand how to create a language through which humans can engage in a conversation about, say, the L.A. riots, it is equally—if not more—important to understand how (or to what extent) we can understand the objects of knowledge in such an event and the ways in which those objects *resist* becoming "normalized" in such a "conversation of mankind."

Bhaskar's analysis of phenomena like the L.A. riots is modeled on scientific experimentation, in which humans "co-determine, or are causally co-responsible for, a pattern of events" (15). As they experiment upon objects or phenomena, scientists meticulously control the conditions they work under, to "identify the mode of operation of structures, mechanisms and processes which they do not produce." When successful, experiments make causal laws, patterns of events, and so on intelligible. Important in this model is the idea that, through creating "constant conjunctions" such as these, scientists are "redescribing" phenomena that *don't* take place in constant conjunctions. We can reproduce a sequence of events to isolate a particular mechanism, but this mechanism can (and does) occur through the same sequence of events *not* produced through human interference, but rather "in nature." These mechanisms (we can think of them as "tendencies") are "intransitive objects of scientific inquiry," objects that act independently of their identification by humans. "Causal laws" are descriptive of the mechanism. The "transitive" dimension—or epistemology—is the specific historical and social form of knowledge (i.e., description) that we have of such objects or mechanisms or phenomena (for another view, see Davenport 158–72.)

The implication of this for the purposes of examining an event like the Los Angeles riots—and in the investigation of linguistic events more generally—is that it isn't necessarily the case that "descriptions" or "redescriptions" of phenomena or mechanisms (like the King beating verdict and the riots that followed it) are purely contingent. We can describe the verdict and the riots (i.e., the events to which we have access); we can inscribe those events with a vocabulary to which we also have access; in so doing we can determine the forms that the riots take on (in terms of genre—newspaper reportage, war correspondence, framed narratives—and in terms of material *content*); perhaps most importantly, we can describe the particular component parts or elements that comprise the riots (that is, their political, legal, social "spins"); and we can do all of this *without* equating those descriptions with "the way the world works apart from our understanding of it." What we—or Seth Mydans, or Bill Clinton, or Benjamin Hooks—may observe and write about the riots may not be "the way it is out there," but those descriptions nevertheless can be said to "rede-scribe" in the transitive dimension (in potentially varying ways) those things that take place as intransitive objects of knowledge, objects that *are* subject to scientific investigation and which *do* operate according to verifiable laws. We require another kind of investigation of the phenomena, one that takes place outside the "conversation" and that first looks at those places where the conversation explicitly fails to make commensurable certain aspects of the phenomena.

This other kind of investigation is precisely a *scientific* investigation. It should be seen as a "three-phase schema," in which a phenomenon is identified, explanations for the phenomenon are constructed and empirically tested, thereby identifying (or "describing") the mechanisms at work. This explanation then becomes the phenomenon to be tested and so on. If in the first phase of this schema we get a regularity through experimentation, it is the *result* of something, and what's imagined in the second phase isn't just imaginary but can come to be known as the "real" (see also Rorty, *Contingency* 18). Mydans's or Wines's descriptions of the destruction caused by the riots are absolutely not "imaginary" (though they are derived from the imagination just as any *scientific* description is). But you *can* move from "knowledge of manifest phenomena to knowledge, produced by means of antecedent knowledge, of the structures that generate them" (Bhaskar 20). So linguistically inscribed knowledge (like the kind we gather as we read the *New York Times*, *Time*, or *Ebony*) can be thought of as knowledge derived from descriptions of phenomena (i.e., the King beating and the verdict and the rioting), phenomena that can be and have been described as structures that generated that knowledge and so on (see Kuhn, esp. 21; Bhaskar 19). Linguistic knowledge has a direct relation to knowledge of phenomena, that is, knowledge that we can think of as being *scientifically derived*, and this relation cannot be left out when we try to understand the resistance phenomena exhibit in written communication (see Bhaskar 23–24).

What's at stake is the degree to which people can change their material circumstances through a redescription of those circumstances. The realist philosophy of scientific inquiry, over and against the Rortyan worldview, implies that scientific inquiry must be understood as having a social component; but that the social component must be understood scientifically: phenomena like the riots, and the inscription of such phenomena, are not simply a function of the social. That social function is also material, and we need to understand how material objects and entities work. For antifoundationalism, redescription (or reinterpretation) is a valuable human act because it leads to human emancipation. By inscribing the complex events that comprise the riots in Los Angeles, the newspapers "created" the riots, at least insofar as the reading public had access to them in a language that would allow them to take part in the descriptive act themselves. But such redescription doesn't change the material constraints by which you are bound because in antifoundationalism's view science is inadequate to the task of fixing, once and for all, the nature of material reality. So even if we wanted to say something about those descriptions' relations to "scientifically determinable reality," science's redescriptions are equally in flux, and so any redescription is apt to be overturned by some other incommensurable redescription, thus voiding any emancipatory properties of the previous one. What you end up with, then, is a "redescription" of the riots in Los Angeles, and of the beating that presumably was its proximate cause, but no way to see how changing that "scheme" is going to change anything else.

I'd like to cite one more example of how the media's normalization of the events in Los Angeles "normalized" the riots. I do so as a way to discuss Bhaskar's materialist analysis of the language used to inscribe the riots as well as of the riots themselves, and to put forward a theory of *change*. This final example—a set of descriptive pieces in the *Times* narrating the looting of several stores, in which a number of the looters were "interviewed" by reporters—serves to show, on the one hand, how even the voices of those taking part in the riots and lootings are themselves "normalizations" further normalized by the reporters inscribing the event and, on the other hand, how the polyvalent languages here can be seen as *effects* of social structures which are complexly overdetermined and must be described not merely in hermeneutic terms as "voices in a conversation," but also as having a *material* (i.e., physical) aspect and material constraints. As Bhaskar notes,

> social structures are concept-dependent, but not merely conceptual. Thus a person could not be said to be "unemployed" or "out of work" unless she and the other relevant agents possessed some (not necessarily correct or fully adequate) concept of that condition and were able to give some sort of account of it, namely, to describe (or redescribe) it. But it *also* involves, for instance, her being physically excluded from certain sites, definite locations in space and time. (174)

Required, first, is the "ontological tenet," in the words of Paisley Livingston, "that there is a mind-independent reality having entities that take part in causal interactions," and an "epistemological tenet," which holds that "these things are knowable, albeit partially and by successive approximations" (90). Science is the way to describe the tendencies exhibited by agents and structures, one that functions both in the transitive dimension (that is, whose *descriptions* are socially constructed) as well as upon intransitive objects of knowledge. It is by suggesting how the utterances that narrate the Los Angeles riots are descriptions of real objects and real structures that we can get past the Rortyan impasse and begin to articulate a positive praxis based on the knowledge such an investigation yields (see Sprinker, vis-à-vis Livingston, 51–52).

In his article dated May 1, Mydans reports that "it was clear from the words of the rioters, as well as black elected officials and others, that their anger ran far deeper than reaction to the acquittal" of the four officers. In the same article, though, his choice of words is telling: though "entire blocks of buildings were left in ruins," some other parts of town "took on the atmosphere of a street party as black, white, Hispanic and Asian residents mingled to share in a carnival of looting." I don't think I'm pushing things here by suggesting that Mydans's use of the term "carnival" evokes the Bakhtinian connotation: an overturning of traditional or sanctioned behaviors with an aim toward outwardly mocking (and subverting) the dominant ideology. What is interesting, though, about the article is that it does not suggest what the "deeper" causes of the riots are. Though certainly sparked by the verdict, community leaders and the rioters themselves suggested that there was more to it than simply letting off steam at the injustice of the verdict announcement. And yet, at least in this article, there is no way to read the riots except by understanding them as a kind of carnival in which the dominant ideology—in this case, the one that has established the legal system and the state which "provides police protection"—is attacked with something like glee. I'm trying to suggest that, though Seth Mydans at the *Times,* and community and city leaders in Los Angeles, understand that there's more going on than just the venting of anger over the announcement of the verdict, they're having a hard time inscribing the complexity of it. Describing this situation by calling it a "carnival" in the antifoundationalist paradigm that conflates redescription with scientific observation (the epistemic with the ontic) runs the risk of obfuscating the complexities involved in the "carnival" atmosphere as simply one of many possible observations of the rioting. But I'd like to suggest, along the lines of Bhaskar's argument, that there are material as well as ideological "constraints" to such a description, and it is these constraints (particularly the material ones) sacrificed by Rorty's antifoundationalism that are crucial to a materialist analysis of the riots themselves.

Such an analysis entails understanding that there are at least two "redescriptions" involved in the narratives that "tell" the riots. The first is that of the rioters themselves. Bobby Green's assessment of the cause for Reginald Denny's beating, "[b]ecause he was white," is one way to understand the highly abnormal event: in his "normalization" of it, you can make sense of the beating by being provided with a rather simple equation: Reginald Denny was white, and those who beat him were black; Rodney King was black, and he was beaten by white police officers; because the white officers were granted a certain license to beat King (and presumably other black motorists) by the verdict, then the young men who beat Denny had a license to beat him because of *his* race. Taking into account the other "normalization," the question that frames Bobby Green's response (why do you think Denny was beaten so severely?), this "conversation" casts the Los Angeles riots—or at least this particular episode—as racially motivated. Both interlocutors are attempting to cope with the utterances (and in this case, actions) of other humans by asking and answering questions that are complexly determined, but whose responses belie that complexity. Now, it is true that for any one person on the street whom you'd ask about the causes of the riots (or of King's or Denny's beating), you'd get several different responses. But these responses are the *effects* of certain physical states and real tendencies that are similarly complex but which are, far from "descriptions," responsible in varying degrees for the utterances themselves, and which must be investigated—regardless of how "partially or by successive approximations"—in order to move past simple redescription and onto some positive praxis. To do so, one would have, for example, to examine the social forms that sanction the "carnival," and how the *forms* the carnival takes can be seen as effects of certain other social forms which in turn must be mapped scientifically.

Reading Michael Marriott's article dated May 1, where the inability to "speak" the riots becomes most clear, you can see not only the Rortyan impasse, but also ways to move beyond it. Entitled "The Sacking of a Neighborhood," the article describes some of the looting on Western Avenue. Among its descriptions are interviews with one young man looting a supermarket, and another walking in the center of Western Avenue. It is not so much the way the interviews are couched; rather, the words of those being interviewed speak most clearly to the problems inherent in the view that it is the contextualization of *discourse* that should occupy the time of people analyzing language events. These words defy easy contextualization:

> Near the ABC supermarket, a young man who would only identify himself by his last name, Master, made several trips through a shattered window with arms full of groceries before discovering that he had a problem. He had grabbed so many boxes of a breakfast cereal, Cinnamon Mini Buns, that he could not close the trunk of his car.
> "I don't even eat this stuff," he said. "I'm going to give it away to people who don't have any food."
> But that, he said, was not why he stole the food. Speaking in hyper-animated gestures, his voice a piercing scream, Mr. Master explained that he looted because he wanted white people across the United States to know how angry blacks

were about the acquittal of four white police officers in the beating of Rodney G. King, and about their general condition in this country.

"This is the '90s," he screamed. "They killed the first King," he said, referring to the assassination of the Rev. Dr. Martin Luther King. "Now they want to mess over the second King," he said, referring to Rodney King. As looters packed their goods in their cars with the unhurried ease of weekend shoppers, Mr. Master looked up from his car's trunk and whispered, "We have been cool too long."

These words, too, resist contextualization:

Along Western Avenue a stocky black man in knee-length shorts and a blue cotton shirt paraded along the median line. Wearing dark glasses and a cap that said "DESERT STORM," he aimed to look menacing.

As cars passed, he would thrust his right arm up in a clenched fist salute; while his left hand rode the inside of his waistband where he said he had a pistol. Its outline could be plainly seen.

"All of this is a statement of unity," said the 33-year-old man who refused to identify himself. "This," he said as he scanned the tangle of police and firefighters and looters against a backdrop of burning storefronts some 20 yards away, "is about the black community coming together."

In each of these two descriptions, one can see two vastly different "impulses" at work. The first is the impulse that might be characterized as the ideological: in Rorty's words, it is equivalent to the attempt "to find the proper set of terms into which all contributions should be translated if agreement is to become possible" (*PMN* 315). This is the impulse of the writer of the article, the attempt to make sense of the language of the unnamed or partially named interviewees (the man with the trunkful of cereal identifies himself as "Master"). In the first description he moves from the language of the first utterance ("I'm going to give [the food] away to people who don't have any food") to the second ("This is the '90s. They killed the first King") with a transition that may or may not have been uttered by Master himself, a transition that marks the connection between the injustice evidenced in the acquittal of the four white police officers and the injustice implied in the hunger of those living in South-Central Los Angeles. There also exists the link between the two "Kings," established by Master and bolstered not only by Michael Marriott, but also by other writers for the *Times* who refer to the riots that erupted after the assassination of Martin Luther King in 1968. In the second description, the unnamed man walking the centerline of Western Avenue is even more explicit: "[T]his is a statement of unity," he yells, though it is unclear what "this" refers to. In the language of both the authors of the articles and of the interviewees themselves, you can see the attempt to "find the proper set of terms" with which to justify looting and protest, and by which to understand the decades-long oppression of an underclass.

But this is the other impulse—the one working against "newspaper writing" or "justification" or any other attempt to rationalize the phenomena described—that is largely extra- or preverbal (and that evidences, in Bhaskar's terms, those objects or events that exist whether we identify them or not). It is the impulse that defies categorization or contextualization and thereby pulls away from agreement altogether. The most obvious signs of the ambivalence in the descriptions are the gestures not only of Master but also of the gun-toting man on Western Avenue. Master is "speaking in hyper-animated gestures," an odd mixture of voice and the body, with his voice sounding, to Michael Marriott at least, like a "piercing scream." But in his use of the assassination of Dr. King to justify his looting of the ABC supermarket for food he doesn't eat, he also inscribes two widely divergent and apparently contradictory desires. It is an expression of anger: the city of Los Angeles, whose legal system let the four officers go and whose police state allowed them to beat a man senseless, must see the rage that such an unreasonable set of actions produces ("he looted because he wanted white people across the United States to know how angry blacks were about the acquittal" and "about their general condition in this country"). It is a reaction to Master's immediate circumstances—he is a black man who, in the words of James Buford, president of the Urban League of Greater St. Louis, felt "powerless and disgusted, betrayed ... by an American dream he had believed in" (Wilkerson)—a reaction that is *not* reasonable if you look for a causal or necessary relationship between the *expression* and the phenomenon that caused the expression. If the looting is in fact a carnival of violence, it is an inversion of the power police officers have in relation to those presumed guilty or violent, one that transgresses the license the state has to control its subjects. But if it is a carnival, it is also highly contradictory expression that refuses translation or a "normalizing strategy:" Master's actions are at once destructive and meaningful, sanctioned (normalized by the media as expressions "like those that followed the assassination of Dr. Martin Luther King" and observed and "contained" by riot troops patrolling the city) and revolutionary (see Stallybrass and White 1–26). And it also speaks to the material conditions perceived by Master, in which "people . . . don't have any food" and would be happy to get any food they could, even if it is, ridiculously, Cinnamon Mini Buns cereal.

It's these material conditions—the "objective constraints that operate on humankind in society and in nature"—that require investigation in order to understand the events in Los Angeles and (possibly) to prevent them from happening again. The contradictions exhibited in the language of Master, of the unnamed man walking Western Avenue's centerline, of the presidential candidates and the others trying to "cope" with what took place in Los Angeles last spring, are the result of structures that are likewise contradictory and complexly overdetermined. The law that protects the residents of Westwood against looters is the same law that allowed four white officers to be acquitted for the beating of Rodney King. The anger that was initially aimed at the "system" that favored whites quickly turned to anger at Korean-American shopkeepers who were perceived as biased against African-Americans (Korean-Americans whose parents may have purchased their stores from the parents of some of the looters in the wake of the Watts riots; see Kim 232n5). As the black community's "statement of unity" for the man walking Western Avenue, the looting was also a statement of the demise of the black community's belief in the "American dream" for James Buford, president of the St. Louis chapter of the Urban League.

What you see, in these passages from the *Times,* is the breakdown of the impulse to make reasonable those things that appear "abnormal" and the emergence of what Homi Bhabha, in another context, calls "nonsense": inscriptions that "baffle the communicable verities of culture with their refusal to translate" (204). To

paraphrase Bhabha, the descriptions here of the events on Western Avenue in South-Central Los Angeles display an "alienation"
between the totalizing language that attempts to make sense of
those events in terms of "riots" or "violence" or "carnival" and the
function of language as expressing those things which are inexpressible, which in Rorty's terms are "incommensurable" but
which, in our attempt to make them commensurable by providing
them with a new context, slip away into something else (see, for
example, Bhabha 203–06). Instead of a way, either in writing the
language of the events surrounding the riots or in theorizing it,
to express those impulses, we need to examine, if only with the
understanding that any data we gather will lead to contingent con-
clusions, the physical constraints that make for the different discourses in the first place.

Realist philosophy sets down four principles that might be followed by antifoundationalism and that can serve as a way to see
how scientific analysis can help generate data with which to examine the events in Los Angeles. First we must recognize, as Bhaskar
suggests, the *sui generis* reality and causal efficacy of social forms,
on a strictly physical criterion, in terms of their making a difference to the state of the material world which occurs in any event
(174). It is, after all, scientists who produce the constant conjunctions through which scientific laws are formulated, just as it is
people who work for the *Times* or *Newsweek* or those who read the
presses or watch the news reports on television who observe and
redescribe "the world." It is those redescriptions, both scientific
and nonscientific, that are then reformulated, retested, and rede-
scribed. We should understand that reinscriptions of the riots in
terms of class, of race, of politics and power aren't just "made-up"
ways of seeing the world, but that they in fact have a *physical* aspect
to them. "Redescribing" these aspects isn't simply a matter of re-
contextualizing the conversation—letting us talk about it in more
or less commonsense terms—but in fact is having a physical effect
on those doing the talking, just as watching the beatings of Rodney
King and Reginald Denny had a physical effect both on the viewer
as well as on the individuals themselves. In the writing and in the
negotiation involved in reading this writing, we renegotiate—in
the scientific sense, re*formulate*—social (and by definition physical)
reality, and in doing so, the social whole will in turn make a difference within the larger (material) world.

Second, we must grant the existence of objective social structures, "dependent on the reproductive and transformative agency
of human beings" (174). These structures aren't created by human
beings, but instead preexist us, and their existence "is a necessary
condition for any intentional act" (174). Inasmuch as we are born
into families, or classes, or neighborhoods (South-Central Los
Angeles, or Kennebunkport, or Columbus), and inasmuch as we
are born physically male or female, we are to this extent always
already inside social structures. And to the extent that we redescribe our material surroundings, we do so as a condition of our
being so circumscribed materially. Put another way, social life always has a material dimension (and, according to Bhaskar, leaves
some physical trace), and it's these physical traces that can and
should be examined scientifically along with linguistic traces. One
of the headlines for an article in the *Times* on May 2 read as follows:
"38 Bodies at the County Morgue Reflect the Diversity of a Torn
City," and the story noted that, in the morgue the previous morn-
ing there were the bodies of 15 African-Americans, 11 Hispanics,
5 whites, 2 Asians, and 5 people of "unknown ethnic origin." Aside
from the irony of the word "diversity" linked to 38 dead bodies,
just the headline on this article suggests that we're not dealing only
with words here: 38 people from perhaps 38 different families living 38 separate lives ended sometime before May 2, 1992, and
there are aspects to those lives—"physical traces"—that must be
examined in order to get past the mystification the language of the
article offers. More to the point, there exist social and economic
"tendencies" that are material, and that preexist our understanding and "description" of them, and these also must be accounted
for as objects that may *disrupt* our capability of describing them.
Antifoundationalism often leaves unexamined the very material
constraints that in many ways determine what gets written and
what gets seen.

Third, Rorty's notion that social interaction consists of "coping with other persons" needs to be reformulated, since we cope
not just with persons but also with social structures and the physical world in which they reside. We need to "find and disentangle
webs of relations in social life, and engage explanatory critiques of
the practices which sustain them" (Bhaskar 175). In reading the
Times, or any description of the world, for that matter, we need to

see language not simply as a medium through which to redescribe "the world," but also as a metalinguistic reformulation of a real set of events or phenomena of which the author has (physical) experience. As a result, we examine not just "the world" as a set of objects of knowledge, but also the author as an agent of social practices which can be examined and analyzed materially and scientifically. We've seen, in the preceding analysis of some of the reports of the riots that were written in the *New York Times,* instances of breakdowns in the narrative that was supposed to make sense of physical occurrences in terms readers could recognize. Instead of suggesting that this breakdown is inevitable (particularly in cases of "abnormal" events which appear by definition to be extra- or prelinguistic in origin), we should see the language as the product of active agents, agents that, in uttering these reactions, produce a materially and socially real set of circumstances that can be examined scientifically. Moreover, we also need to reformulate "coping with nature," because we redescribe the social world *within* the natural world and the ways it works, and we may need to recognize some of these "absolutes" (like the fact of the nonrenewability of natural resources like oil, or like the fact that an underclass exists and has certain characteristics, etc.). The social world and the physical world, both subject to investigation, are inextricably intertwined. By changing one you inevitably change the other.

Fourth, Bhaskar notes that the social sciences are not rendered redundant by writing as "redescription," since we need to be aware of not just motivation and skills but also of "unacknowledged conditions and unintended consequences," both of which can be discussed in scientific as well as in "hermeneutic" terms (177). We may be able to rewrite or redescribe the circumstances that immediately change by uttering "thugs must respect the law," or by critiquing, say, enterprise zones in urban areas. But there are other material circumstances that change, as a result, which we will not be aware of immediately, and these circumstances—because we are unaware of them—cannot be examined hermeneutically, but certainly can be observed and tested scientifically.

Bhaskar suggests a fifth principle: to paraphrase, insofar as human agents desire freedom, it will involve trying to understand (or explain) the character of socially conditioned entities in order that those entities might be changed. That is, it involves "a theory of those [entities'] constraints and, insofar as freedom is feasible, a practice of liberation or liberty preservation" (178). We need not only to understand the linguistic constraints upon human agents, but the physical ones as well; and we need to formulate a theory of change *based upon* such an understanding. Charles Hagen writes in a feature on the video images of the King beating that:

> [A]s the verdict in the case demonstrates, the videotape remains open to interpretation. While most Americans still regard the tape as irrefutable evidence of police brutality, the jury that acquitted the indicted officers obviously saw it differently. This puzzling fact goes to the heart of the matter: that photographic images of all sorts remain essentially ambiguous, and must be anchored in a convincing narrative before they take on a specific meaning. And most images can be made to fit into a number of widely disparate narratives.

"People see what they are conditioned to see," says one wag (Alter 43), and this is just the point: narratives of the same object of knowledge differ. It's not enough to simply try to find a way, hermeneutically, to continue the conversation in order to get as many individuals to participate as possible, because you end up with statements like this, from a *Newsweek* article: "Was the trouble in L.A. a 'riot' or an 'uprising?' Both, actually, but it takes common language and trust to say that." More than "common language" or "trust," we need to understand the *reasons* for doing so through not just the transformation of descriptions, but also through "the transformation of structures rather than just the amelioration of states of affairs" (Bhaskar 178). Only in this way can we get past seeing the riots in terms of redescription and on to suggesting how we can transform the structures that led to them. This last is something antifoundationalism surely cannot do.

Note

I'd like to thank Robert Fulcher, at Mississippi State University, whose seven-page paper, "Richard Rorty's Epistemology and Hermeneutics: Understanding Rodney King *vs.* LAPD," generated the idea for this article; it is with his permission that I have written it. I'd also like to thank Linda Frost, Ellen Gardiner, and Matthew Little for their valuable comments and suggestions.

Works Cited

Alter, Joseph. "TV and the 'Fireball.'" *Newsweek* 11 May 1992: 43.

Apple, R.W. "Bush Says Largess Won't Help Cities." *New York Times* 7 May 1992: A1+.

Bakhtin, Mikhail M. *Rabelais and His World*. Bloomington: U of Indiana P, 1968.

Bhabha, Homi. "Articulating the Archaic: Notes on Colonial Nonsense." *Literary Theory Today*. Ed. Peter Collier and Helga Geyer-Ryan. Ithaca: Cornell UP, 1990. 203–18.

Bhaskar, Roy. *Reclaiming Reality*. New York/London: Verso, 1989.

Davenport, Edward. "The Scientific Spirit." *Literary Theory's Future(s)*. Ed. Joseph Natoli. Urbana: U of Illinois P, 1989. 152–94.

Davidson, Donald. "On the Very Idea of a Conceptual Scheme." *Proceedings of the American Philosophical Association* 47 (1973–74): 1–16.

Dworkin, Ronald. "How Law Is Like Literature." *A Matter of Principle*. Cambridge: Cambridge UP, 1985.

Fish, Stanley. *Doing What Comes Naturally: Rhetoric, Change, and the Practice of Theory in Literary and Legal Studies*. Durham: Duke UP, 1989.

Gross, Jane. "Smell of Fear in Los Angeles." *New York Times* 1 May 1992: 1+.

Hagen, Charles. "Photography View: The Power of a Video Image Depends on the Caption." *New York Times* 10 May 1992: H32.

Kim, Elaine H. "Home is Where the *Han* Is: A Korean-American Perspective on the Los Angeles Upheavals." *Reading Rodney King/Reading Urban Uprising*. Ed. Robert Gooding-Williams. New York: Routledge, 1993. 215–35.

Kuhn, Thomas. *The Structure of Scientific Revolutions*. Chicago: U of Chicago P, 1970.

Livingston, Paisley. *Literary Knowledge: Humanistic Inquiry and the Philosophy of Science*. Ithaca: Cornell UP, 1988.

Marriott, Michael. "The Sacking of a Neighborhood: An Orgy of Looting, a Carnival of Crime." *New York Times* 1 May 1992: A21.

Mydans, Seth. "Los Angeles Policemen Acquitted in Taped Beating." *New York Times* 30 April 1992: 1+.

———. "23 Dead After 2d Day of Los Angeles Riots." *New York Times* 1 May 1992: 1+.

———. "Verdicts Set Off a Wave of Shock and Anger." *New York Times* 30 April 1992: D22.

Rorty, Richard. *Contingency, Irony, and Solidarity*. Cambridge: Cambridge UP, 1990.

———. *Philosophy and the Mirror of Nature*. Princeton: Princeton UP, 1979.

Sprinker, Michael. "Knowing, Believing, Doing; Or Why Do We Study Literature and What Is It Anyway?" *ADE Bulletin* 98 (Spring 1991): 46–55.

Stallybrass, Peter, and Allon White. *The Politics and Poetics of Transgression*. Ithaca: Cornell UP, 1986.

Stevenson, Richard W. "Blacks Beat White Truck Driver as TV Cameras Record the Scene." *New York Times* 1 May 1992: A21.

"38 Bodies at the County Morgue Reflect the Diversity of a Torn City." *New York Times* 2 May 1992: A7.

Wilkerson, Isabel. "Acquittal in Beating Raises Fears Over Race Relations." *New York Times* 1 May 1992: A23.

Wines, Michael. "A Bush–Clinton Exchange on the Riots Turns Partisan." *New York Times* 1 May 1992: A22.

———. "White House Links Riots to Welfare." *New York Times* 5 May 1992: A1+.

Talk About Racism: Framing a Popular Discourse of Race on *Oprah Winfrey*

Janice Peck

On Martin Luther King's birthday in 1992, Oprah Winfrey introduced her talk show audience to the first installment of "Racism in 1992," a year-long, 13-episode treatment of a problem that she said "is alive all over this country." A few months later, South-Central Los Angeles was in flames—the coverage of the "L.A. riots" following the Rodney King verdict framed largely in terms of racial tensions between African-American residents, Korean business owners, and the white police force and jury.[1] Days after the uprising, Winfrey taped two shows on location in Los Angeles that became part of the racism series. In these volatile sessions, intended "to give people who rarely get heard a chance to speak," a diverse L.A. audience talked about the verdict, the riots, the judicial system, and race relations. These episodes are atypical talk show fare, yet share features across the racism series that express what I propose is a popular discourse about race. Produced in and reproduced by the *Oprah Winfrey* show, this discourse draws on a deeper societal "common sense" about race upon which the series is constructed. Hall suggests that among their ideological

© 1994 by *Cultural Critique*. Spring 1994. 0882-4371/94/$5.00.

work, the media "construct for us a definition of what *race* is, what meaning the imagery of race carries, and what the 'problem of race' is understood to be" ("Whites" 35). Based on interpretive analysis of transcripts and videotapes of the 13 episodes, I argue that "Racism in 1992" defines, signifies, and problematizes racism within liberal, therapeutic, and religious frames of meaning deeply embedded in Western history that shape and constrain our understanding of the politics of race.

In keeping with the topical structure of daytime talk shows,[2] the series included the following subtopics: "Racism in the Neighborhood" (January); "I Hate Your Interracial Relationship" (February); "Japanese Americans: The New Racism" (March); "Are We All Racist?" (April); "The Rodney King Verdict I and II" (May); "My Parent Is a Racist" (June); "An Experiment in Racism" (July); "Too Little, Too Late: Native Americans Speak Out" (August); "I Refuse to Date My Own Race" (September); "Unsolved Hate Crimes" (October); "White Men Who Fear Black Men" (October); and "Follow-Up" (November).[3]

Ideology and Discourses of Meaning

Oprah Winfrey is the top-rated daytime television talk show with an estimated 14 million American viewers daily; three-quarters of the predominantly white audience are women aged 18–54. Distributed in the United States and 55 other countries by the King World syndicate, the show has won 13 Daytime Emmy Awards and four NAACP Image Awards (*Oprah Facts;* Freeman).[4] The program's popularity, the intensity of viewers' relationship with the show and Winfrey, and the growing role of talk shows in popular politics, make it a worthy subject for analysis (Gallup and Newport). As founder and head of Harpo Productions, the first African-American to host a national talk show, the first woman to own and produce her own program, and the richest woman in show business, Winfrey is one of the nation's most visible black public figures (Newcomb and Chatsky). Her program has often treated racial issues, and she actively promotes black artistic and educational endeavors. At the same time, her popularity and ratings necessarily cross racial lines—a fact that she can't afford to

ignore.[5] *Ebony* magazine stated in 1991 that a handful of black en-
tertainers like Winfrey, Bill Cosby, and Arsenio Hall have managed
to "transcend race" in terms of their mass appeal ("Television" 52).
In their study of *Cosby* viewers, Jhally and Lewis suggest that such
transcendence involves white viewers overlooking the fact that the
cast is African-American, identifying with the Huxtables instead as
a "typical American family." Black viewers, in contrast, identified
with the show precisely because it's about an African-American
family. My preliminary interviews with female viewers of *Oprah
Winfrey* indicate a similar pattern. So far, white viewers say Winfrey's race is "not important" to them, while black respondents say
it is central. White viewers note, however, that Winfrey's race becomes prominent when the topic is race-related. I believe her
"transcendence of race" requires a more delicate balancing act
than is necessary for Bill Cosby or Arsenio Hall because her program periodically focuses on racial issues. Winfrey must be exqui-
sitely sensitive to the potential for alienating her majority white
audience; this was apparent in her cautious anxiety in the "Experiment in Racism" episode and attests to her awareness of how frag-
ile the "transcendence of race" really is.

Winfrey has been described as a comforting, nonthreatening
bridge between black and white cultures—a perception Cloud
links to popular accounts of Winfrey that minimize and/or de-
politicize her race, presenting her instead as an exemplar of American success.[6] Winfrey herself appears ambivalent on the issue—
sometimes embracing, sometimes minimizing her blackness
(Cloud 16–17). Part of her comforting quality may stem from her
public rejection of black political activism and the Civil Rights
movement (Cloud 8). Her gender may also figure into her broad
acceptance because black women are seen by many whites as less
threatening than are black men. And, as a woman hosting a genre
directed at a female audience, Winfrey is expected to frame the
"topic" of racism in terms of its emotional, interpersonal dimensions, thereby reducing the potential for political conflict. Given
the show's need to please its audience, maintain its "advertiser
friendly" reputation, and not jeopardize Winfrey's mass appeal,
the racism series must seek to bridge or erase divisions among
viewers and participants even as it tackles a profoundly divisive
issue in American society.

The treatment of racism in the series draws on, and is re-fracted through, ideologies of race already present in society; these are part of the material social conditions into which we are born, and within which we acquire racialized identities and identifica-tions, develop an understanding of others based on racial position-ing, and interpret social relationships through racial categories.[7] Both the objects of talk and the speaking subjects in the show are mediated by these ideologies which construct "positions of identi-fication and knowledge" and thus "subjects for action." As Hall says, "We have to 'speak through' the ideologies which are active in our society and which provide us a means of 'making sense' of social relations and our place in them" ("Whites" 32) Further, ideologies "do not consist of isolated and separate concepts, but in the articulation of different elements into a distinctive set or chain of meanings" (31). The choice of elements and the way they're linked play an important role in constructing what's taken to be a "common sense" view of the "problem" of race and its related "solutions." For example, the articulation of racism with an innate cognitive operation implies a different sort of problem and solu-tion than when racism is linked with institutionalized discrimina-tion, or economic exploitation, or a violation of spiritual order. As Miles argues, "the concept of racism is therefore the object of polit-ical and ideological struggle" (4).

My analysis focuses on this process of articulation. I propose that the series constructs an understanding of race and racism for-mulated within a liberal politics, a therapeutic view of human rela-tionships, and a generic civil religiosity. I suggest that these frame-works operate as discourses (in the Foucauldian sense)—as societal "regimes of truth" that work to "speak, classify, name, and establish the dominant and relevant categories of knowledge" (Illouz 233).[8] Further, it is within discourse that elements of an ideology are linked together and their relationship established. As "vehicles of ideology," discourses define participants' contributions in terms of content (what can be spoken, what is the "topic"), relations (how speakers' relationships and interactions are defined), and identi-ties (what subject positions different speakers may occupy in the interaction) (Fairclough 34, 46). The power of discourses resides in their ability to impose these constraints and win participants' consent to abide by them. Power relations are enacted *within* discourse via these constraints, and are exhibited in struggles for control *over* discourse as a "mechanism of sustaining power" (73–74). When a discourse has achieved such social dominance that these constraints are nearly invisible (as is the case with the Western discourse of "the individual"), it attains the status of "common sense" and "will come to be seen as *natural* and legitimate because it is simply *the* way of conducting oneself" (91). Ideologies are most effective when they are least visible, when they have become "common sense." Hall argues that "since (like gender) race appears to be 'given' by Nature, racism is one of the most profoundly 'naturalized' of existing ideologies" ("Whites" 32; see also Miles 3). At the same time, even the most naturalized of ideologies are susceptible to challenge because of "differences in position, experience and interests between social groupings which enter into relationship [and struggle] with each other in terms of power" (Fairclough 88; see also Eagleton 195–96). "Racism in 1992" offers a place to examine the constraints imposed on the meaning of racism by liberal, therapeutic, and religious discourses—and challenges to those constraints—as a site of ideological, and hence social, struggle.

The series did not take a neutral stance toward racism, which was uniformly depicted as "bad," even by participants who betrayed racist sentiments. Public advocacy of racism clashes with the contemporary "official consensus" that racism is scientifically unsound and "morally unacceptable" (Miles 3). (What is said privately, of course, is another matter.) But because the program employs the media narrative convention of dramatic conflict, and given the conflictual history of race relations in the United States, the series necessarily provided a forum for the expression of racist views by many of its 150 guests and more than 2,000 studio audience members. Explicitly racist comments were usually countered by opposing perspectives, however. Less often challenged was what Hall terms "inferential racism"—those "apparently naturalized representations of events and situations relating to race" that "have racist premises and propositions inscribed into them as a set of *unquestioned assumptions*" ("Whites" 36).[9] Inferential racism's relative "invisibility" permits speakers to be "unaware" of the racist implications of their utterances. For example, many whites in the series identified their "not being racist" with their "not seeing color," oblivious to the impossibility of such myopia for people of color in the United States. This equation is based on the naturalization of "whiteness" as the norm against which others are judged. "Whiteness" is defined as the "absence of color" so that "not seeing color" means seeing everyone as "white."[10] For those who do not identify themselves as "white," this move erases—makes invisible—a primary aspect of their experience and social identity. It also implies that they can be seen as "equal" only if they are willing to participate in this erasure.[11] Such instances of inferential racism depend for their invisibility on the premises and assumptions of the dominant discursive frameworks in the show.

Individualism in Liberal, Therapeutic, and Protestant Discourses

Liberalism is based on a belief in the primacy and autonomy of the individual. It envisions human beings as "proprietors" of their persons and capacities and fundamentally motivated by self-interest. Capitalism is viewed as the natural result and extension of this essentialized individualism, and society as an aggregate of such individuals pursuing their interests. The ability to engage in this pursuit without constraint constitutes individuals' rights, and equality becomes the condition in which all individuals have equal access to the means to pursue their private ends. As Hall argues, "in liberal ideology, 'freedom' is connected (articulated) with individualism and the free market" (31).

A therapeutic "mode of thinking about self and society" has become widely dispersed in contemporary American culture, shaping the way we think about ourselves, relationships, institutions, and politics.[12] Also organized around the individual, therapeutic discourse tends to translate everything into individual and interpersonal terms; to expect that any problem can be ameliorated through communication; to emphasize feeling over other modes of experience; to privilege individual experience as the primary source of truth; and to encourage "taking responsibility" for one's own feelings and behavior based on the belief that we are powerless to change anything beyond our own lives.

Religious discourse draws on values from traditional biblical religion to imbue discussion of public issues with a moral authority.

It is strongly influenced by Protestantism, the dominant religious orientation in the United States from its inception. Protestantism is formulated around individual salvation, predicated on a "personal relationship" with God unmediated by church or clergy. A redeemed society is an aggregate of redeemed individuals, but the obligation to be saved resides with the individual whose personal salvation is not dependent on the actions, or the fates, of others. Despite this Protestant inflection, *public* religious discourse is typically generic, avoiding specific doctrines or practices that might generate their own divisions. This generic quality permits the circulation of certain shared values without violating individuals' right to believe as they choose. Religious discourse thus incorporates individualism to accommodate the privatization and plurality of religious belief in contemporary society and the liberal mandate of separation of church and state.

The compatibility and interplay of these three discourses—in the racism series and in society generally—are the product of the intertwined histories of capitalism, Protestantism, and modern science. Protestantism and capitalism, as mutually reinforcing challenges to a feudal religious/economic order, were premised on the liberation of the individual from traditional structures of religious and political-economic authority (Weber; Hill). Liberalism, as a political philosophy and economic theory, elaborated and justified both impulses (Williams 150). Puritan political thought, with its emphasis on the equality of individual souls, supported arguments for the creation of a liberal state (Macpherson). Modern science, which was highly influenced by Protestant values, challenged the feudal metaphysical conception of the natural world. The "new" science and "new" religion were "liberation movements in which an appeal to individualism was encouraged over the oppressive demands" of the old feudal order (Sampson, "Scientific Paradigms" 1335; see also Merton).

As Protestantism envisioned an individual who stood alone before God, capitalism posited an individual who stood alone in the marketplace, and science discovered an individual who stood alone as an object in nature.[13] The product of this historical convergence is a pervasive cultural ethos of "self-contained individualism" (or what Macpherson terms "possessive individualism") that is taken to be a fact of nature—the foundational *cause* of the existing social order rather than a *consequence* of sociohistorical forces. As Sampson argues, the effect is to treat "the given (what is) . . . as though it *ought* to be" ("Scientific Paradigms" 1337; see also Sarason). Once the self-contained individual is "naturalized" and transformed into "common sense," it can then become "implicit in the conventions according to which people interact linguistically, and of which people are not consciously aware" (Fairclough 2). In the racism series, the discourses of therapy, liberalism, and religion are predicated on this naturalized individual.

While these discourses may be separated for analytical purposes, in practice their boundaries are permeable and fluid. The liberal endorsement of individual rights meshes with the religious belief that all individuals are equal before God, and with the therapeutic insistence that every individual's experience must be validated. The boundary between religious and therapeutic discourse has become particularly blurred in contemporary society, owing to the dramatic growth of the "recovery movement" that draws heavily on evangelical Protestantism, and to "New Age" religion that has incorporated ideas from the human potential movement in popular psychology (Kaminer).[14] The latter is based on the primacy of individual self-realization and freedom, founding principles of liberal thought. The interpenetration of these discourses in the racism series is striking where, on occasion, all three might be contained in a single utterance (for example, Winfrey's closing statement in the first L.A. session). This fluidity enhances the persuasive power of these discourses where each can be called upon to reinforce the others. By drawing on the naturalized ideologies of race and individualism in Western history, these discursive frameworks set parameters around the content, relations, and identities in the talk about racism.

Liberalism and the Code of Individual Rights

An overriding sentiment in the series, found across all episodes, expressed by those opposed to racism and those who deny it's a problem, and by persons of different ethnic and racial identifications (though more often by whites), is that people are, first and foremost, *individuals*. In "My Parent Is a Racist," a young white woman who dates other races against her mother's wishes says race "doesn't matter" because "each person is an individual and you get to know them as an individual . . . I don't look at their color or their sex or anything else. It's a person and you learn them as a person." In "The Rodney King Verdict I," a white woman says she doesn't have problems with race "because I don't really see color. . . . I try not to because everybody's an individual. People are so different. Some of them are terrible and then some of them are really nice, of all colors." In "An Experiment in Racism," where the audience was divided into blue-eyed and brown-eyed groups and the former was systematically mistreated in the first half of the show, several of the "blue-eyes" objected strenuously to being judged by a physical trait rather than being seen "as individuals." Their indignation did not subside even when other audience members and guest expert Jane Elliott explained that the exercise was designed to let them experience such discrimination first-hand.

These statements reflect what Carbaugh calls "the cultural code of the individual" based on the "assumption that people are everywhere individuals" (39). Built into this code is the related assumption that rights are the property of individuals—a central element of liberal ideology. Liberalism's articulation of "freedom" with people's right to choose their own beliefs and actions implies that infringements of rights are "a violation against the individual's capacity for relatively free action" (26). This sets limits on the way racism is discussed and the extent to which it can be criticized without transgressing individuals' freedom to think, feel, and believe as they choose. For example, in "My Parent Is a Racist," Ron opposes his daughter's dating a Mexican-American but does not consider it racism (e.g., "bad") because "I don't see where it's causing a problem in my life or anyone else's life." His opposition to interracial dating is also justified in personal terms: "I'm the type of person that believes it's wrong." In the concluding episode, Winfrey asks one of the white guests who had appeared in "White Men Who Fear Black Men" if the show had changed his views about blacks. His reply: "No. I don't think that my thoughts were incorrect. . . . [U]nless we change the name of this country from America, I still believe I have the right to have the beliefs and thoughts I have."

The identification of freedom (and America) with individual rights is further linked with the notion that individual opinions must be respected, regardless of their content. Opinions are the property of individuals, the expression of one's opinion is a natural right, and tolerance of diverse opinions is a necessary safeguard of that right. This is an expectation in public discourse that talk show participants typically abide by. This "code of respect" (Carbaugh 33–38) threatened to break down in the two L.A. sessions and "Experiment in Racism" where emotions were most volatile. In these programs, Winfrey exercised her authority to enforce the code (controlling the microphone, issuing verbal reminders, as in the first L.A. session: "Ladies and gentlemen, we made a vow to each other that we would be heard in this room"). Tolerance of different views is buttressed by the assumption that each person speaks either for "all individuals" (as a universal abstract unity) or only for him/herself, as individuals exercising their rights.[15] Thus it is possible—even necessary—to tolerate racist views in others as long as they acknowledge they don't speak for everyone. For example, when a white male guest calls Native American protests against derogatory sports team names "utterly ridiculous" and "hogwash," an audience member retorts: "I just wanted to say that if he thinks he is representing white people, I don't want to have anything to do with him." The man replies: "I'm representing myself." This enables both speakers to claim validity for their positions within the code of individual rights and respect. In the follow-up show, a young white woman from the "Rodney King" sessions, who had defended the jury's decision and been criticized by other participants, expresses dismay that "everybody was just bashing each other and nobody would listen to every other opinion." She reasserts her original views about the verdict, saying, "Everybody is entitled to their own opinion," to which Winfrey replies: "Absolutely. This is America. You're absolutely right." In another episode, a black woman says her father and brothers are attracted to women who are "docile and white" and is challenged by Winfrey for generalizing docility as a white female trait. Ms. Jefferson: "No, I'm just saying that in my particular instance, that's just what I perceive." Winfrey: "Yeah, I know, which is good, to speak from your own personal experience." If our generalizations are located in our own experience, then, they must be respected because no one is in a position to judge another's experience.

This emphasis on individual opinions, rights, and experience, however, places liberal discourse in a double bind. It becomes difficult to justify the liberal call to correct racially based inequities among different social groups' rights if racism is primarily a problem of and for individuals. Thus, the code of the individual cuts both ways: it can be used to criticize racial stereotyping (defined as a failure to recognize people as individuals), and it can be used to refute the argument that racism is based on, practiced by, and directed at social groups. This double-edge is exemplified in "White Men Who Fear Black Men" when Winfrey asks the white panelists if they "feel a sense of historical guilt . . . because of what's happened to black people?"

> *Joe:* "Not in the least, because I did not commit these crimes. I don't feel that the white race—I mean, how long can we continue to be guilty?"
> *Chuck:* "Well, I have no control over what happened in the past. And I feel I didn't have anything to do with it, just as Joe feels the same way. . . . The black race has no control of what individuals do. That's the way I feel. Just like the white race has no control over individual acts. So why should we feel anything against a race, per se, just because of individual acts?"

The code of the individual was used on several occasions (mainly, but not exclusively, by whites) to challenge the idea that people of color have suffered collectively from systematic oppression. In each case, the speakers cited their own or acquaintances' having overcome personal hardships as proof that blacks or Native Americans are "not taking personal responsibility," are "blaming others," or have "a chip on their shoulders." On one such occasion Winfrey says, "We all tend to individualize what went on in our lives without looking at how racism is systematically carried out from year to year." But this observation is undermined by the overarching individual code that permeates the talk about racism, even by Winfrey. In "Japanese-Americans: The New Racism," white guest Dan Porter accuses the Japanese of "infiltrating" the United

States economy. Winfrey responds, "But isn't what you're saying, though, dangerous Dan? When you say 'they do'—when you start looking at individuals as a group . . . Isn't that very dangerous? Isn't that racism itself?"

Liberal discourse thus produces contradictory definitions of racism. On one hand, the "problem" is framed as unequal rights among different social groups; on the other, the problem is identified as violating *individual* rights by locating people within, or identifying oneself with, those groups. In both cases, the "solution" is posed in individual terms and must not infringe on persons' rights to believe and act as they choose. A consequence of this emphasis on individuals is to remove race relations from a sociohistorical, political context. One's race becomes an individual characteristic, as does one's attitude toward the race of others.[16] Within the discourse of liberalism, then, racism is framed primarily as a problem of individuals and their rights. Indeed, the possession of rights, in American society, is part of the definition of what it means to *be* an "individual." As Carbaugh found in the talk on *Donahue*, in discussing rights violations, "social groups, institutions, and policies, are moved to the back of discourse . . . The state of affairs, as *social* affairs, receive little articulate expression, and if the problem is put into social terms, it quickly succumbs to 'the individual has rights' code" (26).

The primacy of the individual in liberal discourse counteracts and restrains liberal pleas for public policies to redress group inequalities. Lacking a legitimate basis for asking some individuals to give up some of their rights (privileges) to benefit others, particularly when individual rights are also articulated with freedom to pursue one's self-interest in the marketplace, liberal ideology is trapped in a contradiction. This trap generates the need for another framework for defining the problem of racism and formulating arguments for its elimination. Therapeutic discourse takes up this task by defining racism as a psychological "illness" for which individuals, and, by extension society, need "healing."

Therapeutic Discourse and the Disease of Racism

Winfrey's affinity for a therapeutic perspective (she has said that "all the problems in the world" are the result of "lack of self-esteem"), and participants' and viewers' familiarity with this perspective, reinforce the use of therapeutic discourse in talking about racism ("Everybody's Talking" 33). One way racism is translated into an individual psychological phenomenon is by labeling it "prejudice"—a more neutral term that connotes a human predisposition to mistrust the unfamiliar. As such, it can be separated from race (one can be prejudiced against men, or attorneys, or dogs), and universalized as an innate human tendency (everyone has some forms of prejudice). It is aligned with the social psychology concept of stereotyping, seen as a universal tendency to reduce "cognitive uncertainty" by organizing the world into manageable categories (Perkins, Seiter, Henriques). Both concepts translate the political into the psychological: prejudice and stereotyping are simply operations of human cognition that can be corrected by educating people to new patterns of thinking (with better information, we will reject stereotypes and discard prejudices). This way of conceptualizing racism occurs often in the series. In "Too Little, Too Late," Winfrey refers to racism as "ignorance personified" which individuals have a responsibility to correct. Near the end of that episode, Native American guest Michael Haney opines that "maybe we don't have an issue of racism here" but a problem of lack of education. In "My Parent Is a Racist" (where all three guest parents deny they are "prejudiced" while uttering blatantly racist statements), one of the mothers blames their attitudes on ignorance: "When people are sitting here saying they can't know whether we're prejudiced or not, it's because we lack the understanding or the knowledge of it."

Racism is also psychologized by identifying it as an attitude or emotion, usually driven by unconscious motives or hidden anxieties—Winfrey states in one episode that "the whole concept of racism is based in fear"—and connected back to ignorance: we fear what we don't know or understand. In several episodes Winfrey describes prejudice as something that can be "passed from one generation to the next without even knowing it." The series is thus intended to educate people out of these inadvertent psychological category mistakes. Black sociologist Bertrice Berry in "Are We All Racist?" takes this approach: "Anything that is learned can be unlearned," as does black author Kesho Scott in the premiere episode: "White racism is learned and it is a condition. It's part of a social condition and any circumstances can trigger it."

The reference to racism as "a condition" fits well with the therapeutic propensity to locate problems within a disease metaphor. Guest expert Elliott makes this connection explicitly (in "My Parent Is a Racist") when she says that to judge people "by the amount of a chemical in their skin" is to "have a mental problem." The effects of racism are similarly psychologized. In "Too Little, Too Late," Native American Suzan Harjo suggests that stereotyping of Native people "contributes to the low self-esteem of our teenagers, and low self-esteem is the main cause of teenage suicide, and we have the highest teenage suicide rate of any population in this country."

In the therapeutic model, the first step in dealing with one's problem is to admit it exists, a view expressed often in the series. In "Are We All Racist?" Winfrey explains that the program asks this question "because you can't begin to solve the problem unless you admit there is one." In "Experiment in Racism," Elliott admonishes people to "learn about your own racism. First, admit that you have that problem. Then we've got to stop denying it." A therapeutic "breaking out of denial" is enacted many times in the series as people admit to suffering from the "condition" of being racist/prejudiced. This therapeutic confessional mode is most fully displayed in the premiere program among a family of former Ku Klux Klan members. The parents first acknowledge their problem and locate it in their childhood: "We were taught to hate and that's basically what we did. We hated everybody that was not white." They recognize that they passed the disease on to their daughter, who says she too was "taught to hate the niggers, as they were put, and the queers." They examine the painful effects of their pathology on their psyches, "I had so much hatred in my heart. . . . something sort of built up. You get where you can't sleep, the things you do, the things you say. I got to drinking pretty heavy trying to sleep," and on intimate relationships, "It destroys your whole family." And, as in therapy, this revelation of illness is acknowledged by a sympathetic other.

> *Winfrey:* "I have to believe that somebody filled with this much hatred [would] have to have a miserable life."
> *Guest expert Kesho Scott:* "This is an example of one of the ways that we have to understand racism in the '90s as something that does not just hurt people of color. . . . you're seeing how racism hurt them."

Within this perspective, confession is viewed as necessary, and necessarily therapeutic (White). Winfrey confesses (in "Too Little, Too Late") to using the phrase "honest injun" in a television interview and later feeling ashamed when confronted by a Native American viewer. Jane Elliott tearfully admits to being "infected with racism at birth. I want to get over it. It is going to take me the rest of my life to get over it, but I can do it, but I have to choose to do it." As in therapy, overcoming one's illness or dysfunction is a lengthy, painful, and *self-directed* process. The "Follow-Up" episode is organized around this confessional mode as guests, audience members, and viewers from earlier episodes testify how the series helped them stop denying their own problems of racism and move forward in their recovery process. Significantly, several of the white guests who had earlier expressed racist feelings offer as proof of their recovery the fact that they no longer "see color," but now view everyone "as individuals."

When racism is situated within therapeutic discourse, solutions are necessarily framed as "healing"—a term used frequently in the series. In the second "Rodney King" session, actor Lou Gossett empathizes with the audience's discontent, but rejects angry solutions: "If it has to do with violence, I won't join you. I'll understand, but when you get to the healing, please call me." Winfrey extends the metaphor: "We are a country in need of healing." A black panelist in "White Men Who Fear Black Men," who belongs to an organization called "Reality Unlimited" that "develops therapeutic tools in the form of games," says the group is considering creating "a game around race relations."

The framing of racism as an individual psychological dysfunction reflects a general tendency in psychology to "reduce conflicts to subjective misunderstandings, to misperceptions, and to psychological factors within individuals." Such a reduction implies "that merely by changing the way things appear to individuals, the conflicts can be resolved." This view of conflict, moreover, "serve[s] primary ideological functions by eliminating from our analysis the contradictions that exist among groups in the real world" (Sampson, "Cognitive Psychology" 737). Like liberal discourse, therapeutic discourse generates contradictions stemming from its individualistic focus. Because the therapeutic ethos envisions and treats problems almost exclusively at the level of the individual psyche and interpersonal relationships, it has no grounds for formulating a vision of a nonracist society beyond one comprising "healthy" individuals. Based on the view that healthy persons have freed themselves from unconscious constraints, are in a position to "choose" their attitudes and behavior, take responsibility for their own thoughts and feelings, and let go of needs to control the actions of others and situations outside their personal domain, therapeutic discourse lacks a basis for expressing a genuinely *social* ethics (Bellah et al., Lerner). It also legitimizes resistance to such an ethics because the only grounds for moral judgment is one's personal experience. Indeed, to take responsibility for another is to regress into pathology (to be "codependent" or have faulty "boundaries"). The absence of a socially based morality within therapeutic discourse creates a need for another way of defining and problematizing racism, which is taken up by religious discourse.

Religious Discourse: All We Need Is Love

Religious discourse relies on the notions of "understanding" and the equality of persons before God, stressing unity over division in its desire to find a collective, rather than purely individual, basis for moral behavior. The problem of racism is defined as a lack of understanding, a failure to recognize others as divine creations, a violation of the "golden rule," and a resulting spiritual (and hence social) disharmony. It seeks justification by appealing to authorities (God, spiritual leaders, religious teachings), and often employs imperative language—"ought," "should"—to express this vested authority. In the series, arguments against racism are frequently formulated within this framework. In the premiere episode, a black woman in the audience asserts: "God has made all of us equal, no matter what color our skin is." A white female audience member in "My Parent Is a Racist" proclaims: "We are all of different colors and different faiths, but again, we are all human beings and we should love each other just because we're human beings, not because of color." In "Experiment in Racism," Jane Elliott responds to a white man who claims that God created racial differences: "God created one race, the human race, and human beings created racism." A white male in the second L.A. session whose brother was killed in the riots asserts: "I've been raised all my life that if this man here [pointing to a black audience member] cuts himself shaving and I cut myself shaving, the blood in the cup's the same thing; if they lay him and me on a slab somewhere and peel our skin off, unless you're an expert, you don't know who we are, and that we all have a soul that comes from one God."

The emphasis on unity, understanding, and love leads to a rejection of anything that threatens these values, in particular *anger*. Again and again in the series, anger is deemed undesirable, something that may be "understood," but only in order to be overcome. Anger is associated with malaise (physical, psychological, spiritual, social), with disharmony and violence, with a breach of morality, with a breakdown in communication, and ultimately, with racism itself. As the former Klan member asserts, "the Klan or the Black Panthers or whatever the organization is—it's wrong to hate."[17]

This negative evaluation of anger is consistent throughout the series, as is the assumption that it can be eliminated through communication and understanding. The closing sequence of the first Los Angeles session (repeated in the second session) graphically displays this message by counterposing shots of angry South-Central residents with clips of Martin Luther King rejecting violence and Rodney King saying, "We can get along here." This theme is also reiterated in other episodes. During a heated black versus white exchange in "Are We All Racist?" Winfrey breaks in: "One [speaker] at a time, because . . . you can get a lot more said through . . . calmly expressing your feelings than through everybody being angry because the idea behind this show is to promote understanding." Winfrey opens the Los Angeles sessions saying they're intended to help viewers understand "why are black people so angry?" But while South-Central residents are expected to explain their anger, they are clearly not supposed to *be* angry when they do it. In both sessions, when speakers' statements become too heated, Winfrey steps in to defuse them, acting as the "voice of moderation," switching to another speaker, cutting to a commercial. In the second session, Lou Gossett calls for participants to eschew anger in favor of "solutions"—"I don't want you to walk out of here angry." "Experiment in Racism," intended to educate whites about the experience of racist treatment in order to promote "understanding," backfired because so many white audience members took offense at being treated "rudely," being "discriminated against," and being faced with facilitator Jane Elliott, whom they labeled "angry" and "hostile." Several of them walked out during the show, leaving Winfrey visibly shaken.

If anger is bad because it's a barrier to solutions, it can be transcended through "understanding" and "forgiveness." This is expressed by a black participant in the Los Angeles session: "We need to understand each other. OK. We can't point fingers at each other and say we're all wrong or we're all right," and by a white audience member: "like Martin Luther King has stated, it's the renewing of the mind and the spirit, and we have to start a healing process and stop continuing to point a finger, but to look in the mirror and to forgive, start forgiving and loving one another as human beings."

In the series, those who are "prejudiced" are encouraged to forgive themselves for harboring anger and racist attitudes and to seek forgiveness from those they have knowingly or inadvertently harmed; victims of racism are encouraged to release their anger and forgive their transgressors. The widow of a man murdered in 1946 by a white Mississippi mob is asked by Winfrey if she has "reached the point of being able to forgive." The woman replies that she "had to" because living "with all that hate" (toward whites) had made her ill; she had turned this corner by deciding to pray and "leave it in the hands of the Lord." The widow of Medgar Evers appears in this episode and says she had arrived at forgiveness, but since then has "taken a step backwards" because the "old feelings" of anger are "resurfacing." In "White Men Who Fear Black Men," a white woman in the audience proposes prayer as the answer to racial hatred: "We should pray more instead of arguing and fighting. If you want to stop racism, pray and ask God to make the change." The family of former Klan members testify to finding salvation from their racism in God, and later ask their black neighbors' forgiveness for past sins.

Forgiveness, then, banishes anger, promotes understanding and love, and paves the way for unity; these are the solutions to racism within religious discourse. But in its quest for a common moral ground for defining and overcoming racism, this discourse also frames solutions in primarily individualistic terms: to end racism, individuals must change the ways they think, feel, and behave. As Winfrey notes in the premiere program, "true racial harmony" begins "from the heart." This sentiment is echoed by many participants in the series. The white wife of a Native American argues: "We all have to understand that we have got to better our society, and in order to do that, we're going to have to change within ourselves." Suzan Harjo suggests that ending racism against Native people is an "individual choice" involving a willingness to "stop behaving badly to each other." In the first "Rodney King" session, a young white woman argues that racism won't subside "until we decide to look into our hearts" and "take responsibility for our own actions." A black man in the final episode proclaims: "We're finally figuring out if we can talk to each other and find out about the differences, deal with folks one-on-one, we can do a lot better in this country." A white audience member in "Experiment in Racism" proposes that racism cannot be solved "unless we start making a difference and everybody does their own part," to which Winfrey responds, "[E]ach individual is a part of the society. That's how you start to change it." Thus, the solution to racism comes from individuals choosing to understand, overcome ignorance and anger, be fair, seek healing, and love their fellow individuals—all of which are envisioned apart from questions of politics and power. Bellah and Hammond suggest that when a religious perspective emphasizes a "fundamental unity," it tends to formulate any "criticism of existing society" in ways that are "non-hostile, non-confrontational, and often, non-political" (181). The religious discourse in *Oprah Winfrey* follows this mandate.

Dominant Discourses and Repressed Voices

Liberal discourse, organized around individual rights, defines racism as a problem of reason that hinders civic rationality. It labels racism "unfair" and proposes solutions in terms of individuals choosing to extend rights to others to create a *fair society*. Therapeutic discourse is centered on individual health; it defines racism as a problem of the psyche that creates psychological and interpersonal dysfunction. It diagnoses racism "unhealthy" and sees the solution in individual quests for personal recovery that will lead to a *healthy society*. Religious discourse, constructed around individual salvation, defines racism as a problem of the soul/heart that causes separation (from God, from others) and spiritual disharmony. It judges racism "wrong" and poses solutions in terms of individual changes of heart that will lead to a *redeemed society*.

Because these discourses posit reason, perception, and morality as originating in the individual, and society as an extension/reflection of universal mental operations, behaviors, and interests, their understanding of racism is constrained within these discursive walls. Racism will be solved if individuals can be motivated to change their perceptions, feelings, and behavior. In a critique of psychology's dominant cognitive orientation, Sampson argues that its emphasis on the "primacy of inner events and transformations over external events and transformations" leads to an assumption that individuals (and by extension, society) can achieve "harmony" by "abandoning the hope of affecting material reality and learning rather to change themselves." In so doing, such a perspective endorses the social status quo: "Existing arrangements of power and domination are served within a society when people accept a change in their subjective experience as a substitute for changes in their objective reality" ("Cognitive Psychology" 735–36).

I suggest that the problem of and solutions to racism in the series are cast primarily in these terms, and that the popularity of the program (e.g., Winfrey's "transcendence of race") is based on its preference for subjective rather than objective change. It is here, in the subordination of social structures and institutionalized practices to individual choice and perception, that inferential racism is sustained, despite the antiracist intention of the series. As liberal, therapeutic, and religious discourses refract the talk about racism through the naturalized category of the individual, they reproduce the unexamined assumptions that keep inferential racism "invisible." Hall says that "an ideological discourse does *not* depend on the conscious intentions of those who formulate statements within it" ("Whites" 37–38). By constraining the content, relations, and identities in the series, these discourses reproduce racist premises and propositions irrespective of individual participants' positions. The power of the popular media discourse about race resides in its capacity to "constrain a great variety of individuals: racist, antiracist, liberals, radicals, conservatives, anarchists, know-nothings, and silent majoritarians" (46).

If dominant discourses establish the "relevant categories of knowledge," they are also premised on repressed categories of knowledge that generate the need for ideological management. The framing of race and racism in the series tends to repress acknowledgment that as individuals, we are also members of social groups (comprising complex intersections of race, class, gender, etc.) that shape our identities, our relations with others, and our field of social possibilities; that our thoughts, feelings, and actions are themselves products of historical forces that have created structural divisions of race, class, and so on; and that the very concept of the universal, sovereign, abstract individual is also a product of that history.[18]

These discourses are compelling because they draw on, and draw persuasive power from, values that are deeply rooted in American history and consciousness: fairness, equality, freedom, unity, redemption. The racism series speaks *to* these utopian impulses, while it speaks *about* an issue that creates profound anxiety in contemporary society. Jameson suggests that "anxiety and hope are two faces of the same collective consciousness" that find expression in popular culture ("Reification" 144). Popular culture texts, like *Oprah Winfrey,* offer representations of social anxieties at particular historical moments, framed "within careful symbolic containment structures," for the purpose of managing them in the service of legitimizing the existing social order (141). But these anxieties cannot be managed until they are "given some rudimentary expression" (144). In so doing, popular culture products also bring those fears into public consciousness and reveal "our deepest fantasies about the nature of social life, both as we live it now, and as we feel in our bones it ought rather to be lived" (147).

In "Racism in 1992," the discourses of liberalism, therapy, and religion are a means of managing deeply troubling anxieties about racial politics by framing them within the realm of individual rights, health, and morality—thus legitimizing and naturalizing the "isolated individual" on which capitalism depends (Lerner; Sampson "Justice"; Sarason). At the same time, as participants speak *through* these discourses, their talk about racism reveals both an absence of, and longing for, a world of freedom, well-being, community, and love. The tension between what is and what we desire provides a space—"no matter how faintly and feebly"—for the emergence of alternative ways of defining and problematizing racism, and for exposing the exercise of power behind society's dominant discourses about it (Jameson, "Reification" 148).

If ideologies work by articulating elements into a chain of meaning that comes to be seen as "common sense," they are also susceptible to challenge by disrupting the chain. Hall argues that "one of the ways in which ideological struggle takes place and ideologies are transformed is by articulating elements differently, thereby producing a different meaning" ("Whites" 31). Such a breaking of the chain might occur by dislodging equality, healing, and redemption from their individualistic anchor and framing them instead as *social* concerns. Instances of attempts at re-articulation in the series situate racism in a sociohistorical context, posing it as a problem of inequitable access to political-economic wealth and power and pointing to solutions that are collective and political rather than individual and psychological.

Alternative formulations surface primarily, though not exclusively, in the two Los Angeles sessions—not surprising given the urgency of the issue to participants, most of whom are not typical talk show audience members. In these sessions, a few speakers challenge the assumption that we are all simply individuals, irrespective of our place in the social hierarchy.

> *Winfrey:* "But don't we all live in a world together?"
> *Black female audience member:* "Listen Oprah, when you leave your show, you go to a lavish home. Lots of us don't go

home to lavish things. We go home to empty refrigerators, you know, crying kids, no diapers, no jobs. Everybody ain't got it like everybody got it."

These challenges are typically expressed in terms of "we" by speakers who identify with a social collectivity rather than obeying the code of the individual.

> *Black male audience member:* "It [the riot] happened, and it didn't happen for no reason. We as a people—an underclass, an underprivileged people, I should say. You know, we feel a lot of anger, and we feel we're being misrepresented by the media. We've been misrepresented by the government definitely, and definitely the law enforcement."

Also rejected is the assumption that racism and violence are incompatible with the history and core principles and operation of American society. When Winfrey asks the audience why they rioted, a black man responds:

> The reason we did it was because we needed self-satisfaction, we needed self-satisfaction, we had none. We had no satisfaction in what happened to Rodney King. We had no satisfaction in what happened to Latasha Harlins [a black teenager murdered by a Korean grocer who went free]. We've never had satisfaction, 425 years of being unsatisfied, what am I to do? I'm looking at the news and they're telling me my life's not worth a nickel, they're telling me that they can beat me, they can do whatever they want to me whenever they feel like it, and I was supposed to accept this and say, 'Well, we'll just go vote and make it better.' It hasn't been better. We've been voting for years and it's not changing.

When Winfrey, appalled by the looting, asks, "[W]hat's a TV got to do with your life?" the same man replies angrily: "America is a loot. America came over here and genocided the Indians and looted America, split Africa and looted Africa, because you got to take what you want. I'm the rawest businessman in the world."[19] Another participant, a black former L.A. police officer, later argues: "If you want to talk about looting, you want to talk about looting, why don't we talk about the S&L scandal? That was loot-ing. That was a big time ripoff. *That's* looting."

These speakers attempt to loosen the chain that makes racism a problem of individual rights, attitudes, and behavior by re-connecting it to a history of structural inequalities in the American political-economic system. Significantly, they also point to possible links between race and class oppression. Their voices, however, are overshadowed by the pervasiveness of liberal, therapeutic, and re-ligious discourse, and by the code of the individual that makes these utterances simply "personal opinion." None of the above statements were pursued in the show; in every case Winfrey either switched to another speaker or cut to a commercial. In the second L.A. session, Gossett revives the issue of political and economic op-pression:

> *Gossett:* "Racism and violence is [sic] but a mere symbol of a deeper disease in this country and in this world and I think we have to attack the deeper [problem] and it's not rac-ism. It's economics and power and opportunity. So we need to distribute power in some positive way."
>
> *Winfrey* (looking for support from guest Reverend Cecil Murray): "I too am here to try to find some solutions and I think the problem goes even deeper than economics. I think that we are in a moral and spiritual deficit in this country."

Winfrey closes the first L.A. session with a deft blend of the three discourses: "It has been a painful time for this city and for America. . . . I'm hoping that everything that's been said here to-day, that we will take into our hearts and be willing in our own selves to make a difference. There's a time for healing, there's a time for healing. This is our prayer." Her words are followed by the taped sequence of angry South-Central residents, Rodney King's plea for peace, and Martin Luther King's calls for non-violence. In one of these clips, Dr. King says, "[T]he most potent weapon available to oppressed people as they struggle for freedom and justice is the weapon of nonviolence." The choice of this clip was likely motivated by Winfrey's desire to discourage violence and appeal to a diverse viewership. But King's words also challenge the dominant discourses of race in the series. That is, he emphasizes collective "struggle" rather than individual changes, speaks of "oppressed people" rather than of individuals who are discriminated against, and envisions their need as "freedom and justice" rather than as individual rights and personal healing.

Interestingly, the word "justice," uttered only a handful of times in the series, was consistently used to counter liberal, therapeutic, and religious framings of racism. In the first L.A. session, a white male audience member describes the riot as a sign that the United States is "really seriously in a justice war." Later in the show, the black ex–police officer rejects the relativizing code of individual rights: "Justice has only one meaning, not two or three or four or five or six meanings." In "Experiment in Racism," Jane Elliott uses the term to counter the assertion that love and understanding can conquer racism.

> *Elliott:* "But see, I'm not sold on love either."
> *Winfrey:* "Why? Why aren't you sold on love?"
> *Elliott:* "We have had love in this country for 500 years. We have yet to get justice. . . . I'm sold on justice. I think we can have a just society and then people would end up loving one another because we treat one another fairly."

Finally, the term is used to resist therapeutic/religious definitions of healing and forgiveness. In "Unsolved Hate Crimes," Michael Dyson, professor of African-American Studies at Brown University, argues that "healing" is impossible so long as injustice is unacknowledged and sustained. He defines both racism and forgiveness in *social* terms: "We're at the point of racial amnesia, or racial avoidance or racial denial. But once we begin to grapple with the *real* racial history that has been tawdry in this country, then you can start to have forgiveness. Justice is the public language of forgiveness. When we talk about forgiving one another, justice has to be the language we articulate it through."[20]

Conclusion: Rearticulating Race

The limitations of "Racism in 1992" are reflected in its aim, described by Winfrey in the final episode: "We decided to devote one show a month to try and evoke some kind of change in the way people think about the color of each other's skin in this country." Despite occasions of discursive struggle, the series yokes the "problem" of racism and proposed "solutions" to individual perceptions. This is not just a result of Winfrey's own mildly liberal, therapeutic orientation, or of the limits of the talk show form; the ways racism is framed and talked about on *Oprah Winfrey* are also prominent ways it's defined, understood, and problematized in American society generally. Our public and private talk about race is often ambivalent and confused because the lenses through which we view it are partial, in both senses of the word. It's like trying to take a picture of a large heterogeneous crowd with a Polaroid: we get snapshots of individuals frozen in time, lacking the depth of field to show their relationships to each other, their social environment, and their histories.

These limits reflect the contradictions of liberal, therapeutic, and religious discourses, which contain both utopian and conservative impulses. Their liberatory dimension issues from the historical origin of liberalism, modern science, and Protestantism, as challenges to a feudal socioeconomic order formulated in terms of an appeal to individual freedom, reason, and morality. They invoke an egalitarian ethos insofar as they emphasize fundamental similarities that unite individuals. Their repressive dimension is also grounded in their origin as expressions of the interests of an emergent social class (the European bourgeoisie) universalized to encompass humanity "in general." They become conservative forces when that class has achieved dominance within a new sociopolitical order (capitalism). Naturalized individualism then operates to deny or obscure historically structured hierarchies that constitute differences dividing individuals, and that might generate challenges to the legitimacy of that order.

Liberal, therapeutic, and generic religious discourses attempt to resolve this contradiction by repressing the "negative" side of the dialectic—hence their preference for the individual, similarity, and unity. Given that these discourses figure so prominently in the series' talk about racism, the task of "rearticulation" might involve using their utopian elements to expose and critique their conservative consequences. West notes the coexistence in modern bourgeois revolutions of libertarian values, such as individuals' right to speak, worship, and think as they choose, and egalitarian values that "foreground basic social goods—like health care and education and housing and food and employment" (*Prophetic Reflections* 134). In the Winfrey series, the discourses of liberalism, therapy, and religion push the critique of racism into the domain of individual rights, abstract equality, and freedom from the prejudices of others; at the same time, they are haunted by traces of social egalitarian values, democratic strivings, and desires for freedom to take part in the "making and remaking" of the social world (139).

Both impulses are formulated within a universalism that is now under contestation. Critiques of the Enlightenment project (Horkheimer and Adorno) have focused on how its universalizing tendency has been used to exclude or assimilate "problematic" social collectivities (in terms of class, race/ethnicity, gender, sexual orientation, etc.). The "decentering of the subject," the emergence of what has been called the "politics of identity," and the denunciation of "totalizing" or "master" narratives in poststructuralist and postmodern theory are driven by a refusal of this "false universalism." Further, the end of traditional colonialism in the Third World, the "third technological revolution" (West *Prophetic Reflections;* Jameson "Periodizing") that facilitates global transfer of cultural objects, practices, and values, the mass migration of people via the transnationalization of capital, and the growing heterogeneity of national populations have effectively undermined older bourgeois visions of universal culture. As West notes, "[T]here is no way back to these Enlightenment concepts of universality and cosmopolitanism" (122).

What has emerged in its place, according to Wood, is an "ideology of difference" that acknowledges these sweeping sociopolitical changes, and recognizes the coercive character of assimilation and consensus, but that itself deserves interrogation (251). Both traditional liberal universalism and "identity politics" can be seen as responses to the question of the relation of the universal to the particular. Each attempts to answer that question by severing the dialectic—the former by erasing difference, the latter by refusing universality. Further, the individualistic discourses in the Winfrey series, the racist stance they're meant to discredit, and the ascendant "ideology of difference" are different responses to the same sociohistorical developments and forces. All three perspectives provide "practically adequate" explanations of social relations and experiences in a world marked by profound divisions and struggles over what appear to be increasingly scarce material and cultural resources. A discourse or ideology is "practically adequate," according to Miles, when it successfully "refracts in thought certain observed regularities, and constructs a causal interpretation which can be presented as consistent with those regularities, and which serves as a solution to perceived problems" (80). Racist ideology, for example, acquires this adequacy when it "can constitute for some sections of the population a description of and explanation for the way in which the world is experienced to work" (80). While these three perspectives on race and racial conflict are responses to a shared sociohistorical reality, they differ in their conception of causes and solutions. Racist ideology identifies the presence and growth of subordinate racial/ethnic groups as the "cause" of conflict and scarcity, the solution being their containment, exclusion, or elimination. The dominant antiracist discourses in the series blame individual deficiencies of respect, psychological maturity, and spirituality, proposing individual transformation as the solution. Identity politics locates the cause in dominant groups' refusal to recognize, tolerate, and accept the existence of difference; the solution therefore lies in persuading or forcing those groups to see their error and relinquish their illusions of centrality and deserved privilege.

The appeal of these different perspectives does not reside solely in their content; rather, their "practical adequacy" is contingent on their resonating with the specific experiences of different social collectivities (and individuals within them). For example, Wood suggests that both the current resurgence of racism and rise of an official "ideology of difference" in France are related to changes in the global operations of capitalism, as well as a reflection of class divisions in terms of who is most likely to benefit from those changes (254). Similarly, Miles argues that the increase in white working-class racism in England is related to a "decline of capitalist production and the decay of the urban infrastructure" that "coincided with the arrival and settlement of migrants from the Caribbean and the Indian subcontinent"—both of which are "inevitable features of the uneven development of capitalism." When the coincidence of economic decline and migrant settlement are experienced as causally related "a real problem of exclusion from access to material resources and services [occurs], and the search and struggle for a resolution [is] racialized" (81). This analysis might be extended to the Los Angeles riots where mainstream media and public officials focused primarily on racial tensions as the "cause." Davis ("Urban America") proposes that the riots were not simply a product of "natural" or inevitable racial (e.g., "tribal") conflict, but a sign of recognition *across* racial/ethnic differences of a shared oppression. He describes the uprising in L.A. as "the nation's first multi-racial riot" directed at a "redistribution of wealth," and an "insurrection against an intolerable political-economic order."[21] The discussion of the riots in the "Rodney King" episodes short-circuited such an interpretation through an emphasis on individual perceptions and interpersonal relationships—a framing that has practical adequacy for the show's predominantly white, female, middle-class constituency.[22] And for Winfrey, who said in a 1987 interview in *Essence,* "I am where I am because I believed in my possibilities. Everything in your world is created by what you think" (qtd. in Cloud 17). This belief is evident in her response to a black audience member who said he had looted because "that was the only opportunity I had to get something." Winfrey: "Who says you're supposed to have it?"

A number of critics have argued that postmodernism (and postmodern theory), within which the "ideology of difference" is articulated, are products of capitalism's transition from a monopoly to transnational form in the late 20th century.[23] Postmodernism, as an aesthetic and description of contemporary experience, has particular resonance for specific sectors of the population. Wood suggests that the "ideology of difference" is practically adequate for the emergent French salariat class attached to a services/information economy. The "functionally adaptive values" and "ethos" of this "new class," he argues, "consist in the flexibility to handle rapid and constant change in mind-sets and values, an openness to the other, the new, the different—at all levels, from consumer objects to technologies to sexual arrangements" (256). Pfeil proposes that postmodernism is the culture of the American "baby boom professional managerial class . . . a reworking into aesthetic form of its central experiences, preoccupations and themes" (107). The notion of decentered (fragmented) subjectivity, the Foucauldian conception of dispersed, self-reproducing power that "comes from everywhere" with "no definable or limitable sources," the sense that collective identifications are merely fleeting coincidences of decentered recognition or shared "tastes," resonates with the lived experience of this class fraction, which it then projects onto the world in general (106). For West, postmodern culture is the product of an American society balkanized by political preference, race, and subculture, and an outgrowth of "an unwieldy mass culture of hybridity and heterogeneity and a careerist professional class of museum managers and academic professors [trying] to create consensus and sustain some semblance of a common culture as a new political and military imperium" (*Prophetic Reflections* 40).

It seems crucial, then, to ask how the "ideology of difference" is related to the priorities of a transnational capitalist order, and whose interests it serves. Wood proposes that the ideology of difference is directed at "the progressive dissolution of the older ideology of national particularism" that now interferes with the needs of transnational corporate operations. This new ideology is doubly serviceable for the emerging global political-economic order: it helps counter nationalist xenophobia and racism that inhibit the integration of transnational markets and an international reconfiguration of labor forces, while aiding the incorporation of "difference" into the logic of commodification (258, 260). As West argues, "[P]ostmodern culture looks more and more like a rehash of old-style American pluralism with fancy French theories that legitimate racial, gender and sexual orientation entree into the new marketplace of power, privilege, and pleasure" (*Prophetic Reflections* 41–42). While the "ideology of difference" and "identity politics" provide critiques of racism by exposing repressive aspects of traditional Enlightenment universalism, their valorization of difference also vacates space from which arguments for intercollective struggle, identification, and empathy might be formulated. It's a move into a terrain of naturalized power struggles between different collectivities in a world defined by scarcity that contributes to further political polarization.

It is against this background that we might reconsider the talk about racism in the Winfrey series. The "problem" of racism in the show is inflected by awareness of this postmodern ethos of scarcity and identity-based power struggles, and at the same time, the "solutions" proposed attempt to resist and challenge it. That is, despite their individualistic blinders, the liberal, therapeutic, and religious discourses in the series contain utopian sentiments in their quest to find meaningful bridges across social difference. Their appeal is not solely a function of legitimizing the dominant social order—which appears now as a choice between discredited universalism or polarized difference—but also a manifestation, however faint and feeble, of dissatisfaction with it. This utopian impulse or "bridge" implicit in these discourses is formulated through a conception of universality—a belief that there *are* experiences, longings, and needs that might unite human beings, regardless of their differences. Although I criticize the individualistic limitations of these discourses, I believe their appeal—inside and outside the show—can also tell us something about the limits of the "ideology of difference." Careful to avoid a reductive essentialism, West argues for retaining a notion of universality that goes "very deep down—far enough that it makes human connection. If it doesn't make human connection, there will be parochialism, provincialism, narrow particularism" (*Prophetic Reflections* 122). He sees identity politics as one such particularism that "amount[s] primarily to a mode of middle class entree" (122). In the absence of an understanding of human universality, he warns, "there cannot be significant social movements" (124).

Thus, if we are to turn the utopian impulses in liberal, therapeutic, and religious discourse into a critique of their conservative consequences, we might begin by imagining what it would take to make the kind of "deep human connection" West refers to. My sense is that given its infrequent but potent use in the series, "social justice" may be one route to that connection precisely because it implies social interdependence and intersubjective commitment. Certainly, any effort to challenge and oppose racism must take into account the kinds of sociohistorical forces that make racist ideology a practically adequate interpretation of lived experience; it would also involve being able to make human connection with those who are genuinely harmed by a global political-economic order that promotes and benefits from an "ideology of difference." In his analysis of the redefinition of "blackness" in 1980s England, Mercer notes: "no one has a monopoly on oppositional identity" (426). Those of us engaged in cultural criticism would do well to recognize this if we're to find meaningful ways of talking about racism without dismissing large sectors of the populace as hopelessly "backward," and without uncritically embracing identity politics and the ideology of difference.[24] As Miles notes, racism among white working-class people may be as much an expression of their relative economic powerlessness as it is a sign of their power as whites (55). Similarly, the popularity of the right-wing Front National in France among white working classes might be understood as a form of resistance to a political-economic order that exploits working people worldwide (Wood 262–63).

Racism, Hall says, "is not a set of mistaken perceptions," but an attempt to construct an explanation for concrete social/political relations and conditions (qtd. in Miles 82). The same can be said of the dominant discourses in "Racism in 1992." If racist ideology constitutes a practically adequate explanation of those relations and conditions for some people, Miles argues,

> strategies for eliminating racism should concentrate less on trying exclusively to persuade those who articulate racism that they are 'wrong' and more on changing those particular economic and political relations. (82)

The talk about racism in the Winfrey series is fixed nearly exclusively on the level of changing people's perceptions; to do otherwise would call into question the entire sociohistorical edifice that legitimates the series' dominant discourses, as well as the economic logic of the television industry. Analyzing the talk about racism on *Oprah Winfrey* illuminates the ways the "problem" is discursively contained, and the fissures in that containment. It also reveals the limits of merely "talking about racism" in a media forum where differences are allowed, as Cloud notes, "so long as the articulation of difference remains at the level of identity and does not imply political activism . . . against the system that produces racism and sexism" (24).

The task of rearticulating race, then, involves exploring how and why racist (and antiracist) ideologies become practically adequate for specific segments of the population, the specific conditions under which political-economic problems become racialized, and the way class issues are reduced to or displaced onto race. This requires a renewed critical engagement with the question of the relation of the universal to the particular that neither glosses over difference nor eschews universality altogether. I am not hopeful that this task can be carried out within the talk show form, given popular media's tendency to manage rather than illuminate and examine social tensions—not to mention their role in creating an "advertiser friendly" environment. But the analysis of how these discourses constrain the way racism is talked about in one cultural site does give us clues about how they might be challenged in other social locations.[25] As Hall says, cultural criticism that wishes to intervene in social practices might begin by "making visible what is usually invisible"—but should not stop there ("Whites" 47). My analysis suggests that a path out of these discursive constraints would need to articulate racism with issues of economic exploitation (particularly making links between race and class), with social justice, and with collective agency.[26] Such connections move racism out of the shadow of the individual, and into the realm of the social, by exposing the contradictions of the "liberal consensus" that denounces overt racism while reproducing its inferential double that "keeps active and organized racism in place" (49). As the series makes clear, talk, in itself, is inadequate to the task of eliminating racism. But the frameworks through which we talk *about* racism do matter—they powerfully shape what we envision as problems and how we imagine solutions.

Notes

This research was supported with a Graduate School Faculty Summer Research Fellowship, and with a McKnight Arts and Humanities Summer Fellowship, from the University of Minnesota.

1. For an analysis of the riot that exceeds the scope of most mainstream media coverage, see Davis, "Urban America." He notes the significant and underreported participation of poor Latinos (of the first 5,000 arrests, 52% were Latino, 10% white, and 38% black).

2. Topical framing in talk shows organizes the production and promotion of each episode, is used to solicit guests, and creates an interpretive framework for viewers (Peck). By establishing the definition of the day's problem, how it is to be talked about, by whom, and to what ends, topicality is a strategy of *selection* that draws a line between legitimate and "deviant" meanings (Hall "Culture").

3. The series was formally distinguished from regular episodes and linked together thematically through a special opening sequence, modified theme music, periodic display of the series logo, and Winfrey's introduction. The sequence opens with an audio bite of Martin Luther King saying "I have a dream;" it pro-

ceeds with alternating written excerpts from the Declaration of Independence, clips of racial violence, and Winfrey interviewing a white supremacist and a black audience member from past shows. The program's theme music plays beneath the entire sequence; the normally up-tempo signature tune is slowed down, played in a minor key, and altered electronically to create a serious, edgy mood.

4. The program has ranked number one with female viewers ages 18–54 since May 1990 (*Oprah Facts*). Like the audience, the majority of Winfrey's staff is white and female. She says it makes sense for those involved in the production of the show to reflect the audience; she has also defended her hiring practices in terms of choosing the best qualified staff, saying that not to hire someone because s(he) is white would be "reverse discrimination" (Waldron 183). I address the complex relationship of gender to the talk show form as a "feminine" genre, its female target audience, and its compatibility with therapeutic discourse elsewhere (Peck).

5. Winfrey's wide appeal is also attractive to advertisers. In one media buyer's words, the show "is good at generating consistently high ratings while it maintains the aura of being advertiser friendly" (Wells).

6. She was one of three celebrities honored as "outstanding individuals who exemplify the spirit of America" in a 1990 TV special, *America's All-Star Tribute* (Cloud).

7. Miles provides a history and critique of the concepts of race and racism. He argues that because "race" has no scientific basis as a biological typology of human variation, race and racism are ideological constructs, or processes of signification, grounded in "a particular pattern of international economic and political relations" within the history of capitalist development (40). Intrinsic to this history are relations of domination and subordination.

8. I rely here on the "critical language study" approach within sociolinguistics that examines how social power is exercised through and masked by language and discursive conventions (see Fairclough; Fowler et al.; Kress and Hodge).

9. Hall's distinction in some ways parallels that made by writers examining African-American experience in the United States who distinguish between overt/individual and covert/institutional racism (Carmichael and Hamilton; Knowles and Prewitt).

10. For a discussion of this naturalization process and its racist assumptions, see Dyer.

11. In "My Parent Is a Racist," guest expert Jane Elliott illustrated this invalidation for the audience with a "flesh" colored crayon and "nude" pantyhose—both based on white skin tones. At the same time, her equation race = color, even though formulated from an antiracist position, facilitates a reduction of race to personal characteristics or physical traits, thus permitting its subsumption into individualist discourses.

12. For discussion of this ethos in society and in media representations, see Bellah et al.; Lears; Fairclough; Gumpert and Fish; Kaminer; Illouz; and White.

13. Horkheimer and Adorno attribute this process of objectification to the logic of Enlightenment that operates via principles of abstraction, exchange, and substitution whereby first nature, and then humanity, are reduced to the status of objects. Benjamin examines the extension of this logic to the psyche.

14. This fusion is evident in Winfrey's enthusiastic embrace of "recovery" in her program and in her personal life. She's an ardent fan of "spiritual psychologist" Marianne Williamson, who was featured in two episodes in 1992.

15. Carbaugh calls this an "everyone and/or only one kind of talk" (39).

16. This reduction is taken to the extreme when it is translated into "color," where it can be paradigmatically linked to any hue in the spectrum, as it was by

a number of speakers. For example, in "I Hate Your Interracial Relationship" a white woman comments, "I've got two beautiful children. You've got to teach them in the home . . . black and white, brown and green, they're all the same." In the first episode, a former Klan member says his racism was not based on fear: "I really didn't have a fear of nobody. I didn't care if he was black, white, green or yellow."

17. The argument that the motives and anger of both groups is identical is an example of what Miles calls "conceptual inflation," whereby racism is used to explain *all* intergroup conflict. This suppresses or denies the existence of class divisions that produce differential access to power within and across racial categories (55).

18. These repressions can be compared to what Sampson calls "psychological reification" whereby "the forms and contents of human consciousness and of individual psychological experience" are disconnected from sociohistorical processes and given "the status of a fundamental property of the human mind" ("Cognitive Psychology" 738).

19. This speaker, one of the most vocal and articulate participants in the L.A. sessions, was invited back as a panelist in "White Men Who Fear Black Men" (where he was identified as Larry Gillen). This later episode clearly favored psychological explanations of interracial tensions rather than the political-economic explanations Gillen offered in Los Angeles. In this setting, where the four other black panelists were middle-class professionals, Gillen spoke only twice (a total of five sentences). At one point Winfrey said he would be asked to discuss the issue of black men and white police after the commerical break; the subject never resurfaced.

20. The term "justice" is not inherently incompatible with individualist discourse, however, as Sampson shows in his critique of the way justice has been defined and studied within the field of "pure psychology" (*Justice*).

21. West characterizes the riots in L.A. in slightly different terms as "a multiracial, trans-class, and largely male display of justified rage" that "signified the sense of powerlessness in American society" (*Race* 1).

22. The power of these discourses resides in the fact that we live "the social" *as* individuals, experience utopian longings as personal desires, and recognize, on some level, that the "isolated individual" is a "fact" of existence under capitalism. These discourses continue to command our allegiance because they are "practically adequate" explanations of lived experience.

23. For arguments about the relationship of postmodernism to changes in late twentieth-century capitalism, see Jameson ("Postmodernism"), Harvey, West (*Prophetic Reflections*), Wood, and Pfeil.

24. For other critiques of the limitations of identity politics see Bourne, Adams, Briskin, Kauffman, and Cloud.

25. Such sites might include media literacy projects in schools and universities, discussions within community and neighborhood organizations, churches, labor unions, various social movements, etc.—in other words, places where talk is not produced for entertainment purposes or for the packaging of an audience commodity, but aims instead at exploring important social concerns in a context of motivated, but uncoerced, dialogue.

26. William J. Wilson made an early compelling argument that racial discrimination is an insufficient explanation for the persistence and growth of a black "underclass," and that policies aimed at eliminating discrimination based on race do not address the structural economic barriers that keep some groups (of all racial/ethnic identifications) permanently exploited and impoverished (*Declining*,

"Black"). He continues to argue for an analysis that connects race and class *(Disadvantaged)*, as do Miles, Marable, West, Davis *(City of Quartz)*, and others.

Works Cited

Adams, Mary Louise. "There's No Place Like Home: On the Place of Identity in Feminist Politics." *Feminist Review* 31 (1989): 22–33.

Bellah, Robert, and Philip Hammond. *Varieties of Civil Religion*. San Francisco: Harper, 1980.

Bellah, Robert, Richard Madsen, William Sullivan, Ann Swidler, and Steven Tipton. *Habits of the Heart*. Berkeley: U of California P, 1985.

Benjamin, Jessica. *The Bonds of Love: Psychoanalysis, Feminism, and the Problem of Domination*. New York: Pantheon, 1988.

Bourne, Jenny. "Homelands of the Mind: Jewish Feminism and Identity Politics." *Race and Class* 29.1 (1987): 1–24.

Briskin, Linda. "Identity Politics and the Hierarchy of Oppression: A Comment." *Feminist Review* 35 (1990): 102–08.

Carbaugh, Donal. *Talking American: Cultural Discourses on Donahue*. Norwood: Ablex, 1988.

Carmichael, Stokely, and Charles Hamilton. *Black Power: The Politics of Liberation in America*. London: Jonathan Cape, 1968.

Cloud, Dana. "The Rhetoric of Tokenism: Oprah Winfrey's Rags-to-Riches Biography." Unpublished paper. University of Texas, 1993.

Davis, Mike. *City of Quartz: Excavating the Future in Los Angeles*. London: Verso, 1990.

———. "Urban America Sees Its Future: In L.A., Burning All Illusions." *Nation* 1 June 1992: 743–46.

Dyer, Richard. "White." *Screen* 29.4 (1988): 44–65.

Eagleton, Terry. *Ideology*. London: Verso, 1991.

"Everybody's Talking." *First* 30 Nov. 1992: 31–37.

Fairclough, Norman. *Language and Power*. Harlow: Longman, 1989.

Fowler, Roger, Robert Hodge, Gunther Kress, and Thomas Trew. *Language and Control*. London: Routledge, 1979.

Freeman, Mike. "Talk Shows Flourish During May Sweeps." *Broadcasting* 15 June 1992: 11.

Gallup, George, Jr., and Frank Newport. "Oprah is America's Number One Talk Show Host." *Gallup Poll Monthly* April 1992: 43–54.

Gumpert, Gary, and Sandra Fish. *Talking to Strangers: Mediated Therapeutic Communication*. Norwood: Ablex, 1990.

Hall, Stuart. "Culture, the Media, and the 'Ideological Effect.'" *Mass Communication and Society*. Ed. James Curran, Michael Gurevitch, and Janet Woollacott. Beverly Hills: Sage, 1979. 315–48.

———. "The Whites of Their Eyes: Racist Ideologies and the Media." *Silver Linings*. Ed. George Bridges and Rosalind Brunt. London: Lawrence and Wishart, 1981. 28–52.

Harvey, David. *The Condition of Postmodernity*. London: Basil Blackwell, 1990.

Henriques, Julian. "Social Psychology and the Politics of Racism." *Changing the Subject: Psychology, Social Regulation and Subjectivity*. Ed. J. Henriques et al. London: Methuen, 1984. 60–89.

Hill, Christopher. *Reformation to Industrial Revolution, 1530–1780*. New York: Penguin, 1978.

Horkheimer, Max, and Theodor Adorno. *The Dialectic of Enlightenment*. c. 1972. Trans. John Cumming. New York: Continuum, 1986.

Illouz, Eva. "Reason Within Passion: Love in Women's Magazines." *Critical Studies in Mass Communication* 8 (1991): 231–48.

Jameson, Fredric. "Periodizing the Sixties." *The Ideologies of Theory*. Vol. 2. Minneapolis: U of Minnesota P, 1988. 178–209.

———. "Postmodernism; or the Cultural Logic of Late Capitalism." *New Left Review* 146 (1984): 53–92.

———. "Reification and Utopia in Mass Culture." *Social Text* 1 (1979): 130–48.

Jhally, Sut, and Justin Lewis. *Enlightened Racism: The Cosby Show, Audiences, and the Myth of the American Dream*. Boulder: Westview Press, 1992.

Kaminer, Wendy. *I'm Dysfunctional, You're Dysfunctional: The Recovery Movement and Other Self-Help Fashions*. Reading: Addison-Wesley, 1992.

Kauffman, L. A. "The Anti-Politics of Identity." *Socialist Review* 20.1 (1990): 67–80.

Knowles, Louis L., and Kenneth Prewitt. *Institutional Racism in America*. Englewood Cliffs: Prentice-Hall, 1969.

Kress, Gunther, and Robert Hodge. *Language as Ideology*. London: Routledge, 1979.

Lears, T. J. "From Salvation to Self-realization: Advertising and the Therapeutic Roots of the Consumer Culture, 1890–1930." *The Culture of Consumption: Critical Essays in American History, 1880–1980*. Ed. R. W. Fox and T. J. Lears. New York: Pantheon, 1983. 3–38.

Lerner, Michael. *Surplus Powerlessness, The Psychodynamics of Everyday Life . . . and the Psychology of Individual and Social Transformation*. Atlantic Highlands: Humanities, 1991.

Macpherson, C. B. *The Political Theory of Possessive Individualism*. c. 1962. Oxford: Oxford UP, 1979.

Marable, Manning. *How Capitalism Underdeveloped Black America: Race, Political Economy and Society*. Boston: South End, 1983.

Mercer, Kobena. "'1968': Periodizing Postmodern Politics and Identity." *Cultural Studies*. Ed. Lawrence Grossberg, Cary Nelson, and Paula Treichler. New York: Routledge, 1992. 424–38.

Merton, Robert. *Social Theory and Social Structure*. Glencoe: Free Press, 1957.

Miles, Robert. *Racism*. New York: Routledge, 1989.

Newcomb, Peter, and Jean Sherman Chatsky. "The Top 40." *Forbes* 28 Sept. 1992: 87–91.

Oprah Facts. Chicago: Harpo Productions, 1992.

Peck, Janice. "TV Talk Shows as Therapeutic Discourse: The Ideological Labor of the Televised Talking Cure." Unpublished paper. University of Minnesota, 1993.

Perkins, T. E. "Rethinking Stereotypes." *Ideology and Cultural Production*. Ed. Michele Barrett et al. New York: St. Martin's, 1979. 135–59.

Pfeil, Fred. *Another Tale to Tell*. London: Verso, 1990.

Sampson, Edward E. "Cognitive Psychology as Ideology." *American Psychologist* 36 (1981): 730–43.

———. *Justice and the Critique of Pure Psychology*. New York: Plenum, 1983.

———. "Scientific Paradigms and Social Values: Wanted—A Scientific Revolution." *Journal of Personality and Social Psychology* 36 (1978): 1332–343.

Sarason, S. B. "An Asocial Psychology and a Misdirected Clinical Psychology." *American Psychologist* 36 (1981): 826–36.

Seiter, Ellen. "Stereotypes and the Media—A Reevaluation." *Journal of Communication* 36 (1986): 14–26.

"Television." *Ebony* Aug. 1991: 51–52.

Waldron, Robert. *Oprah!* New York: St. Martin's, 1987.

Weber, Max. *The Protestant Ethic and the Spirit of Capitalism.* London: Allen & Unwin, 1976.

Wells, Melanie. "Waiting for the Next Morton Downey." *Advertising Age* 8 Mar. 1993: S-7.

West, Cornel. *Prophetic Reflections: Notes on Race and Power in America.* Monroe: Common Courage, 1993.

———. *Race Matters.* Boston: Beacon, 1993.

White, Mimi. *Tele-Advising: Therapeutic Discourse in American Television.* Chapel Hill: U of North Carolina P, 1992.

Williams, Raymond. *Keywords.* New York: Oxford UP, 1976.

Wilson, William Julius. "The Black Community in the 1980s: Questions of Race, Class, and Public Policy." *Annals of the American Academy of Political and Social Science* 454 (March 1981): 26–41.

———. *The Declining Significance of Race.* Chicago: U of Chicago P, 1980.

———. *The Truly Disadvantaged: The Inner City, the Underclass, and Public Policy.* Chicago: U of Chicago P, 1987.

Wood, Philip. "French Thought Under Mitterrand: The Social, Economic and Political Context for the Return of the Subject and Ethics, for the Heidegger Scandal, and for the Demise of the Critical Intellectual." *Contemporary French Civilization* 15.2 (1991): 244–67.

With His Pistol in *Her* Hand: Rearticulating the Corrido Narrative in Helena María Viramontes' "Neighbors"

JoAnn Pavletich and Margot Gayle Backus

In her collection *The Moths and Other Stories,* Helena María Viramontes exploits the ambiguous cultural space that is brought into being through the placement of a woman in the oppositional narrative position primarily occupied, in the history of Chicano culture, by the male corrido hero. The oppositional moments Viramontes depicts reconfigure the assertive pose of the corrido hero, mediating the corrido's climactic moment of defiance through a series of fantastic and flamboyantly gendered transformations.

The figures of female defiance Viramontes inscribes include a Central American refugee who confronts American immigration authorities with a coffee pot in hand in "Cariboo Cafe"; Amanda, who sews maggots into the side of Don Joaquín, a wealthy, sexually exploitive landlord, in "The Long Reconciliation"; Naomi, who takes up her baseball glove in defiance of patriarchal authority in "Growing"; the unnamed woman who shoots her abusive husband in "The Broken Web"; and especially Aura Rodriguez, the protag-

© 1994 by *Cultural Critique.* Spring 1994. 0882-4371/94/$5.00.

onist of the collection's final story, "Neighbors." In this narrative, Aura Rodriguez is pushed beyond endurance by a complex series of events, including an unanticipated racist assault by the Los Angeles Police Department. She confronts an ambiguously culturally situated adversary who stands outside her (and our) literal and conceptual field of vision. Poised in ambiguous defense of her ambiguous right, Aura Rodriguez takes up an ancient pistol she finds in her basement and assumes, while she simultaneously transforms, the conventional stance of the male corrido hero, with *his* pistol in *her* hand.

Theoretical and Methodological Approaches

In an informal presentation on Viramontes' short story "The Broken Web," Héctor Pérez has pointed to the figurative relationship that exists between the story's opening depiction of the "stone shapes of the holy family" (49), and familial configurations that recur throughout the narrative. In his reading, Pérez emphasizes that the "frozen" family configurations Viramontes depicts may be traced directly to the discursive operation of gender norms, and to the Catholic Church's complicity with and replication of these norms within the Mexican and Chicano communities the story depicts. Pérez's reading demonstrates, in short, that in "The Broken Web" a particular discourse—the discourse of gender difference—functions as a cultural Medusa that freezes, paralyzes, or, to use Louis Althusser's terminology, "interpellates" the story's characters. This gendered interpellation, as Pérez's analysis implies, forecloses alternative possibilities for behavior by or communication between the subjects it constitutes.[1]

Stuart Hall's theory of articulation offers a necessary complement to the Althusserian mode of analysis suggested in Pérez's reading of "The Broken Web." In Hall's words,

> a theory of articulation is both a way of understanding how ideological elements come, under certain conditions, to cohere together within a discourse, and a way of asking how they do or do not become articulated, at specific conjunctures, to certain political subjects . . . it enables us to think how an ideology empowers people, enabling them to begin to make some sense

or intelligibility of their historical situation, without reducing
those forms of intelligibility to their socio-economic or class
location or social position. (Grossberg 53)

Hall understands articulation as the nonnecessary link that *"can
make a unity of two different elements under certain conditions"*
(53).

Hall's model provides an excellent theoretical entré into Chicano culture's complex cultural and ethnic situation relative to European, Indian, and Euro-American cultures, all of which are, in varying degrees, at various moments and for various groups and individuals, present within Chicano culture.[2] Stuart Hall's own position as an Afro-Caribbean intellectual working in and on British culture has undoubtedly sensitized him to the arbitrariness with which certain connections or discourses are promoted and others muted or effaced in the construction of social identity.[3] He has, for instance, spoken approvingly of "emergent ethnicities" that are "constructed in history . . . constructed politically in part." Such consciously constructed and narratively produced identities must, he argues, replace our "dangerous" old notions of ethnicity as "an essence" (Hall 19).

Hall's critique of fixed notions of identity relates closely to Rosaura Sanchez's contention that "cultural boundaries are not necessarily geographical and legal, but rather social, economic and ideological" (81). Both Hall and Sanchez call for analytical models capable of accounting for the fluidity of identity within an increasingly complex global network of cultural and economic relations. We hope, in this article, to contribute to the development of such models. It is our contention that through a gendered representation of the naturalized articulation, conventional to the corrido form, between Chicano patriarchal authority and resistance, Viramontes significantly reframes "tendential historical connections" (Grossberg 54) in the Mexican-American narrative tradition. In so doing, she calls attention to the interpellated nature of gender differences and actively participates in their renegotiation. "Neighbors," the narrative upon which we are focusing, turns upon specific and sometimes daring articulations between various social forces at work against and within Chicano culture. These rearticulations, figured as moments of resistance, draw from and at the same time challenge earlier articulations within the corrido tradition.

The corridic influence in "Neighbors" is manifested primarily in the complex triadic conflict that emerges between Aura Rodriguez, the Los Angeles Police Department, and members of the Chicano gang, the Bixby Boys.[4] Viramontes' text significantly transforms the corrido both formally and thematically, introducing changes in regard to genre, the protagonist, and traditional representations of domination and resistance. Retained are the principal corrido thematics of border conflict, the protagonist's defense of her right against (now multiple) hostile, alien cultures, one of which is nominally her own, and the climactic appearance of the corrido's central icon, the pistol, in the defense of that right. As we will show, in "Neighbors," Viramontes rearticulates what has traditionally been a climactic moment in the border corrido: the "assured defeat" of the hero in defense of his right. Significantly extending the historical corridic representations of women collected and discussed by María Herrera-Sobek,[5] Viramontes mediates the corrido's moment of resistance through a differently gendered and potentially collective narrative figuration. In so doing, "Neighbors" forges new articulations at the same time that it interrogates the ways in which discourses "do or do not become articulated, at specific conjunctures, to certain political subjects" (Grossberg 53).

Articulated Moments Within the Corrido Narrative

The border corrido developed within territory that was once Mexico, but which eventually became Texas, largely in response to the repression that followed the final, decisive assertion of U.S. sovereignty over large portions of northern Mexico in 1848. As Américo Paredes contends, this form of the well-known Mexican folk ballad, composed of a series of octosyllabic quatrains with a characteristic ABCB rhyme scheme, represents an important influence on the later heroic corrido tradition that blossomed within Greater Mexico during the Mexican revolution.[6] Although the corrido figure who defends his right in the face of assured defeat underwent a number of transformations within the Mexican corrido tradition, the border corrido hero, embodied in Paredes' work by Gregorio Cortez, remains latent within the tradition, a residual figure through which the traditional male corrido hero's defiance remains securely anchored to masculine authority.

As the title selected by Paredes for his ground-breaking study of the corrido, *With His Pistol in His Hand,* suggests, an articulated relationship exists between certain supercharged icons and intensified temporal positions embedded within the Texas border corrido. In Paredes' title, the "pistol in [the] hand" of Gregorio Cortez refers synecdochically to Cortez himself, who is, by extension, a synechdochic figure for an idealized precapitalist Mexican-American border culture. It also refers to the expanded and super-intensified *moment* of confrontation between the Mexican-American and Anglo-Texan cultures toward which the whole of the South Texas corrido tradition deployed itself in the late nineteenth to early twentieth century.

The corrido relies for its impact upon the establishment of supercharged, intensified moments in which the cultural consciousness of the Mexican-American people is articulated in a privileged moment of historically determinate conflict, the logic of which asserts or prophecies the *ultimate* reemergence of a coherent and autonomous Chicano culture within what are now North American borders. The supercharged icon of the pistol in the hand of Gregorio Cortez marks the moment at which an overdetermined series of events—each of which emerges with seamless inevitability from a cluster of cultural, social, and economic discourses—culminates epiphanically as events move, finally, decisively, beyond the control of any individual player within the narrative. The culmination of these events offers a moment at which history can be apprehended as an autonomous force momentarily independent of the subjects whose innumerable and ungraspable motivations and actions are ordinarily thought, when conceived of en masse, to constitute its operations. The synecdochic pistol represents the moment when, as Fanon writes, a colonized group passes from "the atmosphere of violence to violence in action," the moment when "the lid blow[s] off . . ." and "the guns go off by themselves" (79). The corrido's epiphanic moment, then, may be understood as both a moment that signals the entrance of history into the course of the narrative, and as a utopian moment that prophetically points toward a future liberation which it constructs as inevitable, and which teleologically confirms the present moment of resistance in its light.

The emergence of this historically and symbolically charged moment within the corrido narrative[7] is invariably signalled through the introduction of highly stylized and culturally charged synecdoches for conflict, which are simultaneously deeply inflected with a specifically Mexican-American construction of male mastery. The articulation of narrative temporality into moments of heightened character *presence* and concomitant intensification of cultural *meaningfulness* within the corrido narrative is negotiated through a central figure reliant upon a culturally specific coding of gender for its impact. Hence, the corrido articulates masculinity with historical agency. The pistol, the rooster, the image of two men facing each other in mortal combat, or, in earlier corridos, cards, gamblers, and fights in cantinas are typical synecdoches for male self-assertion within the corrido. The narrative correspondingly inscribes women, children, and the mother of the corrido hero into a grieving female, domestic space. Together, the moment of masculine self-assertion and feminine grieving confirm the corrido's moments of greatest cultural, political, and aesthetic weight as simultaneously its most powerfully gendered moments.[8]

Such an analysis is borne out through our reading of Paredes' own construction of both the corrido and the society that produced it. While Paredes consistently historicizes the development of the corrido in light of numerous social forces and places the form in dialogue with Scottish, Greek, Russian, and Spanish border balladry, his description of the border culture from which the corrido springs is curiously seamless and uncritical. Paredes describes border social organization as typified by the "family holding or communal village, ruled by patriarchal authority under a kind of pre-eighteenth-century democracy" (242). Paredes' account of a prelapsarian border culture in fact confirms and mirrors the representations of the culture that he identifies in the narrative logic of the corrido itself.

The traditional corrido is comprised of three major narrative elements: the hard-working man who is goaded into violence, the defense by that man of his right, and his assured defeat by capture, exile, or death. In the border ballad, all of these elements are played out within a border-conflict thematic (147). Paredes asserts that these elements are "not only a projection of the border Mexican's reaction to border conflict but a pattern of behavior as well" (118). The quiet, hard-working man, when pushed, will risk his life in the moral defense of his right. Paredes' depiction of this man and his family relies upon an understanding of the patriarchal household as autonomous and as a synecdoche for border culture as a whole. The Mexican-American patriarch embodies absolute authority. As the powerful dispenser of justice and maker of laws, he attempts to ensure for his household, and for the culture which authorizes its configuration, an absolute right to self-determination. Autonomy, patriarchy, and resistance operate together in the narrative Paredes constructs, empowering the patriarch's resistance to external influences through the construction of a subject position whose elevated status (symbolically) protects the community from cultural domination from without.

Paredes' identification of the patriarch as the embodiment of his community is echoed by Ramón Saldívar in his discussion of "El Corrido de Gregorio Cortez." Saldívar argues that Cortez "stands . . . not as an individual but as an epic construction of the society that constitutes him. His fate cannot be disconnected from communal fate" (36). Cortez's fate, and the fate of other traditional corrido heroes is, then, necessarily defeat. As Paredes observes, "[h]is defeat is assured; at the best he can escape across the border, and often he is killed or captured" (149). The convention of the hero's doomed defense, then, emerges at the intersection of two competing constructions of patriarchal authority: Mexican-American patriarchal authority, and the Texas Ranger as he embodies U.S. military potency. Because the Texas Ranger is backed by a well-organized national militia that is redeployed according to the spurious whims of a continually shifting conception of "Manifest Destiny," while the Mexican-American patriarch represents a relatively small population of former Mexican nationals, now isolated within the newly expanded boundaries of the United States, the border corrido's lone male hero is necessarily doomed. The moment of his defeat, a moment nearly contemporaneous with the climactic moment of defiance, marks the moment at which he passes out of a Mexican-American-defined system of representation and into an Anglo-Texan legal system in which he will be represented in Manichean terms as a "Mexican bandit." The isolated corrido patriarch thus enacts the material and representational marginalization of the Mexican-American community at a specific point in history while he simultaneously embodies a resistance that community must, in the name of material and psychic survival, construct as inevitable. The inevitable futility of the corrido hero's defense is, moreover, directly linked to a cultural reliance upon the isolated patriarch as the embodiment of Mexican-American cultural autonomy.

As an emblem of masculine individualist self-assertion, the corrido hero originally circulated as a symbolic form of opposition to the racist forces of the U.S. legal system, just as Américo Paredes deployed Cortez's figure within academic discourse as a strategic means for breaking the deadlock grip within which Walter Prescott Webb and J. Frank Dobie held Texan history. Within the corrido narrative itself, however, Cortez's act of self-assertion is ultimately doomed. Historically, men such as Cortez who did resist were literally doomed mainly owing to the overwhelming force backing the Rangers, who sought to punish them for defending their family and land, but it is also true that the conventional corrido hero is figuratively doomed by the masculinist and individualist stance he is made to take up. Post-Enlightenment individualism and masculinity have both based their claims for ontological centrality and individuality upon a Manichean system of differentiation founded on contrasts between the "autonomous bourgeois white male individual" and an array of racial, cultural, national, and sexual Others. These subjects must remain Other if the construction of masculinist individual agency as dominant *over* others is to be upheld. The corrido hero, in his confrontation with a system that defines itself against the effaced history and subjectivity of Chicano culture, employs the implicit claim to *embody* such a masculinist and individualist subjectivity. This stance raises an impossible contradiction while it exposes the extent to which border culture was affected by and made complicit with a European-based system of Manichean differentiation.

The symbolic importance of the corrido's moment of resistance reinforces and draws from the patriarchal constitution of Mexican-American culture, while it simultaneously enables an interrogation of that very constitution. Thus we see two articulations at work in the corrido: one, between patriarchy and resistance, and the second, between patriarchal authority and defeated opposition. The contradiction between this double articulation points to the ways in which a reliance upon patriarchal authority as assuring cultural autonomy may be crippling rather than enabling for an oppressed group under attack by a hostile culture, even while such a formation may have been historically inevitable. Recognizing the contradictions that exist between the two separate articulations that empower the corrido hero as an emblem of resistance helps us to understand the reasons behind the decline of the corrido itself as an oppositional form. While we can simultaneously appreciate the corrido's continued presence as "a repressed element of the political unconscious . . . exert[ing] symbolic force in the spheres of alternative narrative arts" (Saldívar 41), a rearticulation of resistance to models other than that of patriarchal authority must be engaged to enable the growth of more potentially efficacious cultural forms. Viramontes' "Neighbors" engages such a rearticulation.

"Neighbors": Rearticulating the Corrido

In *The Moths and Other Stories,* Viramontes examines the lines of historical tendention that articulated patriarchal authority with resistance and a doomed oppositionality in the corrido narrative, while simultaneously reformulating this articulation to offer a more heterogeneously gendered and classed moment of cultural/political resistance. The border conflict continues in Viramontes' narratives, but the site of cultural conflict is frequently situated within a differently gendered, as well as raced, human body. Moreover, the fronts which must be protected have proliferated in these stories: border conflict has erupted between genders, classes, and generations as well as at the contact points between national and cultural traditions and races.

Gloria Anzaldúa writes that a "borderland is a vague and undetermined place created by the emotional residue of an unnatural boundary. It is in a constant state of transition" (3). The land that Viramontes' characters inhabit is replete with the tension of raced and sexed bodies in the process of negotiating a terrain that is restrictive as well as unstable in multiple ways. For example, the young woman in "Growing" comes to experience her femaleness through her father's "growing" restriction of her activities (29–38). The mother in "The Cariboo Cafe" experiences the pathetic irony of motherhood in a land where children disappear and mothering, although symbolically central, is materially powerless in the face of very real military force, with very material lines of historical tendention leading north across the U.S. border (59–76). The articulations that Viramontes creates establish borderlands where allegiances are liminal, contingent, and often transitory. Her representational opening of these borders calls our attention to the arbitrary relationship between previously articulated unities within the same cultural parameters and exposes the lines of tendential force that may connect a female subject position with resistance.

Resistance is crucially at issue for Aura Rodriguez, the isolated protagonist in Viramontes' "Neighbors" (101–18). Two parallel plots exist in this story, which is situated in contemporary urban Los Angeles. The first concerns the aged Aura Rodriguez and her struggles with a gang of young men who assemble on the street in front of her house to drink, smoke joints, and play loud music. A secondary plot involves Aura's equally aged neighbor Don Fierro, and his struggles with memories of his son, Chuy, and of a time when his neighborhood was not an "endless freeway [that] paved over his sacred ruins, his secrets, his graves . . ." (106). The two plots are linked through the appearance of a mysterious, large, and unkempt woman who somehow knows Aura's name, but who has arrived to visit Don Fierro.

Aura's isolation from her community frames the story. The first description of Aura situates her "within her own solitude, surrounded by a tall wrought-iron fence" (102). In the last moments of the story she "pray[s] to be left alone" (118). Additionally, the text's reticence in regard to Aura's past reinforces the reader's perception of her as existing in isolation from any identifiable network or community. Aura's alienation from the social structures in her community makes her especially vulnerable to the internecine and generational strife that surrounds her. However, Aura's denial of any need for community is shown to have developed as a survival mechanism that she came to employ as she watched her "neighborhood . . . slowly metamorphos[e] into a graveyard" (102). Just as Gregorio Cortez is gradually isolated from his larger community through the strategic intervention of an alien community that slowly emerged and consolidated around his own domestic sphere, growing increasingly hostile as it grew in strength and numbers, so too is Aura Rodriguez isolated on a domestic island within a larger community she no longer understands. Both Cortez and Rodriguez are residual figures embodying earlier moments in Mexican-American culture; Cortez embodies an ideal of communal autonomy held over from a time prior to U.S. domination, while Aura embodies the hegemonically fostered values and self-perceptions of second generation Mexican-Americans, the group Rodolfo Alvarez has called "the Mexican American generation" (920). Viramontes emphasizes Aura's status as a bearer of residual culture (Williams, Limón) when she tells us that Aura "belonged to a different time" (102).

Frustrated at the lack of respect afforded her by the Bixby Boys who gather outside her home, Aura mistakenly turns to the Los Angeles Police Department for help in resolving her "border conflict." Aura's recourse to the Anglo legal system again emphasizes her powerlessness within her own marginalized community. Her reliance on the LAPD, the modern and equally symbolically charged equivalent of the Texas Rangers,[9] to protect her tragically illustrates the psychic price paid by the psychically assimilated Mexican-American generation. As Alvarez's model predicts, Aura exhibits "a falsely based sense of self-worth" (29); she crucially overestimates the degree of protection that she and other members of the Latino community are accorded under prevailing LAPD standards of enforcement. In other words, Aura retains an illusion that her right to privacy will be protected by an arm of North American culture that, in reality, inscribes her and all members of her race into a system in which they are coded as inferior, criminal, and dispensable. Aura only realizes her mistake when she witnesses the brutality unleashed against the young men by the police: "When the two policemen dragged [Toastie] down the porch steps, she could hear the creak of their thick leather belts rubbing against their bullets. She began to cry" (109). Aura realizes too late that with their shocking assertion of unnecessary force, the police have violently and callously undermined her own safety.

Rubén's last words to her as he is driven away in the police car are, "We'll get you . . . You'll see" (109).

In contrast to and intensifying Aura's growing awareness of her own isolation are the events that she observes taking place at the house of her neighbor Fierro, her last, tenuous, if unavowed, link to a larger community. Aura's deep but utterly passive curiosity concerning her neighbor's mysterious guest, a large, unkempt, unnamed woman, hints at the psychic pain underlying her partly self-imposed exile. The importance of Aura's relationship with her neighbor's visitor is foreshadowed early in the story when Aura first sees the woman:

> Aura stopped sweeping her porch and leaned on her broomstick, not to stare at the woman's badly mended dress or her wig that glistened with caked hairspray, but to watch the confident direction she took, unmoved by the taunts and stares. Aura did something she had not done in a while; she smiled. (103)

In spite of an appearance that should repulse the meticulous Aura, the woman attracts her with her self-possession. Aura behaves empathetically toward the woman and gives her the information she seeks, as she observes that "[h]ard years had etched her chapped and sunburnt face" (103).

Later, from her bathroom window, Aura observes the woman dancing for Fierro. As Aura watches, the woman materially reconnects Fierro to a past he is afraid to forget and a community he had believed was gone. She makes him burritos, which represent a welcome contrast to the tasteless food he eats at the senior citizens center. She also makes him laugh. His laughter expresses "a genuine enjoyment of living"; however, it simultaneously evokes a death rattle and a warning: "The laugh was an unfamiliar sound to Aura's ears, as if a screw had loosened somewhere inside his body and began to rattle" (110). After observing her neighbors' warmth and companionship, Aura goes to bed, "cold under the bleached, white sheets" (110). Fierro's death, foreshadowed in his laughter, is depicted in contrast to Aura's death-in-life. The shroud-like quality of the white sheets articulates, in the Hallian sense, death, whiteness, and coldness in Aura's state of isolation, while it also foreshadows and editorializes on her movement toward the narrative's final, epiphanic moment.

Fierro's visitor plays a crucial role in the narrative's movement. She has arrived in Aura's life as would a figure of Death. At the time of her arrival, Fierro's visitor is disguised, or "masked," in a wig and her feet are, suggestively, blood encrusted. When Aura tells her that Don Fierro is not at home she replies indifferently, "Waiting I know how to do!" (104). The woman inexplicably knows Aura's name and treats Fierro as a mother and a lover. She is, in an important sense, unnameable. As a spatial signifier for an earlier, more cohesive agrarian moment that also embodies a liminal temporal condition, (the movement of life into death), the woman at Aura's door functions as a Bakhtinian chronotope: she impels the narrative diachronically in a manner that addresses its synchronic concerns.[10] Her presence articulates historical Mexican cultural experience with present Mexican-American conditions. Moreover, the sound of Fierro's "rattling" laugh, which she precipitates, foreshadows both Fierro's death and the emergence later in the narrative of additional complex Mexican-American symbols for death. This narrative movement marks the unnamed woman as an allegorical and specifically Mexican-American figure for death.[11]

Aura comes to believe that she alone must defend herself after the Bixby Boys destroy her garden in retaliation for her call to the police. Not only do the young men use excrement to write graffiti on her porch, but her gardenias, roses, and chayotes are all torn from their roots and left to wither in the sun. The significance of Aura's garden lies in its connection to her past, and specifically to a female cultural identity: "Some of her bushes were 20 years old, having begun as cuttings from her mother's garden. She had spent years guiding and pruning and nurturing them until they blossomed their gratitude" (111). The rose bushes the Bixby Boys destroy are associated with Mexican-American forms of boundary maintenance; they represent the domestic sphere as it is defined and maintained by Aura in her role as a bearer of culture and preserver of a culturally authorized domestic space. The destruction of the growing, deeply rooted bushes, which vertically connected Aura with her past, and which horizontally demarcated a beautiful but thornily formidable boundary between her "private"

domestic space and the larger community, leads Aura to reinvigo-
rate other, perhaps less conscious cultural connections and forms
of boundary maintenance. Isolated and insulated by a comfortable,
primarily unconscious identification with the dominant culture,
Aura has remained aloof from the increasingly disorganized and
alienated community surrounding her. She is, however, in effect,
abruptly disinterpellated when her psychic identification with the
white power structure and her living, material connections to her
bodily and cultural past are both radically and simultaneously sev-
ered. She is left, in the wake of such enormous upheavals, so vulnerable, so "coldly" alone against the pachucos, that she finds herself, quite suddenly, willing and able to kill. The traditionally
authorized boundaries within which she has lived out her life have
been destroyed, while the legal "protections" through which the
dominant culture "guarantees" the "rights" of its citizens have also
been exposed as fraudulent. Catastrophically bereft, Aura chooses
to defend her right alone, with a pistol in her hand.

Aura's refusal "to be [a] sacrificial lamb" (112) itself represents
an extension of the corrido hero's determination to reject the selective and pernicious attacks of the encroaching Anglo government. In "Neighbors," however, the encroaching cultural forces
Aura seeks to combat are increasingly ambiguous and complex.
Aura's victimization is set in motion by two competing and mutually antagonistic forces: the racist and masculinist LAPD, an up-
dated version of the Texas Rangers, and the Bixby Boys, whose
sexist and ageist attacks exemplify inequitable power relations
within the Chicano community. While the sexism of the Bixby Boys
is of ancient provenance, their *ageism* is a notable byproduct of the
cultural anomie that results when a community's traditional
sources of coherence are under assault. Confronted with a com-
posite antagonist formed out of the long-standing inequities that
have characterized both the Mexican-American experience in the
United States and the repressive institutional response to Mexican-
American rage, Aura's decision to resist propels her backward in
time, in search of cultural power. Spurred by desperation and her
own "knowledge of struggle" (102), Aura plunges into a female-
gendered Mexican-American past, descending spontaneously into
"the gut of the cellar," which is cluttered with box after box of old
"kitchen utensils, books, photographs" (112). Her gendered famil-

iarity with "kitchen utensils," further icons of a female culture-bearing function that no longer pertains, cannot help her. Neither books nor photographs can provide guidance; in this passage they symbolize, respectively, a bourgeois attachment to education as a form of self-legitimation and the sentimentalized past captured in family photographs. The only item that retains cultural power that has not been drained or debunked by recent events is the pistol, a historic symbol of Chicano self-assertion and heroic defiance.

History is, in the narrative, represented as an unfamiliar space cluttered with foreign objects; Aura is said, for instance, to "examine [the gun] like the foreign object it was" (112). In this "foreign" region, which bears within it residual cultural materials from a "foreign" country that doesn't exist anymore, Aztlán, or the parts of Mexico which are now within U.S. boundaries, Aura figuratively searches in her cultural archives for a source of strength to remake cultural boundaries that are once again failing. From among these archival materials, she selects, not only the pistol per se, but the corridic tradition of resistance the pistol cathects.

As Aura crosses a charged historical boundary by taking up the ancient gun, Fierro crosses the border between life and death. He dies in the presence of his visitor, after enjoying a meal of burritos that she prepared for him. During his last illness, the "hours passed as she sat next to him, rocking herself back and forth, mesmerized in deep prayer" (117). Although Viramontes' omniscient narrator informs us that Fierro remembers his visitor's name at the moment of his death, her name is never imparted to the reader. The woman's attendance on Fierro at his death contributes to her figuration as an abstract narrative space, filled and saturated with specifically raced and gendered meaningfulness. In traditional ways, first in the cooking and serving of burritos, and then in her immersion in prayer, she fills Fierro's last moments with cultural markers which ease his transition across the border into death by explicitly positioning him within a coherent cultural cosmology. Fierro's actual death occurs at the same moment at which Aura takes up a position of defiance, behind her door, poised with the pistol in her hand, waiting for the Bixby Boys. Concomitantly, in her grief the unnamed woman leaves Fierro's body and runs to the only local woman she knows: Aura Rodriguez.

The narrative concludes immediately prior to the epiphanic

moment when "the lid blow[s] off . . ." and "the guns go off by themselves" (Fanon 79). The story's inconclusive and suspended final moment of confrontation between Aura and the mysterious visitor reflects backward upon the complexly interwoven events (or lines of historical tendention) that have led up to it. In this story, unlike the corrido, the synecdochic relationship between the gun, Aura, and the Chicano community is inexact. The narrative structure precludes a simple $x = y = z$ configuration; it emphasizes, instead, the multiple influences that differently constitute individuals according to age, gender, race, and class. Aura cannot figuratively embody her modern-day Chicano community in the sense that Gregorio Cortez figuratively embodied his nineteenth-century Mexican-American border community. Conflict in Viramontes' text occurs within a heterogeneous Chicano community, figured in the characters of Aura, the pachucos, Chuy, whose memory seems to represent the trace of an emergent form of masculinity crowded out by the pachucos,[12] Don Fierro, and the woman who comes to visit him. The figuration of characters in Viramontes' texts, here and throughout the collection, operates to interrogate the myth of a unified Chicano community and to examine the complex forces at work in the composition of that myth.

Aura's moment of resistance is iconographically charged with specific historical articulations of gender and defiance. The mysterious woman's position on the other side of Aura's door, however, complexly rearticulates the corridic moment of resistance. The impending face to face encounter between Aura and Fierro's guest represents the potential reunion of Chicano history and culture with a contemporary Chicana subject in a manner that allows for the preservation of both. On the other hand, Viramontes' closing image implies that encounters between Chicano history and the contemporary Chicana subject are profoundly risky, as well as being, as Norma Alarcón contends in "Traddutora, Traditora," "fraught with paradox, contradiction, and unlikely partners" (85). The tensions inherent in this narrative moment represent a central dilemma in contemporary Chicano experience. Aura fears the representatives of a certain contemporary Chicano masculinity whom she believes are waiting outside her door; her fears, however, threaten to preclude a life-sustaining encounter with a representative of a dispossessed Chicana history. At some level, Aura recognizes her own relationship to this history when she first smiles at the confident walk of Fierro's visitor, and subsequently "reads" the "hard years" etched on her chapped and sunburnt face. While Aura clearly admires the resilience and self-assuredness of the mysterious visitor, however, the woman's grief and loss, which have elicited her sudden, urgent need to connect with Aura, disturbingly mirror the grief and loss of acculturation that Aura has struggled to keep "within her perimeters" (102). Aura is afraid to open her perimeters to the pain of the mysterious woman, whose agrarian, mestiza identity threatens to situate her own pain within an overwhelmingly complex communal and historical context that the Mexican-American generation, of necessity, repressed. Fierro's mysterious visitor is clearly not, however, merely a figure for a rural Chicana or mestiza past which Aura, in her appropriation of the synecdochic pistol, must confront. Rather, as a culturally specific allegorical figure for Death, the woman precipitates in Aura, in the closing paragraphs of the story, a memory—a complex image of rattlesnakes—that powerfully embodies Aura's multivalently articulated narrative and social position. She recalls

> [t]he summer of the rattlers. The Vizcano desert was far away, yet she could almost feel the rattlers coiled up under the brittle bushes waiting for her. As a child she was frightened by their domination of the desert. (117)

The image of the rattlers, called up in Aura's mind by the invisible presence of the woman on the other side of her door, leads in heterogenous directions. The rattlesnakes of the Vizcano desert, prefigured in Don Fierro's "rattling" laugh, function in the story as a first order symbol for death itself, and for the all-pervasiveness and invisibility of death. The narrator's description of the rattlers as "dominant," however, and as striking "if . . . disturbed [with] such force that it was always too late to do anything" (117) historicizes the specific forms of death and social death[13] that loom about Aura at the same time that it conflates the Bixby Boys, especially the lunging (desperate, terrified) Toastie whom Aura "was sure . . . wanted to kill her" (109), with the police, and with Anglo society in general.

The description of Aura's fear as triggered by the snakes'

"menacing appearance, their slickness . . . their *instinct to survive*" (118; emphasis ours) suggests the material and symbolic *relations* between the Bixby Boys and Anglo culture that might account for the narrative conflation of the two: the Bixby Boys, as young members of a more rebellious generation, represent inviting targets for Anglo repression. Their "instincts" for both cultural and personal survival within an environment that they perceive (lacking Aura's generational identification with Anglo values) as hostile lead them to become "menacing" and "slick." These snake-like qualities represent strategies for survival within an alien and harsh (desert-like) environment.[14]

A second semantic/symbolic cluster activated by the image of the rattlers refers specifically to Aura's Mexican cultural heritage. As Gloria Anzaldúa suggests in *Borderlands/La Frontera,* the rattlesnake can symbolize a pre-Christian Mexican spirituality and function as a chronotopic site negotiating (which is to say *problematically* articulating) death and cultural empowerment. When the narrator in Anzaldúa's text tells us that as a child she was bitten by a rattlesnake which "interpellated" her, as it were, or entered her as her animal counterpart (26), the story she tells seems to offer an object illustration of the Nietzschean maxim that what does not kill us only makes us stronger. Both Anzaldúa and Viramontes use the rattlesnake as an object, culturally specific manifestation of Nietzsche's aphorism, organizing Mexican culture, oppression (death), and opposition into a very differently articulated configuration from that by which the corrido articulates similar themes. In the corrido, the articulation of death to resistance represents a gap, a weakness in the articulation. The rattlesnake figuration, on the other hand, links up oppression (or even death) to resistance in a more potentially useful way by suggesting that injuries sustained by the community will inexorably be channeled into future empowerment and resistance.

The narrator's report that "the sight of one [rattler] always made [Aura] immobile because she had no protection against their menacing *appearance*" (117; emphasis ours), is also powerfully suggestive. The articulation of the rattler, whose menacing appearance *immobilizes* Aura with Fierro's already death-articulated visitor, suggests that behind Aura's door stands a richly heterogeneous Medusa-figure who bears within her person both opposition and repression, both an assertion of cultural presence and, in her invisibility and the invisibility of the rattlers, the simultaneous admission of cultural absence.

The woman at Aura's door represents a sort of compromise between the Freudian Medusa who, representing female "castratedness" from the viewpoint of the biologically male, figures lack (212), and the Cixousian Medusa who figures female *presence* and bodiliness (885). From the Freudian point of view, the woman behind the door is associated with the "invisible" rattlers and the abysmal Bixby Boys. Her hairspray-caked wig also figures both lack (an artificial appendage might be replacing something unnaturally absent), and concealment (what can be under it?), while at the same time its "flopping black cotton" (103) evokes the possibility of writhing, serpentine tendrils. Cixous' celebratory reading of the Medusa allows us to account for the ways in which the figure of the unseen woman also represents a repressed Chicana presence which, though denied, is nonetheless present and on the verge of visibility. The woman at the door is imbued with an indisputable corporeal presence; she in fact makes "a spectacle" of herself. Her blood-caked feet, her confident disregard for the neighborhood's reactions to her, the fact that she mysteriously *knows* Aura, and her "rummaging through her bags like one looking for proof of birth at a border" (103) all establish her as a powerful, magical, transgressive, and culturally specific figuration for Chicana immanence. And while the future, in Viramontes' story, is unquestionably unwritten, the unseen woman with the "caved in mouth" hovers at the threshold of our vision, an ambiguous harbinger of death, revolution, and a specifically Chicana future, within which residual forms of culture-bearing and boundary maintenance may give rise to emergent forms of collectivity and resistance.

Rearticulating the Interpellative Medusa

The Gringo, *locked into* the fiction of white superiority, seized complete political power, stripping Mexicans and Indians of their land while their feet were still rooted in it.
                                        —Gloria Anzaldúa (emphasis ours)

Anzaldúa's portrayal of the economic and military seizure of Texas, and the narratives of white superiority that underwrote those crimes and that "locked" white America into untenable and costly fictions, casts ideology as a sort of Medusa that freezes all of us, through a Manichean series of hypostatizing binary articulations, into subjects. In *The Moths and Other Stories,* Viramontes depicts crucial moments in this process of articulation, as well as moments when such articulations are subverted, resisted, or empowered with unexpected or unintended meanings. Viramontes focuses her narratives around those who are disempowered within the symbolic order—those who have few opportunities for self-representation—who must live out their lives figured within the gaze and narrative constructions of others. These narratives are imbued with historical as well as contemporary political meaning through patterns and icons recognizably charged with the rhythms and intensificatory logic of the corrido informed by new and potentially oppositional articulations.[15]

While the traditional corrido's epiphanic moment communicated itself as monolithic, absolute, and simultaneously emptied out and filled with inchoate meaningfulness, modifications to traditional Mexican-American narrative structures introduced in the work of contemporary writers such as Viramontes, along with Arturo Islas, Los Hermanos Hernandez, Gloria Anzaldúa, Cherríe Moraga, and a host of others, rely upon the slips, gaps, and dissonances within the dominant culture's system of Manichean binary oppositions to saturate the historically charged moment with heterogenous and multiply vacillating, tense, and undecidable interpretive possibilities. As in the corrido, the supercharged moment in contemporary Chicano literature remains the historical moment, the moment at which events move momentarily and decisively outside of the sphere of any one person's influence. The sensitized moment within a new generation of Chicano/a narratives places the overdetermined nature of the historical moment in direct dialogue with the event's irreducibility to any single, readily decodeable meaning. It is significant to note that this narrative development is emerging at a moment of intergenerational crisis when, as Lora Romero observes, many theorists of minority cultures have constituted themselves as *postmovement* intellectuals who "distance themselves from the social movements of the 1960s and 1970s—and . . . have routinely invoked the fantasy of a population that is 'non-intellectual'" (136). If, as Romero observes, in the 1980s a generation of minority cultural theorists situated themselves as "[p]ostmovement authors . . . able to theorize minority culture and politics in a way that would have been impossible in the tumult of the 1960s and 1970s" (136), it is important to note a symmetrical countermovement, discernible in the work of Viramontes and other theoretically oriented Chicano/a authors, which evinces a passionate curiosity concerning quotidian strategies of survival for differentially situated Chicano/a subjects, and a concomitant interest in the present moment as affording promising opportunities for new forms of political intervention. These writers share with Américo Paredes, and other "*pre*movement" intellectuals and activists, a commitment, however differently perceived and represented, to the on-going and historically informed reinvention of a Chicano culture capable of surviving and productively addressing evolving modes of hegemonic domination.

The tense, ambiguous narrative epiphanies of Viramontes' short stories exemplify the ways in which these contemporary Chicano/a cultural producers are figuratively reuniting history with subjectivity in defiance of a broader cultural consensus that situates the moment of historical opportunity in the past and the production of political strategies and intellectual analyses exclusively in the academy. Viramontes' astute reformulation of historically and culturally charged narrative moments corresponds to Hall's model of rearticulation, and concretely supports Hall's contention that such rearticulations can intervene in and respond to specific historical and cultural moments. Viramontes accomplishes her rearticulations with minute attention to the heterogeneous groupings and loyalties which invariably exist *within* a minority culture. Her heterogeneous reworking of the corrido narrative allows for a closer and far more theoretically enabling analysis of the means by which we are all constituted as subjects as well as for the production of new and more powerfully oppositional and inclusive articulations within the constraints of the interpellating process. In her rearticulation of the Mexican American oral tradition, Viramontes has, in the mirror-like shield of her fiction, reorganized, reframed, and reconstituted cultural identity, and appropriated the dangerous power of the interpellative Medusa for her own oppositional ends.

Notes

We are deeply indebted to the following scholars, all of whom have made indispensable contributions to this article: Ramón Saldívar and Lora Romero each read and responded helpfully to several versions of this project; Barbara Harlow, José Limón, Ann Cvetkovich, and Susan Dauer all provided useful feedback to various drafts. Héctor Pérez was characteristically generous in sharing his knowledge about specialized debates in Chicano studies; Lisa Jadwin and Bernadette Brick provided vital assistance during the final stage of the manuscript's preparation; and Wahneema Lubiano's analysis has fundamentally informed our own approaches to literary representations of gender, class, and ethnicity, and we dedicate this article to her.

1. We have chosen the Althusserian term interpellation, described at length in his essay "Ideology and Ideological State Apparatuses," to specify the phenomenon of a discursively constituted freezing or paralyzing of the subject. In choosing Althusser's term, which precisely captures our sense of the subject as irretrievably embroiled within and constituted through ideologically configured systems of representation, we hope to retain the explanatory force of his model while modifying it to allow for the possibility of agency.

2. Gloria Anzaldúa has characterized the Chicano cultural condition as one of "mestizaje." In her description of the south Texas Valley where she grew up, Anzaldúa briefly enumerates the complicated, uneven, and undemocratic sequence of historical and cultural relationships that have shaped this region and its inhabitants. "[T]his land [and its people] ha[ve] survived possession and ill-use by five countries: Spain, Mexico, the Republic of Texas, the Confederacy, and the U.S. again" (90).

3. In an address delivered at Hampshire College in the spring of 1989, Hall pointed out,

> [i]f you ask my son where he comes from, he cannot tell you he comes from Jamaica. Part of his identity is there, but he has to *discover* that identity. He can't just take it out of his suitcase and plop it on the table and say 'That's mine.' It's not an essence like that. (19)

4. We do not wish to suggest that the corrido is a necessary master work to which all Chicano/a writers inevitably turn. The influence that the corrido has had on contemporary Chicano/a artists, both formally and thematically, has been well established by Ramón Saldívar, José E. Limón, and others. That the thematic of border conflict and resistance should remain important 100 years after the border corrido's emergence speaks more to the consistency of exploitive power relations in North America than it does to the intrinsic tenacity of the corrido form within Chicano culture. Although the Hallian articulation between the corrido form and cultural expressions of resistance is not inevitable, for the moment the corrido continues to exert a significant influence on oppositional cultural productions within the Chicano tradition. This influence, moreover, is not confined

exclusively to poetic production. As José Limón argues in his discussion of the corrido's influence on Chicano poets writing from 1965 to 1972, the corrido "may still exert its own persuasive influence on a third and future social drama." In Viramontes' work, experimental narrative prose is clearly grounding itself in corridic conventions as a means of accounting for new "social drama." New forms of social drama are themselves emerging out of the internal divisions and strife within the Chicano community that have developed in response to long-standing political, social, and cultural repression.

5. It is important to acknowledge that some of the corridos collected and analyzed by María Herrera-Sobek in *The Mexican Corrido: A Feminist Analysis* represent significant earlier breaks within the dominant corrido tradition. In her chapter on "the soldier archetype," for instance, Herrera-Sobek observes that on the occasions when a woman is allowed to occupy the defiant space of the male corrido hero, she is sometimes "permitted a weakness that is taboo for male protagonists" (96). In the corrido "De Agripina," Doña Agripina, a Mexican land reformer who fought against those who wished to extend the powers of the Catholic Church "con sus armas en la mano" (with her weapons in her hand), is, in contravention to corrido convention, allowed a moment of confusion and fear when she realizes that she and her comrades will be decimated if reinforcements do not arrive quickly. Shortly prior to the arrival of the backup troops that did indeed save the historical Agripina and her comrades, the corrido depicts her asking a comrade anxiously whether he has seen any sign of reinforcements. While such moments are usually stylized out of existence for the male corrido hero, as Herrera-Sobek observes, "the corrido's succinct description of a woman with weapons in her hand and yelling aggressively places our Agripina in a special dimension" (95). As Herrera-Sobek's analysis implies, even in the traditional corrido context the presence of a female subject in the position of the corrido hero brings a new and ambivalent "dimension" to the corrido narrative.

6. According to Paredes, *El Corrido de Gregorio Cortez* set the model for the twentieth-century Lower Border corrido. He moreover observes that in later corridos, the role of the Texas Ranger is "extended not only to possemen but to border patrolmen, immigration officers, prison guards, and even to Pershing's soldiers when they are in pursuit of the border raider Pancho Villa." He also contends that "it is not too much to suggest" that the influence of the Lower Border corrido, and of *El Corrido de Gregorio Cortez* itself, extended to the Greater Mexican heroic corrido, a form "which began ten years after Cortez rode his famous ride" (150).

7. Related concepts of narrative intensification include M. M. Bakhtin's chronotope, in *The Dialogic Imagination*, and Paul De Man's theory of allegory, in his essay "The Rhetoric of Temporality."

8. The corrido both narratively and thematically assigns its greatest symbolic weight to the male protagonist, who, though vanquished in the end, is constructed within the narrative, *through his conformity to a specifically Mexican-American set of cultural ideals and gender roles,* as a personage of historical consequence and moral substance whom his Anglo persecutors cannot rival. These roles are not in any way simply equatable with Anglo-American sex/gender dichotomies. Cf. Norma Alarcón, "Making Família From Scratch" 147–155, and Ramón Saldívar, *Chicano Narrative* 22.

9. Our recognition of the equivalence between the Texas Rangers and the LAPD as supercharged icons of white cultural supremacy draws from a keynote address delivered by Barbara Harlow at University College-Galway's conference

"Gender and Colonialism" in May 1992, in which she foregrounded the role of
the LAPD in "Neighbors."

10. Alvina Quintana describes similar chronotopic resonances in the work of
Denise Chavez in her article "Politics, Representation and the Emergence of a
Chicana Aesthetic."

11. Clarrissa Pinkola Estes, in *Women Who Run With the Wolves: Myths and Stories
of the Wild Woman Archetype,* poetically conflates a series of stories that she has
heard in her travels in the southwestern United States and in Mexico concerning
La Loba, a female figure associated with a larger group of death-related personas
Estes calls "the bone people" (26–27). Estes's recapitulation of these stories provides a concentrated folkloric background to Viramontes's depiction of Fierro's
guest:

> There is an old woman who lives in a hidden place that everyone
> knows but few have ever seen. . . .
>
> She is circumspect, often hairy, always fat, and especially wishes to
> evade most company. . . .
>
> They say she lives among the rotten granite slopes in Tarahumara
> Indian territory. They say she is buried outside Phoenix near a well.
> She is said to have been seen traveling south to Monte Alban in a
> burnt-out car with the back window shot out. She is said to stand by
> the highway near El Paso, or ride shotgun with truckers to Morelia,
> Mexico, or that she has been sighted walking to market above Oaxaca
> with strangely formed boughs of firewood on her back. She is called
> by many names: La Huesera, Bone Woman; La Trapera, The Gath-
> erer; and La Loba, Wolf Woman.
>
> The sole work of La Loba is the collecting of bones. She is known
> to collect and preserve especially that which is in danger of being lost
> to the world. (27)

12. Don Fierro's son, Chuy, with his "almost womanly slender fingers" (104)
and his "good heart" (115), figures an alternate masculinity crowded out by another example of a masculinist overreliance on violence. However, this alternative
remains an inchoate potential in Chuy's ghost. It saturates the landscape of Don
Fierro's memories and continues to exist in the cane Fierro whittles on Aura's
porch from the 2 × 4 Chuy used as a defense against his attackers—a material
transposition from weapon to helping hand.

13. Cf. Patterson.

14. The pachucos gather near Aura's home, slithering slowly to "a cooler location" (118) to "lose themselves in the abyss of defeat" (102). Just as a desert is
characterized by the lack of water, the symbolic order is, for the pachucos, characterized by its fundamental lack of significatory agency; they experience American
society as "an abyss of defeat," in which their subject position is coded in terms of
lack relative to what Audre Lorde has called "the mythical norm."

15. In the Chicano literary tradition that has taken shape over the past twenty
years, the "sensitized" moments in which the cultural and the historical are articulated through supercharged images have expanded and taken on a multiplicity
of new forms. In some cases, as in the late Arturo Islas's *The Rain God,* in which
the death of Felix organizes and energizes the entire second half of the novel
(111–80), the sensitized moment may be expanded to accommodate and account
for many generations of historical-cultural conflict so that a single, heightened
moment may articulate an even broader range of social, historical, and cultural
discourses. Gender codings continue to play a significant role within the construc-

and 15) when they began. At that age they were especially conscious of and open to cultural motifs from the world around them: their families taught them movement and language from their particular heritage; television, the one-eyed baby-sitter, taught them advertising techniques; currents running within their communities taught them something about politics and the history of their oppression.

Contemporary phenomena like advertising and popular culture and current social movements like Black, Latin, and Red Power resonate in the work and attitudes of subway painters. This blending is defined below as "creolization," and several innovators among this group of rebellious artists creolize images and ideas from the society around them to create their work. Because this movement was created spontaneously by adventurous teenagers, it appears to have no clear-cut precedents. My interviews with writers and my research, however, have shown that this art form is part of an African-American and Caribbean "Creole" cultural continuum.

Creolization as an Attitude

The concept of creolization is sometimes used among anthropologists to explain the formation of new products of multicultural interaction.[1] Here "creolization" is used as a metaphor for what happens when a new language is created by the merging of two or more languages. Basic to the creole process is the meeting of two or more cultures. Often there is a relationship of domination/subordination between them.[2] In this meeting, elements from different cultures are combined because they have a meaning or a function useful to a particular person or cultural group. The end result is the creation of a new tradition distinct from either one, yet having elements of both.

A cultural product tells us something about the ideas and philosophical orientation of its producers. The paintings of New York City writers often reveal the sophisticated receptivity of writers towards their environment, and their sense of comradeship with their peers. Writers grew up within the kaleidoscope of cultures of which Chinatown, Little Italy, Spanish Harlem, Greenwich

tion of these sensitized narrative moments as moments that are charged with meaning, filled to bursting with presence and intelligibility. The moment's appropriation of gender as a discourse, however, within the work of Viramontes, Islas, Anzaldúa, Moraga, the Hernandez Brothers, Rocky Ramirez, and many others, no longer relies on a simplistic Manichean reading of transcendental and binary gender codes. Instead, gender as a discourse is empowered within the epiphanic moment, as it is typically read against and through both Chicano and Anglo binary oppositions of gender, race and sexual orientation.

Works Cited

Alarcón, Norma. "Making Família From Scratch: Split Subjectivities in the Work of Helena María Viramontes and Cherríe Moraga." *Chicana Creativity and Criticism.* Ed. María Herrera-Sobek and Helena María Viramontes. Houston: Arte Público, 1988. 147–55.

———. "Traddutora, Traditora: A Paradigmatic Figure of Chicana Feminism." *The Construction of Gender and Modes of Social Division. Cultural Critique* 13 (1989): 57–87.

Althusser, Louis. "Ideology and Ideological State Apparatuses (Notes Toward an Investigation)." *Lenin and Philosophy and Other Essays.* Trans. Ben Brewster. New York: Monthly Review, 1971. 127–86.

Alvarez, Rodolfo. "The Psycho-Historical and Socioeconomic Development of the Chicano Community in the United States." *Social Science Quarterly* 53 (1973): 920–42.

Anzaldúa, Gloria. *Borderlands/La Frontera: The New Mestiza.* San Francisco: Spinsters/Aunt Lute, 1987.

Bakhtin, M. M. *The Dialogic Imagination: Four Essays.* Trans. Caryl Emerson and Michael Holquist. Austin: U of Texas P, 1981.

Cixous, Hélène. "The Laugh of the Medusa." Trans. Keith Cohen and Paula Cohen. *Signs* 1 (1976): 875–93.

De Man, Paul. "The Rhetoric of Temporality." *Blindness and Insight: Essays in the Rhetoric of Contemporary Criticism.* Minneapolis: U of Minnesota P, 1983. 187–228.

Estes, Clarissa Pinkola. *Women Who Run With the Wolves: Myths and Stories of the Wild Woman Archetype.* New York: Ballantine, 1992.

Fanon, Frantz. *The Wretched of the Earth.* Trans. Constance Farrington. New York: Grove, 1963.

Freud, Sigmund. "Medusa's Head." *Sexuality and the Psychology of Love.* Ed. Philip Reiff. Trans. Constance Farrington. New York: Macmillan 1963. 212–13.

Grossberg, Lawrence. "On Postmodernism and Articulation: An Interview with Stuart Hall." *Journal of Communication Inquiry* 10.2 (1986): 45–60.

Hall, Stuart. "Ethnicity, Identity, and Difference." *Radical America* 23.4: 9–20.

Harlow, Barbara. First Plenary Lecture. Gender and Colonialism Conference. University College, Galway, 21 May 1992.

Herrera-Sobek, María. *The Mexican Corrido: A Feminist Analysis.* Bloomington: Indiana UP, 1990.

Islas, Arturo. *The Rain God: A Desert Tale.* Palo Alto: Alexandrian Press, 1984.

Limón, José. *Mexican Ballads, Chicano Poems: History and Influence in Mexican-American Social Poetry.* Berkeley: U of California P, 1992.

Lorde, Audre. *Sister Outsider: Essays and Speeches*. Freedom: Crossing Press, 1984.

Paredes, Américo. *With His Pistol in His Hand: A Border Ballad and Its Hero*. Austin: U of Texas P, 1958.

Patterson, Orlando. *Slavery and Social Death: A Comparative Study*. Cambridge: Harvard UP, 1982.

Pérez, Héctor. Presentation in Ramón Saldívar's graduate seminar, "Cultural Studies: Ethnicity and Gender." University of Texas, Austin, 6 Dec. 1990.

Quintana, Alvina. "Politics, Representation and the Emergence of a Chicana Aesthetic." *Cultural Studies* 4 (1990): 256–63.

Romero, Lora. "'When Something Goes Queer': Familiarity, Formalism, and Minority Intellectuals in the 1980s." *Yale Journal of Criticism* 6.1 (1993): 121–41.

Saldívar, Ramón. *Chicano Narrative: The Dialectics of Difference*. Madison: U of Wisconsin P, 1990.

Sanchez, Rosaura. "Ethnicity, Ideology and Academia." *Cultural Studies* 4 (1990): 294–302.

Viramontes, Helena María. *The Moths and Other Stories*. 1985. Houston: Arte Público, 1992.

Williams, Raymond. *Marxism and Literature*. Oxford: Oxford UP, 1977.

Creolizing for Survival in the City

Ivor Miller

In the early 1970s the New York City subways burgeoned with a new art form. While Norman Mailer and a handful of writers and photographers celebrated the phenomenon, others saw it as an attack on society. By the mid-1980s New York City's young guerrilla artists had developed their craft to produce full car murals that became a tourist attraction for visitors from around the world. To regain control over the subways, New York mayors Lindsay and later Koch initiated and sustained multi-million dollar campaigns to erase the paintings and arrest the painters. While the passionate and bold murals have vanished from New York's subways, the art form has become a world-wide phenomenon with adherents in Europe, Australia, New Zealand, and all major U.S. cities. In New York the original painters, who are mostly male, still call themselves "painters," "aerosol artists," "graffiti artists," or "writers," and the most dedicated of them continue to create their work in public spaces and for art galleries.

Since the beginning of their movement in 1971, New York City subway painters have used diverse cultural ideas in their creative processes. Most of the great painters were young (between 12

© 1994 by *Cultural Critique*. Spring 1994. 0882-4371/94/$5.00.

Village, and the Lower East Side are a part. Their familiarity with cultural diversity helped them transform their segregated society into a city-wide community that included hundreds of creative youth. Initially, they communicated their awareness of each other by painting signatures on the trains. From the South Bronx, and of African-American and Caribbean descent, PHASE 2[3] says:

> We communicated when we were just doing signatures. Back when STAY HIGH 149 was painting, everybody used to like his signature, so we used to write it on the trains. We would write his name, say "149," write our name next to his and point to his name. Then later we would see he wrote our name, and then write something next to it. (March 1989)

Originally, groups of writers met at certain train stations to watch the latest style innovations and to form painting crews. Many passionately recall the individual creativity that was encouraged within a unified group of writers. From Upper Manhattan, and of Puerto Rican/Brasilian descent, CO-CO 144 affirms that aerosol culture was a spontaneous response to a need for multi-cultural unity:

> The movement broke barriers. We were at a point where after the 50s and 60s there were the gangs, and you couldn't go into a neighborhood, neighborhoods were put into pockets like Black Harlem, Spanish Harlem, and the Upper West Bronx. This movement is something that broke negative barriers and created unity. It did so many things at one time. It was totally pure (positive). . . . Our intentions weren't to deface property. It was a call for unity—even amongst people who weren't writers. A lot of people that I met would be surprised to meet me. "You're CO-CO 144?" and there you'd strike up a conversation, and they would look up to you and say how great you are, and where they'd seen your name and how many times. It wasn't to fluff yourself up like a rooster and be egotistical, it was something real nice, very positive and constructive.

Perhaps the most dramatic aspect of the writing movement was its creation of an interracial youth culture at a grassroots level. As writing groups formed, each painter brought his or her own cultural style and perspective to the art. When a new piece rode by on the rails, other writers would study it, incorporating the styles or images they liked the best into their own work, and a fresh style would be born later that night in the train yard. In this way the complex layers of the creole process continued to intertwine. New styles appeared constantly on the trains.

Comradeship between writers formed because they needed mobility to get their names up around the city, and there was safety in numbers. Thus to move through the grid of neighborhoods divided by rival gangs, writers formed "crews" that could move together, and could watch out for each other while painting in the train yards. The communication that existed through the call and response of train paintings and within the groups who made them helped create an integrated culture not reflected in adult society. The powerful self-identity "ALL CITY"[4] writers created through painting gained such momentum that it literally dissolved the rigid segregation enforced by gang structures in many barrios.[5] From the South Bronx, and of African-American Deep South descent, AMRL/BAMA speaks:

A lot of what happened back then cannot be explained easily because it was like a coming together of minds. To me I always look back and think how amazing it was, because you had a bunch of guys with the same kind of mental attitude going out to do something. When it was really rolling, two years after it began, we're talking about three or four thousand writers that could communicate peacefully all over the city, and shared ideas. And that kind of activity was not happening during that time, there were too many gangs out there and all that madness, and yet these cats came out of nowhere, didn't even realize what they were doing, and created a major network in the city, communication from Brooklyn to Manhattan in a day, without the use of a phone. It was really tight.

It is not clear whether this integration was an influence of the consciousness created by the Civil Rights movement with integrationist ideals, the spontaneous result of youth needing to express a shared inner city, multi-cultural experience, or whether integration was found through a common desire to rebel against an uncaring system. It is clear that youth from a broad spectrum of cultural heritages came together to form a complex rite of passage. Urban youth, growing up in segregated neighborhoods, acted upon their visions of an integrated society, and many had to struggle against the long-standing prejudices of their families and neighborhoods to do so. PHASE 2 speaks:

> We're not living in an atmosphere that tells us to love your brother, and harmonize with everybody, or teaches us how to deal with somebody that speaks Spanish, or Arabic or something or another. Because where I come from, you judge people's personalities depending on where they come from. You don't judge them as people. You say, "Well, what do you expect from a [so and so], he's this color, or from that part of town . . . Yet this art brings all of the cultures here together as one. Maybe if this art was not from a "ghetto,"[6] there would be a different approach to the art from our society. If it wasn't just a bunch of kids who weren't expected to make anything with their lives anyway. All this art came up from the gutter. This art brings the masses together. (June 1989)

The painters, in a spontaneous surge of creative energy, succeeded for a time in creating an integrated culture (Fig. 1). They developed unwritten rules for the evaluation of their work. What counted among writers was how innovative and powerful one's style was, not what one looked like. From Queens, and of Ecuadorean descent, LADY PINK says:

> Writers came from all ethnic backgrounds, all classes, and the police knew to look out for a group of kids who were racially diverse—those were the writers. If a gang was all black or white the police wouldn't bother them. In the early '70s race wasn't an obstacle for a writer to join a crew, gender wasn't either. That set in later. Barriers break down quickly when you go down into the subways. It's like being in Vietnam. After you come out, you have a link, a comradeship. Once you were a writer, you were respected, you could go anywhere in the city. You were known, you had friends and connections, even if you had never set eyes on them before. It was a family.

At a time of life when youth need to explore the world, ask questions, and express their new thoughts and perceptions, a lot of

Fig. 1. "The Crazy 5's," circa 1972, at Co-op City, the Bronx, with Blade in center. From the collection of Blade.

their energy was spent struggling with poverty, fighting the boredom of unchallenging school classes, and defending gang territory. From the Lower East Side, and of Puerto Rican descent, LEE reflects:

> A lot of people don't realize the impact the writing movement had in the neighborhoods, because the gangs were still around. The gangs kept neighborhoods apart, the city was a jigsaw puzzle of gangs keeping turf and territorial rights. So this movement brought people together: blacks, Puerto Ricans, whites, Orientals, Polish, from the richest to the poorest, we were equals. We took the same energy that was there to stand by your block with bats or guns and flying colors all night long, and used it to go painting, to create.
>
> Without the movement, I would never have met a writer like ALE [Fig. 2]. Look at the respect we give each other, it's immense. You don't get that anymore, because this country still seems to be sleeping on the fact that we are human beings. Just because of the color of our skin and our backgrounds are different, doesn't mean that we should be kept apart. This society thrives on violence and discrimination. What is a 100%

Fig. 2. "ALE 1," circa 1972. Aerosol paint on MTA train. From the collection of Blade.

human being supposed to look like? It is what comes from the insides that matters, you know?

New World Creoles

Throughout the African Diaspora creole cultures have been created as a response to the imposition of the European masters' culture upon African slaves. The creation of African-based creole forms (in music, food, religion, and language) tend to be characterized by the creative ability of Africans to infuse European cultural forms with African and African-derived worldviews.[7] Maya Deren writes of the creole process that created Haitian Vodun:

> Voudoun . . . is, in fact, a monumental testament to the extremely sophisticated ability of the West African to recognize a conceptual principle common to ostensibly disparate practices and to fuse African, American Indian, European and Christian elements dynamically into an integrated working structure. Where, at first glance, it might seem that Christianity had triumphed over Voudoun, it becomes clear, on closer study, that

Voudoun has merely been receptive to compatible elements
from a sister faith and has integrated these into its basic structure, subtly transfiguring and adjusting their meaning, where
necessary, to the African tradition. (56)

Aerosol art was born from similar creolizing processes that gave
the world Afro-Catholic religions like Haitian Vodun, Cuban San-
tería, and Brazilian Candomblé; Southern creole and Cajun cooking; and urban musical forms like Salsa, Latin Jazz, Be-Bop, and
Hip Hop music. Unlike postmodernist strategies, which emphasize
the dismantling and breaking up of traditions, creolization tends
to synthesize existing fragments together into a seamless whole.
Jelly Roll Morton and Sidney Bechet, two early jazz innovators,
explain that jazz was born from multi-cultural interactions:

> "We had all nations in New Orleans," said Jelly Roll. "But with
> the music we could creep in close to other people," adds Dr.
> Bechet. ". . . Jazz was the hybrid of hybrids and so it appealed
> to a nation of lonely immigrants. In a divided world struggling
> blindly toward unity, it became a cosmopolitan musical argot."
> (Lomax 100)

The various ethnic groups in New Orleans sought a common reference point so they could interact in positive ways. The musical
blending that created jazz was an answer to this need.[8]

Creolization often requires that the cultural producers be
receptive and spontaneous in grappling with new ideas.[9] Artist
PHASE 2 believes some creole forms are created by the ingenuity
of people who need to constantly create food, language, and life-
styles from the meager materials and resources that are available
to them:

> We live here in Babylon and we learn what we learn from here.
> But a lot of us take what we learn and become inventive with
> it. When we came over here from Africa, we took what we were
> given and did what we could with it. We were never given so
> much anyway. They gave us the guts of the pig, and we made
> it into some type of southern gourmet dinner. It's always been
> that way, we get seconds all the time. Even with the second-
> hand education we receive, we have created a new form of
> painting. (May 1989)

From Harlem, and of African-American/Native American descent, VULCAN agrees with PHASE 2 that sophisticated cultural achievements can be created with minimal resources and determination.[10] His description demonstrates the parallels between the creation of Southern cuisine and Northern aerosol art:

> Everything that we did with the spray can was done by trial and error. There were no teachers. There were no books, no schools. I grew up reading comic books. I was never taught to draw. The only thing I wanted to draw was pieces, letters, and draw them wilder and wilder. We evolved from spray painting one simple letter into these complicated styles.

Like the guerrilla artists they are, writers devoured images from the myriad popular culture forms around them. AMRL/BAMA speaks:

> I think half the guys who were writers learned how to read and draw better through comic books than schoolbooks. They were into those underground comics and they were seeking good art. And when I say good art, I mean we related to everything being art. So we could look at a Captain Crunch ad and see something that you could steal for your piece.

Creolization is a strategy for cultural survival that has been dramatically accelerated by colonialist expansion in the past 500 years.[11] Indigenous cultures the world over have been forced to grapple with the imposition of European systems and ideas. Today, United Statesian economic exploitation and cultural imperialism often work together to expand the world market. Even within segregated, working class, inner city neighborhoods of the United States, propaganda bombards residents, feeding them Western ideals of beauty and behavior, trying to turn them into consumers. Many inner city poor people creolize aspects of the dominant culture as a strategy to maintain both an individual and a group identity. They use creolization as an effective strategy to maintain their cultural integrity.

Trains, spray cans, and pop culture are all products of industrial societies that coerce people to work, or get them to buy products. Writers take these industrial artifacts, designed to be passively consumed by them, and actively reshape them to create their own culture. In fact they literally reshape the spray-can nozzles in original ways in order to meet their creative needs;[12] they infuse the trains with their spirits by painting their signatures on them; and they create personal statements using advanced advertising techniques from the ads imposed upon them by Madison Avenue.

PHASE 2 describes how the images that influenced writers were transformed on the trains:

> They try to make you think that everybody's influenced so much by these Pop artists, Futurists, Surrealists and Vaughn Bodé,[13] but the creative guys are going to *feed* off of Bodé, they're not going to copy his art to the letter. It's good to be able to copy something, but it's even better when you can take something and make it your own. That's basically what I think has been done with writing at this point, it's *our* writing now, you see what I'm saying? Whereas when we were babies growing up, learning the ABCs, now people have to learn *our* ABCs. (July 1989)

The disruption of African and African-American cultures produced by slavery, immigration, and poverty has left gaps in self-knowledge, history, and family structure that young black writers have tried to fill. Yet urban writers from all ethnic groups have a common history of dislocation from their ancestral lands and cultural fabric. They all fill gaps in their lives by participating in the creation of their youth culture. By constantly recreating their own local culture as a means of self-identity and group affirmation, many writers reject the assimilation demanded by mass marketed culture. PHASE 2 speaks:

> Here in the USA I think it is vital for people to be culturally aware of their heritage, because people try to take it away from you every day of your life, and make you become a part of the mainstream, as opposed to what you already are. (July 1989)

Aerosol art springs from an attitude of constant rebellion against assimilation. Seeking to advertise the uniqueness of their identities, writers developed an inclusive culture based on creative principles. From the Lower East Side, and of Cape Verdian descent, SPAR reflects:

> We were kids faced with a world that said "It's got to be done our way. You've got to live with it." So we as kids just wanted to change that.

One strategy writers use to reject society's authority is to reinterpret images from the popular culture around them. Images from advertising and television constitute some of the "materials at hand" that artists use as building blocks to create their own culture. The most obvious images are those gleaned from Times Square neon signs, from psychedelic posters, from television, and from other public advertising. Infusing color and rhythmic structure into Roman lettering, writers distort the alphabet to project their names. At its height the movement created an artistic rite of passage that included thousands of inner city youth in a multiethnic culture of rebellion and creativity.[14]

The creole process requires the ability to recognize the point where two cultures, the marginalized and the mainstream, meet. In New York City, artist AMRL/BAMA explains the fascination of many early writers with mass culture visual ideas:

> Writers used to flip for company logos, because they would get ideas from them, to the point where you would see a serious looking B-Boy walking around with a Good Housekeeping magazine, or any magazine that carries a lot of ads. What was this kid doing reading that magazine? He wasn't reading it, he's looking at the ads, looking for styles, and the better magazines had the better ads. There used to be a place on 42nd street that sold magazines from all over the world, and we used to hit that place! German magazines had great ads, especially during the 70s. We were looking at, say, aspirin ads, and they were not like the ones we had here. We were taking, not just from everything here, but looking out and finding what was really that classy art, and we were advertising our name, we looked at the advertisers to find out how they do lettering. . . .
> The point is that they were soaking in all this inspiration. These guys were very intelligent, and knew how to assess the things that they saw.

Out of necessity writers built a culture around themselves, using their own aesthetic form to project their identities. We have seen how writers synthesize pop culture in their work. Now we will see how African and African-American aesthetic concepts are reinterpreted in this new visual form.

African-American Concepts in Aerosol Art

Some basic aesthetic ideals shared by writers of all heritages seem to have African-American origins. The importance of individual style, of juxtaposing brilliant colors within a rhythmic framework, and of maintaining a "cool" composure in the midst of intense or even dangerous activity are important in many African and African-American aesthetic forms.[15]

Dozens-like competition, a basic element in African-American performance forms, is a fundamental dynamic between writers, AMRL/BAMA recalls:

We were competing in a give and take, sharing kind of way. We were getting off on each other. The hard competition was there, but there was no negative thing in there.

Living in the inner city, the majority of writers have little knowledge about their cultural heritage, where their ancestors came from and how they lived. Yet it is clear that an African-American cultural heritage provides a base from which many writers construct and improvise their pieces. Some writers, like SPAR, consciously study the relationship of West African style to aerosol aesthetics:

The media makes a form like this seem totally new, yet it is connected to our history. You listen to Cab Calloway, if that's not Hip Hop, then . . . what is? It's not like somebody saw some Africans dance and then created burning [an early form of break dancing]. It just developed. It was not self conscious. It's related to the group effort. It's related to ancient days, the dancers, the people scratching records like the old drummers, and the artists, who decorated houses and made costumes.

Whether consciously partaking in African-American traditions or not, many writers work within cultural sensibilities that have been

Fig. 3. "Break" by Freedom, circa 1982. Aerosol paint on cement. Photo by Ivor Miller.

passed down for generations in the Caribbean and the United States.[16]

By creating a visual art form using the interaction of motion, word, and rhythm, writers have transformed the dance, voice, and drum rhythms SPAR speaks of into visual elements. Some writers describe the stylized letters as human forms in motion (Fig. 3), an image heightened by the movement of the trains. The human voice becomes visual in the "shout" of the name riding across the city-scape on elevated trains, and the musical meter becomes the rhythmic patterns used to structure aerosol paintings.

Visual rhythm shapes the letters writers use to spell their names and statements. Reinventing the Roman alphabet to project African-American ideals of rhythmic style, some master painters have developed scripts with dancing characters, rhythmically pulsing and coming to life with the movement of the trains. Listen to LEE:

> Have you ever seen Wild Style? The letters are movements. They are actually images of people. The way some Rs are styled, they look like they're dancing. Some of the letters look like they're hitting each other, and the Fs, they look like

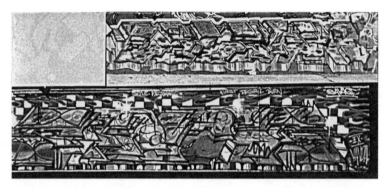

Fig. 4. Two panels by Vulcan; bottom panel is "Savage," 1987.
Aerosol paint on cement. Credit IGTimes.

they're trotting along. And the movement of the trains brings
them to life. It's an instantaneous communication. It's not only
that you're saying "Yah, I'm Bad because I did some Wild
Style," some of the writers were expressing their spirit. . . . [I]n
the '70s you were considered nasty if you could make Wild
Style lettering that was unreadable to even writers. But I think
writers didn't look and see what kind of figure was being created from the painting. Because it wasn't letters anymore,
there's something else in there. It's not words, it's not a name
anymore, it's more of a living thing that you have created, because every letter has a character to itself, and the writing on
the subways definitely showed that. The way some of the letters were trucking, and some of them looked like they were
dancing across the cars. And that's why the paintings did come
to life when the cars moved, and the movement was a big part
of it. Art in motion. It brought a whole spectrum of color and
meaning to it. But it's done unconsciously.

Structural form in the work of some writers recalls traditional
African-American quilt making (Fig. 4). Rhythmic sense, the juxtaposition of hot and cool colors, and the use of off-beat phrasing
are evident in both forms.[17] In fact some paintings appear to be
visualizations of Hip Hop rhythms (Fig. 5), with heavy funk and
polymetrical patternings—the electric neon progeny of Ghanaian
Kente cloth and traditional African-American quilting. VULCAN
speaks:

Fig. 5. "Heliz," by Heliz, 1992, in Queens. Aerosol paint on cement. Photo by Ivor Miller.

> I think about rhythm a lot in my paintings. I try to make things balance, and I can see if things fit or if they don't. Some ideas might be artistically or stylistically good, but might not fit into a whole package. The whole painting must be strong, and rhythm has a lot to do with it.

PHASE 2 creates complex structural designs, like visualizations of jazz improvisations. He does this by building off the lines created by letters, making visual rhythms (Fig. 6). In this way his letters are no longer phonetic symbols but have been expanded into abstract ideas. He says:

> Language to me is infinite. If somebody created it, you can create yours. English is just semi relevant. Words have just been made up [and applied arbitrarily]. If there is a god, he didn't make these words, and say this is officially this, and this is all it can be. Twenty-six letters aren't enough for me. To me letters are nothing but tools to go beyond to something else.
>   Letters are structures that you can build off of. Do you look at a building and say, "What does this building mean?"— or do you say, "That's a beautiful building"? Do you have to

Fig. 6. By Phase 2, in Hawaii, 1989. Aerosol paint on cement.
Credit IGTimes.

be able to read hieroglyphics to be able to appreciate them? I
can relate to hieroglyphics as a form, and the form relates back
to me in terms of my African (Alkebu-lan)[18] roots. I don't sit
there trying to figure out what it says. It has poetry of motion
just being there.

Many of my letters tell a story, they are always moving
forward. They almost represent motion, and almost represent
individuals. It's not even a theory: I look at them and that's
what I see. (March 1989)

In his raps, recording artist Kool Moe Dee displays a parallel attitude of building rhythmic images with language, of using letters
and words as structures. His attitude toward language reveals a
close relationship of rhythmic rapping to aerosol rhythmic lettering, of individual style in spoken language to innovation in complex Wild Style signatures:

I don't write I build a rhyme
I draw plans draft the diagrams
An architect in effect.[19]

The Incorporation of Pop: Super Heroes as Self-Portraits

The injection of rhythm into the Roman alphabet is one facet
of the creole process developed by subway painters. The way writ-

ers creolize images of super heroes and self-created characters into their signatures is yet another. Sometimes used like power symbols on the shields of Plains Indians, these characters are symbols that depict the painters as powerful and potent beings. In indigenous American lore "these signs told who [the shield bearer] was, what [he] sought to be, and what [his] loves, fears and dreams were. Almost everything about [him] was written there reflected in the Mirror of [his] shield" (Storm 9). LEE speaks of the self-revelation that writers both sought and gained by making visible these symbols:

> Many paintings with characters were like self-portraits of the writers. A painting was more than just a name, writers probably wanted to take a look at themselves when the train rolled by, they wanted to get as close to looking at themselves as they could. It was a mirror in a way.

One of the original pop culture symbols used on the trains was "the Saint" icon from the television show of the same name (Fig. 7). Used by the African-American painter "STAY HIGH 149," a.k.a. "VOICE OF THE GHETTO," it suggested the sleekness, intelligence, and secretive powers of a world class undercover agent.[20]

Some writers gained fame by associating their names with popular icons. Others visualized their self images and sources of personal power by depicting original symbols related to their ethnic heritages. PHASE 2 has incorporated ancient Egyptian symbols into his work (Fig. 8). Creolizing images from pop culture that relate to an ancient past is one way PHASE 2 creates an identity based on Egypt as his ancestral homeland:

> I paint profiles in some of my work. Some people might say they're Egyptian, but they're not really, yet they go back to my roots. It's instinctive. In fact since I was a kid, the relationship with Egypt and Africa, subconsciously, was right there. I remember a cartoon with Bugs Bunny, and my man Bugs had an Egyptian head-dress on, and he's doing the King Tut [dance]. It blew my mind. I've always said that I'll go to Egypt and there's going to be some ancient statue that will resemble me. I know this. People can believe what they want, but the spirit never dies. (May 1988)

Fig. 7. "Stay High 149" by Stay High 149, circa 1971. Aerosol
paint on wood. From the collection of Freedom.

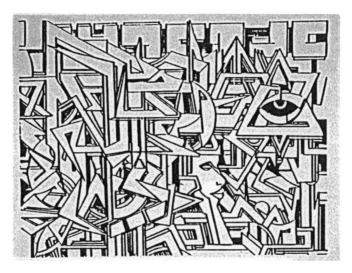

Fig. 8. By Phase 2, circa 1990. Ink on paper. Credit IGTimes.

CO-CO 144 has integrated Taino ritual images into his signature. He has created a cultural identity out of icons relating to his homeland (Fig. 9):

> I have incorporated many meanings into my name, and the way I incorporated the Taino petroglyphs into my signature is one of them. The continued use of writing my name in my paintings is important to me. Although the letters are now an abstract form, the name is still there. It's in the face of the embryo I painted in some of the Taino paintings I did.
>
> When I was painting the Taino works, I was feeling that I wanted to express myself and my culture in a certain way. Since I was in Puerto Rico, where these petroglyphs were created, it was a way for me to introduce my work. And it was a new experience for Puerto Ricans to see urban, aerosol art. At the time I didn't make a conscious connection between the Taino paintings and aerosol as underground work, but it's funny that my work evolved from the underground subways, and then here I'm combining it with something that was done 700 years ago that was also done underground. It's like history repeating itself.

From Co-op city in the Bronx, and of African-American descent, BLADE is inspired by science fiction, and creates characters

Fig. 9. "Pensamientas Indigenas," by Co-Co 144, 1985. Aerosol
paint on canvas.

Fig. 10. "Aerosol Armada," by Phase 2, circa 1990. Collage. Credit IGTimes.

out of his own experience. Raised in an African-American tradition that emphasizes dreams and visions as a mainstay of the creative process,[21] BLADE gets much of his imagery from dreams:

> All my characters are original. For some reason I just think of these things, and I'm able to create them, even if I'm in the middle of a dream at 3 in the morning. I guess you could say that I have a lot of science fiction dreams. A lot of people ask how I could have possibly thought of that, but that's the way I saw it, and some of my dreams move. I had a dream of myself once as flying through the clouds up into the black part of the skies. So I drew a character doing that. It was so strong, I thought I was really flying through the clouds. Many of my characters are self portraits.

The sci-fi images used by writers have multiple ramifications: they can represent mythic and archetypal heroes, yet also project into an idealized future where science has obliterated poverty and social judgment based on skin color (Fig. 10). Robots and fantasy beings have bright neon skin or armor and live forever in a glittering, new world. Hip Hop historian David Toop says that popular

icons are used to represent both universal archetypes and culturally specific hero types in Hip Hop culture:

> If the association seems far fetched, it's partly because the im-
> agery has changed so dramatically—the mythological trick-
> sters and heroes are replaced by electronic-age super heroes
> recruited from . . . science fiction . . . re-run television series,
> video games, comic books and advertising. The central heroes,
> of course, are the rappers [and writers] themselves. (28)

"Say It Loud": The Incorporation of Black and Latin Power into an Art Form

Writers testify to the reality of their lives through their art.
EZO, of Puerto Rican/German descent, is one of the few aerosol
painters to write a manifesto outlining the underlying political
concerns of many inner city painters. He states that:

> PHASE 2, SHARP, LADY PINK, FUTURA 2000 and others
> are some of the few artists who share a common idea: to use
> their anger to chip away at the misconceptions that are woven
> in our daily lives to entrap and confuse. What are these mis-
> conceptions? To begin with, the idea that our society has the
> ability to repair itself in its present condition; that our situation
> is tolerable and will continue to be so if it's left alone. (Whip-
> pler 1)

Protest and self-affirmation are inherent in both the music and
visual art of this inner city Renaissance. Grand Master Flash
and the Furious Five came out with "The Message," "Survival,"
and "New York, New York." Melle Mel rapped the apocalyptic
"World War III," with lines like "War is a game of business" and
"Nobody hears what the people say." Writers painted names like
"CRIES OF THE GHETTO," "SLAVE," and "SPARTACUS," and
eventually dominated the subway system with whole car paintings
depicting the violence of their lives: images of guns, gangsters, and
political statements like "HANG NIXON!" abounded. To this day
Hip Hop continues to be a vibrant and profound expression of
inner city black and Latin culture and concerns.[22]

Writers saw a lot of problems and injustices in the world they were born into, and with the surging optimism of youth were determined to change what they could in their environment. Subconscious though it may have been, the large scale, collective motivations of writing culture reflected some of the important issues of the day. From Washington Heights, and originally from the Dominican Republic, JON-ONE says:

> Aerosol is definitely something from the era of the sixties and seventies. It was a very rebellious time in history. The first generation of writers, MIKO's generation, they were going outside and tagging on ice cream trucks when everybody else was rebelling against riding on the back of the buses. They had the Vietnam War protests, JFK was president. From those times until now, aerosol has become an established art form.

The popular consciousness raising and self-affirmation exemplified by music like James Brown's "Say It Loud, I'm Black and Proud"; the community organizing and teachings of the Black Muslims, who practiced name changing to reflect spiritual transformation, and who made the fluid styles of Arabic lettering familiar throughout inner city black communities; the Black Panthers and their militant stance toward societal revolution; the Young Lords Party and their merging of community action groups (Luciano); and Dr. M. L. King and the SCLC with their ideals of all races and heritages harmoniously living and working together were all impetus[23] and inspiration for young writers. The anger and frustration youth felt around them from their parents and communities, the resilience and hope for new possibilities that came with the emergence of new black, Latin, and Native American consciousness, were translated into a green light for artists without tools, without canvas, to paint it loud, to create their art, by any means necessary. The "subterranean guerrilla artists," as LEE calls them, invaded the city's nerve center, the subways. Painter and gallery curator Renny Molenaar, originally from the Dominican Republic, reflects on the need for visibility many writers and, by extension, their families and communities felt:

> Graffiti is the one way, the only way that we have made our presence felt. Whether it's the art or the tagging. The govern-

Fig. 11. By AMRL/BAMA, circa 1987. Aerosol paint on canvas. Credit IGTimes.

ment has always acted as if we don't exist here. Millions of us [Latinos] have migrated here, and the black people who have been here for centuries. They make believe that we don't exist. Third world people. You walk into the trains and WHAM!, you know our presence is here. We are not present in business, the government, in the movies. We were nowhere, with some exceptions. This is one of the few ways to make our presence known (Fig. 11).

CO-CO 144 gives us his perspective:

I knew all those [political movements] were going on. Although I didn't understand why Puerto Ricans were living in exile and marginalised, I could feel the pressures of the environment. Society started conditioning people to believe the stigma that a Puerto Rican is a dishwasher, or a black is a shoe-shiner. Unconsciously that is one of the reasons that we wrote. You go downtown today and you see that most of the doormen are Puerto Ricans or Dominican. I think that growing up and seeing these things, we wanted to express ourselves and say hey, "This is CO-CO and this is what I'm about, and I'm not going to be another waiter or a dishwasher." Unconsciously it was a way of screaming out and saying, "This is me, and I'm not your household doorman!"

Current ideas of black and Latin consciousness motivated inner city artists to create their art by any and all means necessary. This new generation grew up with the pride and the power of their awakening to political and collective consciousness, and expressed these attitudes using African-American and Afro-Caribbean cultural styles as a point of departure. James Brown, funk music, hot/cool color juxtaposition, off beat phrasing, Latin Catholic icons (Fig. 12), and more were creolized into these grassroots expressions of contemporary inner city life.

Self-Worth and Group Consciousness: A Resistance to Cooptation

The work of many writers is intrinsically rebellious. Writers tend to explore the environment around them and respond directly to their observations. Several writers recall the joy they found in painting, simply because it was done for free. Many subway paintings were created as a public gift, a rare thing in a society where even the earth, the water, and time itself are bought and sold. JON-ONE says:

> It kept me going every single week, wanting to paint another train, wanting to make people happy to ride the train. You walk around the city and everything costs money, everything is expensive, and here you ride the train, somebody's painting on it for free. It's bugged out![24]

To this day many resist categorization by the art dealers and gallery owners, refusing to gear their work to a consumer market. CO-CO 144 speaks about United Graffiti Artists (now United Urban Artists),[25] the first organized group of writers, and how they resisted cooptation:

> When we got organized at UGA this awareness developed about who we were, what we were about, and how to value ourselves. Because to a certain extent we were labeled as

Fig. 12. "In Memory of Julissa," by Chica, 1988, in the Lower East Side. Aerosol paint on cement. Photo by Ivor Miller.

"those ghetto kids." When you value yourself you begin to value the things you do.

We did have offers from certain companies, and we felt at that time, of not selling out, of not becoming another Peter Max. We didn't want to get involved in one commercial product and then in all kinds of products and commercial companies that want to play you out and then—there goes your art.

For example we were offered something by a carpeting mill. They wanted to do carpets with names on it. We wondered: where they would put a carpet with a name on it? It would be a fad, with matching curtains—"make your house look like a subway station." Why do that? What's more important—money, or the integrity of your art? We wanted to be fine artists. We wanted to keep the content of our art.(1989)[26]

The Future of Aerosol Art—Its Assimilation into Mainstream Culture and Its Continuation as a Grassroots Art Form

Through the organization of art dealers in the early 1980s, many subway painters became famous as "graffiti" artists in New York City and eventually in Europe. Here the work was captured on canvas; the motion of the train paintings were halted. The art became "Westernized" and acceptable to the upper strata of society. Originally from Ecuador, LADY PINK writes:

> There seems to be considerable contradiction between the nature of what was produced by the 70s graffiti writers and what is now being created by the 80s artists.
>
> Painting on canvas or a gallery's walls removes the element of risk, of getting one's name around, of interaction with one's peers and one's potential younger rivals. The pieces in galleries cease to be graffiti because they have been removed from the cultural context that gives graffiti the reason for being, a voice of the ghetto.
>
> Authentic graffiti cannot exist in the sanctuary provided by the galleries and museums. (STOOPID FRESH)

Some collectors had tags painted on their living room walls; others hung canvases in their homes depicting painted subway cars. Some artists who had little or no connection with writers and their culture became famous as "graffiti" painters. Jean-Michel Basquiat, Kenny Sharf, and Keith Haring became known to international audiences as representatives of the culture. Yet the more they painted, the less the public knew anything at all about subway painting culture. JON-ONE says:

> Look at the whole hypocrite scene, you don't have to be blind. Who made the whole spray can movement? Yet in the multi-million dollar business, who is recognized as aerosol writers? Jean-Michel Basquiat and Keith Haring, and they never even painted trains. And you talk about graffiti to anybody, and they go "Oh, ya, I know Keith Haring, he does really nice graffiti." He never even painted a train, you know?

Why Haring, Basquiat, or Sharf became famous while hard core writers like PHASE 2 didn't is both complex to say and simple to understand. PHASE 2, a working-class person who cares for the integrity of his art more than for money, rejected many gallery offers. He reflects:

> We created an art form that came from the letter. The medium that it belongs on is the subway. There is nothing that can compare to it being on the trains. What's so crazy is that these guys deny their history to jump into something that's easier, for the dollars. They deny their birthright. It didn't come from outer space or the galleries. It can be shown in galleries, but that's for the advancement of art, to educate. It belongs on the trains. (March 1989)

Other writers, like PHASE 2, were culturally unprepared to deal with the gallery business world. They couldn't just paint 100 pieces for a certain date to fill an order. They were young, capricious, and rebellious, not ready to fit their work "into" a market. Haring, on the other hand, was middle class, and culturally prepared to pick up on what galleries wanted. For him, aerosol painting was one style among many that he could accept or reject in his work as gallery demands changed. Because they were subway painters, PHASE 2 and other writers aren't considered artists in the way that Haring was:

A large percentage of the galleries aren't interested in you as an artist if your work isn't "in." It's a business, but it's never projected that way until the chips are down. When I start painting on another level, evolving my work, they start saying, "Well, this isn't really subway art. This stuff is great, but we can't use it." I say, at least a vampire leaves you with eternal life, these people just suck you dry and leave you for dead. (March 1989)

Writers like PHASE 2 have no choice about accepting or rejecting their culture because it's an integral part of their identity. "Writers do what they do because they have to. It's a way of life," says VULCAN (Walker 66–67).

Disregarded by, disillusioned about, or simply uninterested in the galleries, many artists continue to this day to develop and paint new styles in their barrios. Of African-American Deep South heritage, KASE 2 says:

There's always going to be plenty of more styles to come. I've got Futuristic Style already in my mind. Just by looking out my window [from the 10th floor of a project building in the South Bronx] and seeing all that stuff out there, that gives me ideas. Seeing everything, the bridge, the buildings, the trees, the antennas, the pipes and the poles on the roofs. Everything I look at gives me an idea, but I keep it as an abstract. . . . I can get an idea for a signature from looking out at the city.

After a ten-year campaign to erase all train paintings, in 1988 the MTA succeeded. Using razor-tipped fences, guard dogs, and a police force, the Transit Authority kept writers from the trains. Thus writers began to paint walls and canvases to keep their form alive. Meanwhile, through picture books and video tapes made about the original subway painters, young artists from Europe, Australia, and New Zealand now take inspiration from New York City masterpieces. Says VULCAN:

While the trains are now clean here in New York, all over the world there are thousands of kids who do this art, and they get attention and shows, and are being hailed as artists in their own countries. This is in Australia, England, Norway, Denmark, California, New Zealand. I get letters from all over the world. Sometimes I just look at my mail and don't believe it. A few years ago nobody in Australia had ever heard about subway paintings in New York, and now I'm getting letters and phone calls from there! It's a world wide thing. We, the writers from New York City gave other writers from around the world a program to follow. (1989)

JAY-ONE, a writer originally from Guadeloupe, now lives in Stalingrad, a poor section of Paris. He explains why writing has evolved among working-class kids:

Hip Hop came to Paris, mostly in breakdancing and rapping in 1983, through movies like *Beat Street.* My friend SKI and I were designers, so we chose to do graffiti style. We are about six to ten people in Stalingrad who inspire and push each other.

It's the same between minorities and middle class people all over the place. In Berlin it's the Turkish, in Stalingrad the Moroccans, Tunisians and Algerians, and in New York the Puerto Ricans. You need some kind of soul to do graffiti, you need some kind of violence inside of you. That's why Spanish and Black people are doing this, because they've got something to say. Living in Champs Elysées you have everything you want, and you don't really care about expressing yourself. You just take, and have nothing to give. In Stalingrad we have something to say, we minorities have to do something.

We bring what's inside ourselves, our experience, and put it on the walls. In Paris we feel that the competition is not really between artists, it's between the society and us.

Aerosol art, like the blues, jazz, and black and Latin dance, is now a worldwide phenomenon. How it will be interpreted by new generations remains to be seen. Already established artists and art world figures are coopting ideas from the movement. As her father once exploited the design of indigenous masks of Africa to create his masterpieces, Paloma Picasso has capitalized on the indigenous culture of New York City to come out with a new line of palladium and gold jewelry called "Gold Scribbles"[27] (Figs. 13 and 14). Musician Malcolm McLaren used "graffiti" lettering styles on the cover of his 1983 album "Duck Rock" (Island Records). According to some writers, mainstream artists like Frank Stella have used letters,

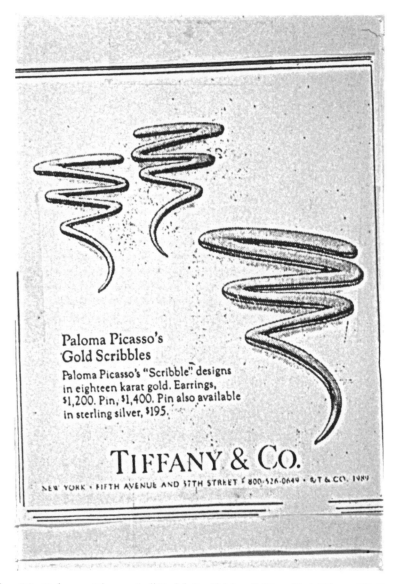

Fig. 13. Paloma Picasso's "Gold Scribbles." *New York Times* 20 Oct. 1989: A3.

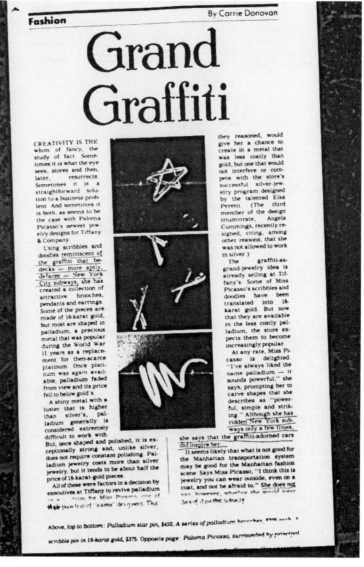

Fig. 14. "Grand Graffiti," on Paloma Picasso. *New York Times Magazine* 20 Nov. 1983: 168.

color, and ideas of movement from aerosol culture in their own paintings and sculpture.[28] Some writers' work is copied outright. Of both Jewish and Antiguan heritage, SHARP says:

> I've seen advertising where models are out in the street advertising a product, and behind them is a building with a piece of mine that I didn't do, that doesn't exist anywhere in the world; it was done by an airbrush artist who copied it to make it look "rustic." If you look at Paula Abdul's video "Opposites Attract," there is a graffiti piece in that. I've seen my pieces used in video games.

The fresh ideas and raw energy of today's youth cultures are continually infusing our mass culture with off-center pulses that keep the rest of *us* alive and feeling, and not falling into a suburban drone. They are cultural rebellions that seek to unbalance the power structures of our society. Writers constantly reinterpret mainstream culture by using its images and its tools, such as spray cans and advertising, to express their own worldviews. The work of these artists demonstrates a wealth of cultural ingenuity and a capacity for resilience that keeps inner city youth culture a creative and enduring force.

How rap phrases and tagging will be incorporated into American middle class life in the following years, the way blues rhythms and Motown lyrics have infused new life into the mass culture grapevine, remains to be seen. I hope that aerosol art will be understood not as a "fad," or a mindless "attack" on society, but as an inspired art form. Without understanding the African-American and creolized elements of contemporary youth cultures we can't truly understand ourselves, for these cultural influences are intrinsic to the makeup of our cultural heritage and future as United Statesians.

Notes

I would like to thank both John Szwed and Eric Perkins for sharing their ideas and bibliographies. I would also like to thank Jill Cutler for her generosity as friend and editor.

1. "Scattered here and there in anthropology recently, there have been intimations that this world of movement and mixture is a world in creolisation; that

a concept of creole culture with its congeners may be our most promising root metaphor"(Hannerz 551).

2. "'Creole' also supposes a situation where the society concerned is caught up in 'some kind of colonial arrangement' with a metropolitan power, on the one hand, and a [tropical] plantation arrangement on the other, and where the society is multi-racial but organized for the benefit of a minority of European origin" (Brathwaite 10).

3. Writers are identified in the upper case by the names they use as signatures.

4. This is a term writers use for those whose names are up in all areas of the city.

5. For a personal account of teenagers living in Harlem during the gang era, see Thomas 51–59.

6. PHASE doesn't like the term "ghetto," because he feels it is pejorative. For people who live in poor barrios and projects, this is their home and their community, and he calls it just that.

7. "[M]any aspects of Afro-American adaptiveness may themselves be in some important sense African in origin" (Herskovits 141–42; see Mintz and Price 48). See also Szwed and Marks on the transformation of the Quadrille dance and music form in the Caribbean.

8. For examples of similar creole processes in the creation of Cuban/Puerto Rican music in New York City, see Glasser.

9. As one author has said of Rastafarian culture (which incorporates ideas from European, African, and Jamaican cultures), "much of the vitality and creativity of the Rastas stem from their openness to new ideas and progressive forces" (Owens 24).

10. Many anthropologists would also agree. "[P]eople in Afro-American societies, even within the context of oppression that pervaded them, quite literally built their life-ways to meet their daily needs" (Mintz and Price 44).

11. "[T]he persistent process of [cultural] transfiguration . . . is the reaction of any group of people to oppression" (Brathwaite, "Commentary Three," qtd. in Craton 151).

12. For examples of this, see Cooper and Chalfant 33.

13. Vaughn Bodé was an underground comics artist whose colorful, bold, and sexual characters inspired many writers.

14. For a discussion on aerosol culture as a rite of passage, see Feiner and Klein 50.

15. "[A] basic West African/Afro-American metaphor of moral aesthetic accomplishment [is] the concept *cool.* The primary metaphorical extension of this term in most of these cultures seems to be *control,* having the value of *composure* in the individual context, *social stability* in the context of the group"; according to Warren D'Azevedo, the Gola people of Liberia admire the ability "to reveal no emotion in situations where excitement and sentimentality are acceptable . . . to do difficult tasks with an air of ease and silent disdain" (qtd. in Thompson, "Aesthetic of the Cool" 41).

16. "[S]o far as their culture is concerned, all Americans are part Negro" (Woodward 17).

17. See Thompson, *African Art in Motion,* 10–13, for a discussion of off-beat phrasing in West African cultural forms, and Thompson, *Flash of the Spirit,* 207–22, for off-beat phrasing design in the Americas.

18. "Land of the blacks," according to PHASE. Alkebu-lan is an ancient, pre-European contact, name for Africa (see Ben-Jochannan xxvi).

19. Kool Moe Dee, in "I Go To Work."

20. With the global impact of mass culture, it isn't unusual that "Fela Anikulapo-Kuti, or Fela for short, the creator of Afro beat music, political radical and hero of Nigerian popular culture," used the same image. Fela says: "I'd given myself a nickname just for fun: 'Simon Templar' . . . You see . . . I had read this novel—The Saint—whose main character was named Simon Templar. This guy was very, very clever" (Moore, qtd. in Hannerz 556).

21. For examples of dreaming in African-American creativity, see Ferris and *Who'd A Thought It* 70.

22. See Slovenz for a discussion of rap, and by extension, aerosol art, as a community based, what some might call "folk," art form.

23. See Childs for an excellent discussion of the organizational approaches used by various African-American resistance groups, and why some are effective and others not.

24. Many words that writers use are derived from African sources. For example, "bug —'enthusiast,' . . . esp. as final element in compounds, e.g., jitterbug . . . Cf. Mandingo-baga . . . denoting person as final element in compounds, e.g., Mandingo jita-baga . . . Note also black West African English baga, 'fellow'; convergence with English bug/bugger and cat" (Dalby 178).

25. See Castleman for a brief history of U.G.A., which was formed in 1972 (117).

26. Burlington Industries gave UGA a $150,000 offer to design rugs (IG-Times).

27. Thanks to Jaime Ramirez (MICO) for this info.

28. Thanks to CRASH and DAZE for this info.

Works Cited

AMRL/BAMA. Tape-recorded interview. July 1989.

Ben-Jochannan, Yosef. *Black Man of the Nile.* 1970. New York: Alkebu-lan Books, 1971.

BLADE. Tape-recorded interview. Dec. 1988.

Brathwaite, Edward Kamau. *Contradictory Omens: Cultural Diversity and Integration in the Caribbean.* Kingston: Savacou Publications, 1974.

Castleman, Craig. *Getting Up: Subway Graffiti in New York.* Cambridge: MIT P, 1982.

Childs, John Brown. *Leadership, Conflict and Cooperation in Afro-American Social Thought.* Philadelphia: Temple UP, 1989.

CO-CO 144. Tape-recorded interview. Nov. 1989.

Cooper, Martha, and Henry Chalfant. *Subway Art.* London: Thames and Hudson, 1984.

Craton, Michael, ed. *Roots and Branches: Current Directions in Slave Studies.* Historical Reflections. Directions, No. 1. Toronto: Pergamon, 1979.

Dalby, David. "The African Element in American English." *Rappin and Stylin Out: Communication in Urban Black America.* Ed. Thomas Kochman. Urbana: U of Illinois P, 1972. 170–86.

Deren, Maya. *Divine Horsemen: The Living Gods of Haiti.* 1953. New York: McPherson, 1970.

Feiner, Joel S., and Stephan Marc Klein. "Graffiti Talks." *Social Policy* Winter 1982: 47–53.

Ferris, William. "Vision in Afro-American Folk Art: The Sculpture of James Thomas." *Journal of American Folklore* 88.348 (1975): 115–31.

Glasser, Ruth. *¿Que Vivó Tiene La Gente Aqui en Nueva York?: Music and Community in Puerto Rican New York 1915–1940*. Berkeley: U of California P, forthcoming.

Hannerz, Ulf. "The World in Creolization." *Africa* 57 (1987): 546–59.

Herskovitz, Melville J. *The Myth of the Negro Past*. 1941. Boston: Beacon, 1958.

IGTimes 2 (Spring 1984).

JAY-ONE. Tape-recorded interview. Dec. 1991.

JON-ONE. Tape-recorded interview. Dec. 1991.

KASE 2. Tape-recorded interview. June 1988.

Kool Moe Dee. *Knowledge Is King*. Zomba Recording, 1989.

LADY PINK. Tape-recorded interview. May 1988.

LEE. Tape-recorded interview. July 1989.

Lomax, Alan. *Mister Jelly Roll: The Fortunes of Jelly Roll Morton, New Orleans Creole and "Inventor of Jazz."* 1953. Berkeley: U of California P, 1973.

Luciano, Felipe. "The Young Lords Party 1969–1975." *CARIBE* 7.4 (1983): 1–33.

Mintz, Sidney, and Richard Price. *An Anthropological Approach to the Afro-American Past: A Caribbean Perspective*. Philadelphia: Institute for the Study of Human Issues, 1976.

Molenaar, Renny. Tape-recorded interview. 1988.

Moore, Carlos. *Fela, Fela: This Bitch of a Life*. London: Allison and Busby, 1982.

Owens, Joseph. *Dread: The Rastafarians of Jamaica*. Kingston: Sangster's Book Stores, 1976.

PHASE 2. Tape-recorded interviews. May 1988, Mar. 1989, June 1989, and July 1989.

SHARP. Tape-recorded interview. Feb. 1990.

Slovenz, Madeline. "'Rock the House': The Aesthetic Dimensions of Rap Music in New York City." *New York Folklore* 14.3–4 (1988): 151–63.

SPAR. Tape-recorded interview. Apr. 1988.

"STOOPID FRESH: Queens and Hip Hop Culture." *Jamaica Arts Center.* Jamaica. 1990.

Storm, Hyemeyohsts. *Seven Arrows*. New York: Ballantine, 1972.

Szwed, John, and Morton Marks. "Afro-American Transformation of European Dance Cycles." *Dance Research Journal* 20 (Summer 1988): 29–36.

Thomas, Piri. *Down These Mean Streets*. 1967. New York: Vintage, 1974.

Thompson, R. F. "An Aesthetic of the Cool." *African Arts* 7.1 (Autumn 1973): 40–43, 64–67, 89.

———. *African Art in Motion*. Berkeley: U of California P, 1974.

———. *Flash of the Spirit*. New York: Random House, 1984.

Toop, David. *The Rap Attack: African Jive to New York Hip Hop*. London: Pluto, 1985.

VULCAN. Tape-recorded interview. June 1989.

Walker, Morgan. "Aerosol Kids" *Thrasher Magazine* August 1991: 66–67.

Whippler, Joseph F. (EZO). "Urban Expressionism Manifesto." Unpublished essay, 1987.

Who'd A Thought It: Improvisation in African-American Quilting. San Francisco: San Francisco Craft and Folk Art Museum, 1987.

Woodward, C. Van. "Clio With Soul." *Journal of American History* 56 (1969): 5–20.

White Skin, Black Masks:
Colonialism and the Sexual Politics of *Oroonoko*

Susan Z. Andrade

> The discourse of post-Enlightenment English colonialism often speaks in a tongue that is forked, not false.
>
> —Homi Bhabha[1]

In focusing on white, middle-class, heterosexual women, hegemonic feminist literary theory has generally presumed that centuries of gendered oppression have left such women naturally sympathetic to the oppression of all people. Much of this criticism has failed to recognize that differently oppressed groups in given historical moments often have conflicting political agendas that preclude ready alliances between struggles or easy understandings between individuals. One might say that feminist literary criticism set out first to deliver female characters, then women's texts, from patriarchal silence. By coaxing women's texts into giving up their true or latent meaning—the articulation of the female subject—such criticism elides the contradictions embedded in each text. This same principle represents female agency in the terms of a European figure against the ground of a woman of color. In so doing, it both excludes the multiplicity of interests that gave rise to each discursive formation and intrudes its own interested discourse.[2] Simply put, any reading structured so tightly around a single principle such as the subjecthood of women must thereby exclude other interpretive categories. By this logic, categories such as race or class, which are deemed marginal to this formulation, must be assimilated into (rather than accommodated by and explored in) the necessarily static model. There can be no room for the heterogeneity of the many facets of subject constitution.[3]

This essay concerns an early woman-authored novella, written toward the beginning of England's prosecution of imperial expansion, none of whose main characters represented fully formed subjects in that time or place. *Oroonoko: or, the Royal Slave*, the story of an African slave/prince, was published in 1688, the year before Aphra Behn's death. Feminist critics have celebrated the fact that Behn's novella gave voice to dispossessed African slaves. Yet, however sympathetic members of one marginal group might be toward another, they must contend with the results of inherent differences. For when giving voice to the abject status of another may threaten their own interests, members of a privileged (but also oppressed) group may vacillate between identification and disavowal. By focusing on the contradictory desires of the white female narrator of this novella, member of a group both marginal to and dominant in the colonial order, my reading strategy confronts the ideological contradictions and political struggles between various subjugated groups. Reading the instability of power and profound ambivalence inscribed in this colonial discourse foregrounds the imperial—and sexual —history of the English novel as well as of the place of this novel within the currently emerging Anglo-American feminist canon.

As early as 1929, Virginia Woolf in *A Room of One's Own* hailed Behn as England's first professional woman writer, and contemporary feminist critics celebrate Behn's wit and poetry as well as her sexual and political activity.[4] Indeed, her poetry offers one of the most powerful literary challenges to the male-dominated libertine tradition of late seventeenth-century England. Significantly, however, feminist scholars generally either have ignored the text for which Behn is best known or, in addressing it, have denied the significance of the race relations depicted within. Both Rita Kramer and Judith Kegan Gardiner mention *Oroonoko* as proof of Behn's opposition to slavery but focus their essays on her life or poetry. Even Laura Brown's more recent essay, which does analyze the novella and is informed by recent works in anticolonial cultural criticism, downplays altogether the racial relations between the white female narrator and the black title character. However, critics who attend more carefully to the category of race contend that *Oroonoko* reads as an argument for maintaining the institution of slavery.[5] It is between these two perspectives, which have little in common besides agreeing on Behn's importance to the development of the contemporary novel, that I propose to insert my discussion of *Oroonoko*. The novella takes place first in Coramantien, Africa, where Oroonoko is a cultivated prince and heir to the throne.[6] It then moves to Surinam, America, where he has become a slave. Both sections are recounted by an educated British woman, sensitive both to the brutality of African slavery and to the indignities of women's oppression.[7] The Coramantien narrative resembles a chivalric romance: Oroonoko, a noble and handsome warrior, falls deeply in love with the beautiful Imoinda. They become secretly betrothed. Although able to defeat many times his number on the battlefield, he runs into difficulty when his grandfather, the king, decides to make Imoinda his consort. (Imoinda remains a virgin, however, because the old man is impotent.) Oroonoko manages to slip into her room, and they consummate their relationship. Upon discovering them, the old king condemns Imoinda to death. In his grief, Oroonoko is tricked by an unscrupulous English captain who sells him and his attendants into slavery and takes him to the New World. To his immense surprise, he discovers that Imoinda is alive and well in Surinam; they are soon reunited and married. Oroonoko now begins to demand his freedom. The narrative tenor changes as he issues his demands, then leads a failed slave rebellion against the plantation owners. Oroonoko and Imoinda are promised freedom if they surrender, and they do. Instead Oroonoko is brutally whipped. He swears vengeance on the colonists, deciding to kill Imoinda first, in order, the text asserts, to protect her from the possibility of rape afterwards. She agrees. Upon her death, however, he becomes so disconsolate that he is paralyzed, unable to exact any revenge. The colonists find him some days later weeping over her body and execute him by slow dismemberment.

I will examine the slippage between the Europeanized African prince and the brutish slave by focusing on the question of power with respect to the white female narrator and by reading her ambivalent implication in imperial domination, the literary expression of female subjectivity, and the sexual dynamics of miscegenation. Then I will explore the racially and sexually coded function Imoinda has in the novella. My argument is that the difference between the heroic, princely Reformation courtier Oroonoko embodies while in Coramantien and the savage and uncontrollable creature he becomes in Surinam can best be explained by reading his proximity to the narrator. Only after she confronts in the flesh, as it were, the brave Oroonoko whose inherent nobility is incompatible with his status as slave does he first appear violent. The dialectic subtending the narrative is based on gender and race relations as they impinge on sexuality, and therefore, as Michel Foucault reminds us, on power. The narrator's continual vacillation toward the subject of her story results from a complicated (and often conflicting) set of colonial and gendered dynamics. Taking a cue from Homi Bhabha, I want to illustrate the multiple and contradictory types of narrative alternations inscribed here, to explore the twin poles of recognition and disavowal which shape the colonial order.[8]

The relationship I chart between the white female narrator and the black male character, though mirroring the discourse of its own age, also reflects an ambivalence generated by the discursive field of two important precursor texts: Shakespeare's *The Tempest* and *Othello*. Each of these dramas serves as a kind of negative model of interracial relations available to our female narrator. *The Tempest*, a paradigmatic text for those working in colonial and postcolonial literatures, especially those of Africa, the Caribbean, and Latin America, offers the example of Miranda, who, as the father's daughter, obeys the patriarchal injunction not to have sexual intercourse with the native Caliban.[9] She retains her virginity and marries instead one of her own race chosen by her father, thereby helping him regain his dukedom. (Let us not forget, however, that Caliban admits to attempting to rape Miranda, in order, he says, to populate the island "with Calibans", i.e., potential challengers to Prospero's power.) Desdemona, on the other hand, asserts her sexual desire, defies the father, and becomes the native's wife. Her body, however, ultimately becomes the battleground on which Brabantio and Iago war with Othello and serves as a warning to those white women who would run the risk of committing miscegenation.[10] Peter Stallybrass states that in the first half of the play, Desdemona is "an active agent" with a (Bakhtinian) Rabelaisian freedom of bodily space. Following this logic, in the second half, the worse Iago's insinuations, the more she is "purified" from her former sexuality, the sexuality which had made her compatible with the excessively coded Othello.[11] In fact, it has been suggested that Othello probably provided a model for Oroonoko.[12] The narrator's changing responses to Oroonoko constitute an attempt to negotiate between the stances of Miranda and Desdemona, and she eventually chooses the former.

It is Miranda—not Prospero—who offers Caliban language, thereby teaching him to express himself through the only discursive system she knows, that of the father.[13] Similarly, through the telling of her tale, the narrator of *Oroonoko* is able to give voice to the native male. This linguistic concern with power is worked into the recurring figure of the "Female Pen" our narrator wields. On the one hand, she tells us that she is from an important colonial family, the daughter of a man who, but for his untimely death, would have been Lieutenant Governor of Surinam (48). On the other, she is very self-conscious about her lack of power as a woman: "his Misfortune was, to fall in an obscure World, that afforded only a Female Pen to celebrate his Fame . . ." (40). However, although her pen is that of a mere female, it is powerful enough to generate plays that are performed in London.[14] On the first page of *Oroonoko*, she acknowledges that she controls the depiction of the character about whom we will read: "I shall omit, for Brevity's sake, a thousand little Accidents of his Life, which, however pleasant to us, where History was scarce, and Adventures very rare, yet might prove tedious and heavy to my Reader, . . ." (1). Within this literary text, then, the narrator has tremendous power, and it is her participation in imperial culture, which was drawn to the peoples it dominated, which concerns me here. Attraction to oppressed peoples is completely consistent with the ideology of

European dominance, and that identification as well as refusal fuels this relation.

Even a conventional close reading of *Oroonoko* disputes the claims made by Gilbert/Gubar and Kramer by demonstrating that the text is clearly not an antislavery narrative, since the narrator unblinkingly accepts the slave industry and the title character's active participation in it. As a prince in Coramantien, Oroonoko himself owns many slaves and sells more to European traders. Once in Surinam, his language and actions continually confirm the implied dichotomy between the essential nature of those who are slaves and those who are free human beings. Before he learns that Imoinda is still alive, Trefry, a sympathetically rendered slaveowner, tells Oroonoko of a beautiful female slave who scorns the admiration of slaves and owner alike. Oroonoko's response is that Trefry should claim his property:

> 'I do not wonder' (*reply'd the Prince*) that *Clemene* should refuse Slaves, being, as you say, so beautiful; but wonder how she escapes those that can entertain her as you do: or why, being your Slave, you do not oblige her to yield? (42)

Even Oroonoko, the sufferer of slavery, upholds the system of power relations it organizes. I will return to this unproblematic treatment of the body of the black woman and the violence done to it.

Once he discovers that Clemene is really Imoinda, Oroonoko unsuccessfully offers Trefry gold or "a vast Quantity of Slaves" in exchange for his own and Imoinda's freedom (45). And he marks his difference from other slaves in additional ways. Toward the end, he expresses his shame about the failed slave uprising, not for having fallen short of his goal, but for having consorted with inferiors: for, "what he had done in endeavoring to make those free, who were by Nature Slaves, . . ." (66). Thus it is not the practice of enslaving Africans that the text attacks, it is that of enslaving this particular individual—who happens to be African.

It is no wonder then that when the fair white narrator of the novella sets out to speak the words of the native, she is automatically caught in the contradictions of imperialism, for embedded in her discourse is the *a priori* acceptance of Oroonoko as savage. All of the description of his nobility in Africa specifies the non-African nature of his mental and physical attractiveness. Even critics uninterested in ideological analysis acknowledge that Oroonoko "functions in the story as an embodiment of just those values affirmed by European societies under the influence of Christianity and the humanistic tradition."[15] I would add that Oroonoko's "European" qualities are not fixed. He is described as European-like, that is to say in positive terms, primarily in the beginning when he poses no threat to the narrator. He reverts to the savage African at the end. In the following passage, the narrator indicates that Oroonoko's attributes (such as those of "real Greatness of Soul" and "refined Notions of true Honor") are *due* to his contact with Europeans:

> Some Part of it we may attribute to the Care of a *Frenchman* of Wit and Learning, who . . . took a great Pleasure to teach him Morals, Language and Science; . . . Another Reason was, he [Oroonoko] lov'd when he came from War, to see all the *English* Gentlemen that traded thither; and did not only learn their Language, but that of the *Spaniard* also, with whom he traded afterwards for Slaves. . . . He had nothing of Barbarity in his Nature, but in all Points address'd himself as if his Education has been in some *European* Court. (7)

Likewise, Oroonoko's physical state is described as that of a blackened or "ebonized" European, his Otherness domesticated for European consumption. Moreover, here the narrator specifically elevates him above the other Africans and alienates him from them:

> His face was not of that brown rusty Black which most of that Nation are, but a perfect Ebony, or polished Jett. . . . His Nose was rising and *Roman,* instead of *African* and flat: His Mouth the finest shaped that could be seen; far from those great turn'd Lips, which are so natural to the rest of the Negroes. The whole Proportion and Air of his Face was so nobly and exactly form'd, that bating his Colour, there could be nothing in Nature more beautiful, agreeable and handsome. . . . His Hair came down to his Shoulders, by the Aids of Art, which was by pulling it out with a Quill, and keeping it comb'd; of which he took particular care. (8)

Even if we accept Brown's reading that this erasure of difference might function to encourage a readerly response perception of Africans as similar to Europeans, and therefore worthy of a similar respect (48), we must acknowledge that the above passage depends on a fundamental difference between Oroonoko and other Africans. Moreover, insofar as he is not entirely like the colonizer (white but not quite, to paraphrase Bhabha) Oroonoko's mimicry can constitute only a partial representation. The distortion of the imperial lens becomes more evident as he moves down in power and across the world.

Until his arrival in Surinam, Oroonoko almost always acts with impunity. Coramantien is the only site within the narrative where his dramatic and knightly acts pose no threat (to our narrator).[16] Although he transgresses the law that forbids him his grandfather's consort, he is not reprimanded. He always wins in battle; even when his side is losing, his entrance into the fray turns the tide. Once in Surinam, however, these noble qualities do him no good. He is able neither to free himself from slavery nor to revenge himself on those who enslave or whip him. Were he to succeed in any of these ambitions, it would fundamentally threaten the political and economic order in which the narrator is invested.

The two diverging approaches to the narrator's treatment of Oroonoko are predicated on the unease that such a heroic figure generates. In his reading of colonialist tropes, Abdul JanMohamed calls this ambivalence a product of imperialist duplicity that operates through the economy of its central figure, the Manichean allegory. JanMohamed says that "the exchange function of the allegory remains constant, while the generic attributes can be substituted infinitely (and even contradictorily) for one another" (64). In other words, the values of the master/slave axis remain fixed, the European master—or mistress—always occupying the dominant or valued position, the native slave always subordinate or disdained. While the values of the axis remain fixed, the correspondences of each half can, and do, change; in effect, it is impossible ever to move out of the subaltern position. Similarly, within the novella, the narrator attempts to negate Oroonoko's difference and depict him as European. This is her most frequent rhetorical move, until he begins to demand his freedom. After Oroonoko rebels against his subordinate position as slave and threatens hers as mistress, however, she begins to depict him as volatile, excessive, and distances herself from him. Unlike Othello, Oroonoko has not yet freed himself from slavery. As a European-like prince, however, neither can he logically continue to accept the institution or its constant humiliations.

The most salient change in description of Oroonoko occurs after he marries Imoinda, renamed Clemene as he is now Caesar. Of this renaming, Carol Barash suggests that the title character's original name is even more problematic: "as if he were born always already colonized, his 'African' name, Oroonoko, bears the mark of the river [Orinoco] that cuts through Surinam" (283). (I would add that by conflating his African history with a South American geography, not only is Oroonoko always already colonized, but the validity of his claim to Africa is linguistically denied.) Not wanting the child that the pregnant Imoinda is carrying to be born into slavery, Oroonoko now begins insistently to demand the freedom Trefry has promised him. Of course he will not obtain it from the colonists. In the following passage, the narrator resorts to an ambiguous "they," giving no pronoun reference, denying her own complicity in Oroonoko's slavery.

> They fed him from day to day with Promises, and delay'd him till the Lord-Governor should come; so that he began to suspect them of Falshood, and that they would delay him till the time of his Wife's Delivery, and make a Slave of that too; for all the Breed is theirs to whom the Parents belong. (45)

The narrator exhibits a growing discomfort with Oroonoko's interrogation of his place as property within a slave economy. Robert Chibka sees this wavering as a linguistic sign of her gendered alienation, a reading that supports the general feminist reception of this text. I believe along with Barash, however, that this hesitation is more clearly a result of her increasingly open affiliation with the plantation class.[17] Later, drafted by the colonists to mediate between themselves and Oroonoko, the narrator acknowledges that he promises never to harm either her or his captors:

> However, he assur'd me, that whatsoever Resolutions he should take, he would act nothing upon the *White* people; and as for myself, and those upon whose *Plantation* where he was,

> he would sooner forfeit his eternal Liberty, and Life itself, than
> lift his Hand against his greatest Enemy on that place. He be-
> sought me to suffer no Fears on his account, for he could do
> nothing that Honour should not dictate . . . (47)

Nevertheless—and here the slippage shows—Oroonoko's demand for freedom, however appropriate for a noble prince, makes
the narrator very uneasy. Directly after the above meeting with
Oroonoko, she advises the colonists to restrict his movements and
to spy on him, this despite her friend's promise to do no harm to
the whites.

> After this I neither thought it convenient to trust him much
> out of our view, nor did the Country, who fear'd him. . . . [H]e
> should be permitted, as seldom as could be, to go up to the
> Plantations of the *Negroes,* or if he did, to be accompany'd by
> some that should be rather in appearance Attendants than
> Spies. (48)

At about this time in the narrative, after the narrator has established Oroonoko's difference, but before he initiates the slave rebellion which will forever consign him to radical alterity, a curious
textual shift takes place. The narrator, her female friends, and
Oroonoko participate in a series of "diverting adventures." Positioned at this particular narratological moment, the shift functions
to contain temporarily Oroonoko's increasing volatility. The adventures unfold in a marginal and privileged space where relations
of labor and property are suspended. In each of the adventures,
Oroonoko and the white women depart the plantation and ven-
ture into as yet undomesticated territory. By leaving behind the
site of the racially determined master-slave binary, they are able to
participate in the nonracialized and abstractly gendered world of
gallant knights and courtly ladies—the same landscape that Oroonoko once inhabited in Coramantien. (The difference here is that
the narrator and her friends replace Onahal and Imoinda in the
role of the ladies. The narrator says of Imoinda at the end of this
section, almost as an afterthought, that she "was a sharer in all our
Adventures" [58]; however, Imoinda as subject or agent is never
specifically mentioned in any of the exploits.)[18] Through these stories, especially through that of his slaying of an invincible tiger that

seven bullets in the heart had previously failed to kill, Oroonoko briefly regains his status as a princely figure.

This narrative truce is short-lived, however. Only a few sentences later, in one of the more ideologically transparent passages of the text, the narrator again rewrites Oroonoko from (European) prince to (African) savage. I cite at length from this important passage and will refer to it again:

> So that obliging him to love us [women] very well, we had all the Liberty of Speech with him, especially myself, whom he call'd his *Great Mistress;* and indeed my Word would go a great Way with him. . . . [The narrator informs us that she notices Oroonoko's changed, more thoughtful, behavior] and told him, I took it ill he should suspect we would break our Words with him, and not permit both him and *Clemene* to return to his own Kingdom, . . . He made me some Answers that shew'd a Doubt in him, which made me ask, what Advantage it would be to doubt? It would but give us Fear of him, and possibly compel us to treat him so as I should be very loth to behold; that is, it might occasion his Confinement. Perhaps this was not so luckily spoke of me, for I perceiv'd he resented that Word, which I strove to soften again in vain. . . . (46–47)

Although she calls herself his friend, the narrator takes great pleasure in Oroonoko's name for her, "Great Mistress," linguistic acknowledgment of the explicit difference in their status as well as of an implied sexual relationship. She also asserts that she has influence, or power, over him. This power depends on his belief in the colonial order; any suspected loss of belief threatens the plantation economy and deeply disturbs the narrator. That in fact her power is in doubt becomes obvious in the next few lines. When Oroonoko questions whether he will be set free, the narrator "has Fear of him" and threatens to lock him up, to confine him even more than his slave status would ordinarily warrant. Her loss of control means that Oroonoko reverts to the unwitting and unconscious agent of menace resulting in her paranoia as she tries to guess his sinister intentions.[19] The interchange above takes place during the only scene in which the narrator and Oroonoko confront each other in the flesh. As such it is determined by the dynamics of gendered, racial, and, as we shall see, sexual power, that of a colonial/white woman versus that of a male/African slave.

Later, when she hears of the slave uprising, the narrator flees, frightened not by the masses of unknown slaves, but by (her friend) Oroonoko:

> You must know, that when the News was brought on *Monday* Morning, that *Caesar* had betaken himself to the Woods, and carry'd with him all the *Negroes,* we were posses'd with extreme Fear, which no Persuasions could dissipate, that he would secure himself till Night, and then would come down and cut all our Throats. This Apprehension made all the Females of us fly down the River, to be secured; and while we were away, they acted this Cruelty; for I suppose I had Authority and Interest enough there, had I suspected any such thing, to have prevented it: . . . (67–68)

This passage is offered as explanation for why she was not able to prevent Oroonoko's punishment, a whipping and the rubbing of chili pepper into his wounds, punishment administered after the colonists promise clemency. Because she fears Oroonoko will kill her, the narrator flees. He is whipped because of her absence, and she is absent because she does not trust his promise not to hurt her. Attempting to hold together the conflicting narratives of the noble slave/prince with that of the plantation society in which she is invested, the narrator engages in increasingly convoluted rhetorical twists which only expose even more her ultimate allegiance to the latter. Moreover, the two main characters' proximity to each other above testifies to how their bodies are differently inscribed in discourses of pleasure/desire and domination/power. In the scene above and the later, even more brutal, scene of Oroonoko's dismemberment and death, the narrator removes herself from the site of violence and thereby from the responsibility for it.[20] In this manner, the text repeats the phenomenon of recognition and disavowal: both decrying the cruelty of slavery while evading the onus of having to act against it.

Thus far I have mapped out some of the tensions between the white female narrator and the black male character, tensions which most feminist critics have until now ignored.[21] In order to reconcile the assumptions of earlier feminist readings of the text with the narrator's obvious doubt and fear of Oroonoko, I will reexamine Oroonoko's shifting location within the text: his occupation of a somewhat precarious gendered and racialized position between the narrator and Imoinda, between gallant knight and uncontainable savage. Brown's essay offers a point of departure for my argument.

Focusing on the category of gender, Brown states that the generic codes of heroic romance help to normalize Oroonoko's radical alterity. Within the genre, the desirable woman serves invariably as motive and ultimate prize for male adventures (49).

> This narrative must have its women: it generates female figures at every turn. Not only is the protagonist represented as especially fond of the company of women (*Oroonoko* 46), but female figures—either Imoinda or the narrator and her surrogates—appear as incentives or witnesses for almost all of Oroonoko's exploits. (50)

However, Brown neglects to mention that for the text the "desirable woman" is more often the narrator, not Imoinda. For example, after having killed a tiger, Oroonoko offers its cub to the narrator by laying it at her feet (51). And later, before he undertakes the hunt for another, more dangerous tiger, he flirtatiously asks the (white) women what they will give him in return: "*What Trophies and Garlands, Ladies, will you make me, if I bring you home the Heart of this ravenous Beast, that eats up all your Lambs and Pigs?* We all promis'd he should be rewarded at all our hands" (51). In the rare instances outside of Coramantien when Imoinda is figured as the desirable woman, she functions metonymically either as negative mirror image or surrogate to the narrator. Brown's reading, invested primarily in reading Oroonoko as allegory of Charles II, cannot adequately encompass the sexual dynamics of Oroonoko's racial difference from the narrator. Neither can it address the effacement of Imoinda by the narrator. My contention is that only by interpreting the interaction of race and gender at this historical juncture can we understand the functioning of this particular sexual triangle.

The widespread sexual relationships, voluntary or forced, between black women and white men in the seventeenth-century

New World were based on grossly unequal power relations. These relations generated a hegemonic discourse of displacement which insisted on black female supersexuality. This argument is not new.[22] I would like, however, to shift this interracial sexual axis and examine an area of discourse which has received much less scholarly attention: white patriarchy's control over the erotic life of white women in slave societies. Historical work from the British Caribbean and the Southern United States testifies to a related move by which white men displaced their anxieties about the sexual availability of black women onto their relations with white women. The intense familial surveillance of white female virtue resulted in what some historians have called a stultification of sexual expression on the parts of planter-class women.[23] As we shall see, this context is of particular importance to the feminist reception of the work of a sexual radical such as Behn.

Most Behn scholars assume that Oroonoko embodies an ideal Reformation courtier. (That both Brown and Goreau see in Oroonoko a resemblance to the dashing Charles II supports my point.) Few, however, acknowledge that as such, he constitutes—or may well constitute—an object of sexual desire for the heterosexual narrator. After all, Oroonoko is by far the most gallant, courageous, and handsome man of the novella; Trefry comes in a distant second.[24] Unlike the other men of the novella, Oroonoko is not only brave and strong, but prefers the company of women.[25] I contend that the tension between the narrator and Oroonoko we have noted is partly due to inexpressible desire, for within the context of the late seventeenth-century British Caribbean, sexual desire between a white woman and a black male slave is taboo.[26] Behn's bawdy poetry and dramas critical of arranged marriage make clear her daring in challenging restraints on women's sexuality. In such an environment as the Caribbean, however, her uncloaked explorations of this particular interracial sexual dynamic would not only have challenged her other political and economic values; they might have resulted in personal censure. While the female characters of Behn's other works often struggle to assert—even flaunt—their sexuality, the otherwise outspoken narrator of *Oroonoko* may never articulate desire for this ideal male because, unlike her male compatriots, she bears the additional burden of safeguarding racial purity. As reproducers of the race, it is white women who bear

the patriarchal injunction against miscegenation.[27] The imperative
to preserve whiteness coincides here with a taboo against white
women's expressing any desires that do not support their racial
and reproductive function. Desire that attributes phallic power to
a black man is the most dangerous because in one step it threatens
to undo the sexual and economic laws of the plantation.[28]

Racial mixing through the bodies of black women, however,
does not appear to be an issue in this novella. Though the narrator
is highly conscious of sex/gender hierarchies, she has no scruples
representing the common rape of black women. Even Oroonoko's
advice to Trefry that he claim his rights and compel the unknown
beautiful slave to yield to him is preserved without comment by
the narrator. In response, Trefry says that he has considered force,
but is ultimately unable to bring himself to do it:

> *I confess* (said *Trefry*) *when I have, against her will, entreated her with
> Love so long, as to be transported with my Passion even above Decency,
> I have been ready to make use of those Advantages of Strength and
> Force Nature has given me: But Oh! she disarms me with that Modesty
> and Weeping, so tender and moving, that I retire, and thank my Stars
> she overcame me.* (42–43)

With Trefry's gallant gesture, the text shifts the location of possible
rape from the European to the African. After all, it is Oroonoko
who initially suggests rape to Trefry. Similarly, Trefry's rhetoric
above empowers the black woman in a curious manner, suggesting
by "she overcame me" that Imoinda, who is, after all, a female slave
with few resources, can successfully persuade her master not to
rape her.[29] Although this means that the romance conventions are
still in place, since Imoinda has sexual contact only with Oroonoko, it also means that Trefry will not have sexual relations—
voluntary or forced—with her. I will return to this point again.

Given the heightened racial tensions surrounding the development of this (quasi)romantic relationship, the figure of Imoinda
takes on special meaning. The black woman functions here as synecdoche to the narrator; her marriage to Oroonoko serves partly
as a stand-in for the implied (and unspeakable) romance between
him and the narrator. The text offers several examples of how the
two women occupy the same position vis-à-vis Oroonoko. For ex-

ample, Beverle Huston points out that the narrator's entrance into the text occurs immediately after Oroonoko is reunited with Imoinda, thus metonymically identifying the former woman with the latter (34). As the designated recipient of Oroonoko's desire, Imoinda permits the narrator to participate in otherwise forbidden sexualized relations. Another example of a metonymic identification between the two involves women and violence—again invoking *Othello*. At the time of the slave rebellion, the narrator worries that Oroonoko will come down and cut her throat. Significantly, however, not only does he never do her any harm, but he ends up cutting the throat of Imoinda, her only rival.[30]

Through this displacement, the text transposes a gendered hierarchy to a racial one, consigning the African woman to the same passive position against which the European has herself railed. Imoinda, serving as the acquiescent receptacle of Oroonoko's love and sperm, is defined almost exclusively through her body. Chibka calls her voiceless, always associated with "body language": "From the 'powerful Language' (17) of eye contact with Oroonoko, to her dance before the king and the stumble that betrays her preference for Oroonoko, to her final submission to his dismembering knife, she is confined largely to physical movement or stasis" (527). In contrast, the relationship between the narrator and Oroonoko is elaborately verbalized. Here again is an example of her flirtation with him during their adventures in the wilderness. Note how marital boundaries are playfully transgressed: "we [women] all had the Liberty of Speech with him, especially my self, whom he call'd his *Great Mistress;* and indeed my Word would go a great Way with him . . ." (46). Even their dalliance is linguistically based.

Within the limited realm of the corporeal, Imoinda's physical characteristics, the only details of her identity are vaguely drawn. In contrast to the earlier-cited description of Oroonoko, for example, one which illustrates his uniqueness, the description of Imoinda offers no specific information whatsoever about her legendary beauty. She is rendered exclusively in terms of her effect on the men around her:

[T]o describe her truly, one need say only, she was Female to the Noble Male; the beautiful Black *Venus* to our young *Mars;*

as charming in her Person as he, and of delicate Virtues. I have seen a hundred White Men sighing after her, and making a thousand Vows at her Feet, all in vain and unsuccessful. And she was indeed too great for any but a Prince of her own Nation to adore. (9)[31]

Not only is the black woman constituted entirely through her body, but she is represented both as "blank darkness," to appropriate the title of Christopher Miller's book on Africanist discourse, and as an object of desire available only to one man. Given Imoinda's essential, though unexplained desirability, the narrator's early prophecy of her romantic destiny takes on special meaning: "She was too great for any but a Prince of her own Nation to adore." As corporeal complement to the narrator's disembodied voice, the black woman functions as that which points to a lack in the narrative. But like other repressions, it is produced by the very taboo on white women and black men that forbids it. The sexual threat (and possibility) that Oroonoko represents to the narrator is thereby contained early in the figure of Imoinda and reinforced throughout the narrative.

There is one important moment during which Imoinda forcefully departs from her usual submissive behavior. While visibly pregnant, she accompanies Oroonoko and Tuscan into the thick of battle during the slave uprising, fighting with them long after the other slaves give up. She wounds the governor with one of her poisoned arrows; in fact, she is the only slave named who inflicts such harm on a colonist. Were it not for the quick action of his Indian mistress sucking out the venom, the narrator informs us, the governor would surely have died (64–65). I read as significant that Imoinda's most visible exhibition of agency occurs at the instant when blackness is inscribed as most dangerous to the whites. The text briefly rewrites her from subservient woman to violent African, her blackness subsuming her femininity at the moment her agency physically threatens the highest representative of plantation power in Surinam.

The prevailing sense of Imoinda's personality remains vague, however; and this indeterminacy contrasts sharply with the gruesome specificity of her murder. The juxtaposition of the independent and articulate European narrator with the pregnant African who gladly submits to the patriarchal knife is yet another method by which the former disposes of the threat that the latter represents.[32] As the apparent object of Oroonoko's desire, Imoinda may lay legal claim to his name and child, as the narrator, confined by her racial status, cannot. With that in mind, I cite from Imoinda's death scene:

> [W]hile Tears trickled down his Cheeks, hers were smiling with Joy she should die by so Noble a Hand, and be sent into her own Country (for that's their Notion of the next World) by him she so tenderly loved, and so truly ador'd in this: for Wives have a respect for their Husbands equal to what other People pay a Deity; and when a Man finds occasion to quit his Wife, if he loves her, she dies by his hand; if not, he sells her, or suffers some other to kill her. (72)

In a text preoccupied with the status of Woman, the African (woman) is decapitated under the guise of cultural relativism, sacrificing her body so that the narrator may explore—literarily if not literally—new sexual territories. As corporeal synecdoche to the narrator's disembodied voice, Imoinda functions as a surrogate. My point is that Imoinda, far from being an insignificant figure, is absolutely necessary to the ideology of the text. She first prevents the white woman from committing miscegenation, and then becomes the willing martyr whose death protects the narrator from the fate of Desdemona.

Like Othello's dramatic degradation from magisterial general to crazed wife-murderer, a gesture which also renders him impotent, Oroonoko also moves from being a noble and rational hero to being a violent savage, self-destructing at the end. Similarly, his intractable (and foolhardy) codes of honor both make him endearing and help contribute to his inevitable downfall. Although Oroonoko does not doubt his wife's fidelity, like Othello, he is also consumed by the possibility of being cuckolded. Moreover, the novella proves that like the African of the Shakespeare drama, this African is also capable of killing his beloved wife in the name of such a masculine honor.

Othello's presumption of ownership of Desdemona's body provides the rationale for her murder. While Imoinda willingly allows her life to be taken, she does so at the behest of her husband, who worries that "she may be first ravished by every Brute" (71). By linking Oroonoko's fight for honor (his primary claim to superiority over the continually duplicitous Europeans) with his attempt to control his wife's sexuality, the novella suggests a subtext at once proto-feminist and *pro*-slavery. It recasts the commodification of blacks into that of women (i.e., sexual slavery) and replaces Africans with women at the bottom of the master-slave binary. Appropriating the metaphor of slavery to express the oppression of white women is not inherently pro-slavery. However, the imbrication of masculine honor (here embodied as black) with violence against women and their sexual agency undermines the moral force of much of Oroonoko's truthtelling.

Some feminist readers of Desdemona (Karen Newman and Ania Loomba in particular) recognize that in her assertion of sexual desire and her contravention of racial/sexual taboos, the European woman removes herself from patriarchal protection, thus making herself vulnerable to murder.[33] Desdemona's desire for what is taboo is undone and denied in the latter part of the drama, where she reverts to a passive and innocent (i.e., desexualized) victim. Our plucky narrator is part of the corpus of a writer who celebrates (white) women's sexual expression and who, conversely, cannot draw the portrait of a woman who, because she asserts sexual will, makes herself vulnerable to dishonor and ultimately, to death. Thus the figure of Imoinda as a sexual surrogate. She will suffer Desdemona's punishment—inscribed here as inevitable. Similarly, these readings of Behn I have been calling hegemonic deny the narrator's desire, and her fears of being both ostracized from and trapped within a plantation libidinal economy. Because they haven't wanted to acknowledge the possible contradiction of political agendas (Desdemona versus Miranda, so to speak), they have continued to uphold Imoinda as occasional sexual surrogate, occasional extension of the narrator.

I read the text's increasing violence as an attempt to negotiate an uneasy closure between competing political and libidinal discourses. Within the logic of the latter, the elimination of his wife and child makes Oroonoko finally available to the narrator. By the same token, however, Imoinda's absence means that the European woman is no longer sexually protected from the threat of miscegenation. Within the discourse of political economy, Imoinda's death

at Oroonoko's hands means that he has transgressed a fundamental law of the slave order. Since the destruction of life is the destruction of valuable property, in this instance property about to
reproduce, and since Oroonoko's exploded volatility now might
threaten the colonists, he must be put to death. He acknowledges
this by disemboweling himself. The colonists confirm it by castrat-
ing and hacking him to bits.[34] Because there is no time for the
earlier, inappropriate, sexual tensions to reappear and because he
no longer represents a threat to the Europeans, the narrator's description of his slow death can be unambivalent and sympathetic.

My concern here is not to discredit Behn at the moment
when, thanks to feminist reexaminations of the English canon, she
is being acknowledged as a legitimate literary foremother. Instead,
agreeing with Nancy Armstrong who "insists that the history of the
novel cannot be understood apart from the history of sexuality"
(9), I believe that *Oroonoko* should be accorded its rightful status as
precursor to the contemporary novel. My point is that here the
construction of sexuality, as well as of race and gender, is imbri-
cated in and ultimately supports, however ambivalently, the colonial order in which the text was written. In the rush to recover
Behn, feminist critics have generally neglected *Oroonoko*'s constantly shifting sexual dynamics and have utterly ignored the figure of Imoinda. By sanitizing the novel and failing to acknowledge
the link between power and desire, these critics have perpetuated
the assumption that we read for/with the narrator, rather than for/
with Imoinda—failing altogether to notice the incoherence of this
particular female figure. A reading such as mine, while supporting
Behn's claim to literary legitimacy and acknowledging her importance as a writer addressing subjects of sexual radicalism, takes into
account her cultural biases and complicity with attitudes of colonial nationalism.

Notes

Research for this essay was helped by a Ford Foundation Grant from the
Center for Afro-American and African Studies at the University of Michigan. My
thanks to Nancy Glazener, Rhonda Cobham, Gregory Diamond, and Elizabeth
Bohls for their generous comments.
    1. "Of Mimicry and Man: The Ambivalence of Colonial Discourse" (125).
    2. This, for example, is what happens in that classic of feminist poetics, *The*

Madwoman in the Attic, which, without acknowledging the centrality of colonialism, takes for its radical trope the figure of a white Caribbean woman whose insanity results from geographic/racial contamination. See also Julia Kristeva's *Des Chinoises,* translated as *About Chinese Women,* which locates a gendered category of opposition in the interstices of European and hysterical avant-garde discourse. Curiously, however, the *sémiotique* appears to permeate all aspects of Chinese culture, which Kristeva represents as monolithic. As the site that managed to evade the Law of the Father, China thus serves as the transparent passageway through which (European) women can locate the feminine pre-Oedipal. For Gayatri Spivak's powerful critique of both texts, see respectively, "Three Women's Texts and a Critique of Imperialism" and "French Feminism in an International Frame."

3. This kind of analysis also encourages the conflation of categories of the marginal or oppressed; an example is the historical tendency among many male cultural critics to represent the violence of colonialism as that of emasculation (read: feminization) of male natives. Not only does such a move pejoratively code femininity, but it is incapable of addressing the gendered and racial violence to which female natives have been vulnerable.

4. See Woolf 66–69. For contemporary feminist readings, see Sandra Gilbert and Susan Gubar's introduction to the section on Behn in their edition of *The Norton Anthology of Literature by Women.* See also Judith Kegan Gardiner, Rita Kramer, Katherine Rogers, and Elaine Campbell. Campbell's brief essay, which belongs to the mainstream (i.e., hegemonic) tradition that celebrates Behn and defends the veracity of her Surinam travels, is ironically published in an anthology titled *A Double Colonization.*

5. See Lucy Hayden, Dorothy Hammond and Alta Jablow (25–27, 40), and Lemuel Johnson (50, 86, 102). None of the above, however, are feminist in their analysis.

6. Coramantien, also spelled Coromantyn or Koromantyn, was the name given in the New World to ethnic groups like the Ashanti, who came from the interior of the African Gold Coast, now Ghana. These slaves had a reputation for being very proud and rebellious, and often led maroon uprisings. Behn herself calls them a "very warlike and brave" nation, "being always in hostility with one neighboring Prince or another" (3). For more information on such uprisings, see Barbara Bush. Also see Richard Price, *The Guiana Maroons* and *Maroon Societies.*

7. Although this text does not necessarily represent the narrating self as autobiographical, most critics read the narrator to be Behn. Similarly, I will not be reading any ironic distance between the two.

8. Bhabha is not the first to recognize this aspect of colonial ambivalence, although I am especially indebted to the rigor of his work. Winthrop Jordan in his encyclopedic *White over Black* has written of colonial ambivalence on the part of the English: "desire and aversion rested on the bedrock fact that white men perceived Negroes as being *both alike and different* from themselves" (137). Moreover, like Robert Young, I am doubtful about the usefulness of such a Freudian paradigm as Bhabha's for thinking through all of colonial discourse, in part because, as he himself acknowledges in "The Other Question," he assumes that the colonial and colonized subjects are male (see Young's chapter on Bhabha). Nevertheless, in the reading of a novella so clearly preoccupied with colonialism and sexuality, Bhabha's model is important indeed.

9. Thanks to Lemuel Johnson for suggesting this to me.

10. Ania Loomba points out that even if she is passive, as in *The Tempest,* the white woman's contact with the alien male would pollute her. In *Othello,* the prob-

lem arises precisely because Othello is not a rapist and Desdemona not an unwilling participant in their sexual relations (52).

11. However, Stallybrass's analysis elides entirely the category of race *qua* race in *Othello;* he reads the title character (in a class analysis) as a "social climber." The reading of the mapping of gender and sexuality onto the bodies of women in Renaissance England provides only a beginning of the kind of analysis I suggest here.

12. See Hammond and Jablow. I am not concerned here with the issue of the authenticity of Behn's writings about Surinam. Notably, those who dismiss Behn's claim to truth are mostly male, those who uphold her truthfulness mostly female and feminist. For a prototypical example of the former position, see especially Ernest Bernbaum. For the latter perspective, see especially Campbell, Angeline Goreau, and Rogers.

13. The following exchange occurs in act I, scene ii, where Miranda and Prospero confront Caliban with his attempted rape: "I pitied thee, / took pains to make thee speak, taught thee each hour / one thing or another. When thou didst not, savage, / know thine own meaning, but wouldst gabble like / a thing most brutish, I endowed thy purposes / with words that made them known" (354–60). His ungrateful response is: "You taught me language, and my profit on't / is, I know how to curse. The red plague rid you / for learning me your language!" (364–67).

14. The only play she mentions by name, however, is Dryden's *The Indian Queen* (2).

15. See Frederick Link 140–41.

16. Later I will discuss one instance when, once in Surinam, Oroonoko is able to become a knightly figure again. This is a unique narrative moment, however.

17. Chibka says: "In a long conversation with 'Caesar,' she manipulates pronouns brilliantly to place herself half in and half out of the community of Europeans" (522). However, Barash (who is a feminist critic) points to how this renaming coincides with the narrator's change in position vis-à-vis the slaves: "In calling Oroonoko and Imoinda once they reach Surinam, 'Caesar' and 'Clemene,' the author/narrator assists in rendering her characters as slaves. From this point on, the narrator considers herself a slave-owner, using the pronoun 'we' rather than 'they' when referring to those who govern the colony" (283). Thanks to Barash for allowing me to read her chapter in manuscript form.

18. For example, on several occasions, the narrator specifies which four people visited the Indian towns, which six participated in the adventure with a tiger (50), etc. Imoinda is never listed in that company.

19. I am indebted to Young's discussion of Bhabha's concept of mimicry for this formulation.

20. As we have seen, she runs away the first time because she's afraid he will harm her. The second time, when it's clear that he is physically restrained and will soon die, she becomes ill and takes to her bed.

21. At the time I wrote this essay Brown's article and Barash's chapter were the only feminist pieces I knew of which assumed colonialism and race relations to be a significant feature of *Oroonoko,* though neither propose the kind of reading I am suggesting here. As this essay goes to press, however, I have learned of two more essays: one by Moira Ferguson, the other by Margaret Ferguson. Both—particularly the latter—offer densely historicized readings of racial and colonial relations in this novella, and I consider their work to be important complements to my essay.

22. The number of black feminist critics who have addressed this phenomenon is too long to list here. Critics who examine these relations specifically in the Caribbean include Barbara Bush, Winthrop Jordan, and Elsa Goveia. For a parallel, though different perspective, see Hortense Spillers' "Mama's Baby, Papa's Maybe." See also the novel *Heremakhonon,* by Guadeloupian Maryse Conde, which implodes this overdetermined discourse, and my reading of it, "The Nigger of the Narcissist."

23. See John D'Emilio and Estelle Freedman's "Race and Sexuality" in *Intimate Matters.* See also Eugene Genovese's *Roll, Jordan, Roll* and Jordan.

24. Lore Metzger, who introduces the Norton edition, mentions for example that during Behn's lifetime, rumors circulated that "she had had a love affair with the hero of the story" (x). But Goreau comes closest to articulating the dangers of such an interracial romance. While discussing the diverting adventures section, she calls Oroonoko "the perfect Arthurian knight . . . in the guise of black slave." She then goes on:

> How does Aphra [sic] define herself in relation to this? The narration
> of these deeds is evidently to the purpose of demonstrating Oroo-
> noko's 'manliness'—in the same way a knight's honor is proven by
> his physical prowess. She portrays herself as sharing many of his ad-
> ventures, but never implies any doubt of the propriety of her actions;
> . . . (62)

25. Despite his "Spirit all rough and fierce" which had too little action "great enough for his large Soul, which was still panting after more renown'd Actions" (47), the narrator says that Oroonoko "liked the Company of us Women much above the Men, for he could not drink, and he is but an ill Companion in that Country that cannot" (46).

26. I suspect that this interdiction is one reason why, in his dramatic adaptation of the novella (*Oroonoko,* 1696), Thomas Southerne rewrites Imoinda as a white woman (the narrator as a character disappears). Of the historical context of Behn's time, Jordan compares interracial relations in slaveholding U.S. societies (where lower class white women could and did sleep with black men and occasionally married them) with those of the British Caribbean, where interracial sex was much more rigidly proscribed: "In the West Indian colonies especially, and less markedly in south Carolina, the entire pattern of miscegenation was far more inflexible than in the other English colonies. White women in the islands did not sleep with Negro men, let alone marry them" (140).

27. Reading the success of lynching in the Reconstruction United States, Hazel Carby points to another instance when competing interests have worked against a united feminist agenda: "[W]hite men used their ownership of the body of the white female as a terrain on which to lynch the black male. White women felt that their caste was their protection and that their interests lay with the power that ultimately confined them" (270).

28. Reading U.S. pre-Civil War legal discourse concerning miscegenation, Eva Sacks points out that in many states, "marriage between a white woman and a black slave would produce legally free children, thereby depriving the slave-owner of potential slaves—a reduction in the stream of future earnings capitalized in the black body" (43).

29. Given the vulnerability of black slave women in the British Caribbean, Imoinda's success represents a rare phenomenon indeed.

30. Jordan points out that sexual tensions often "bubbled to the surface especially at moments of interracial crisis when the colonists' mundane control over

their Negroes appeared in jeopardy. During many scares over slave conspiracies, for instance, reports circulated that the Negroes had plotted killing all white persons except the young women, whom they intended 'for their own gratification.'" He also points out that these charges were ill-founded at best, "for there is no evidence that any Negro in revolt ever seized any white woman 'for their own use'" though they had opportunity to do so" (152).

31.   Later in Surinam, the narrator describes Imoinda as a beautiful example of the exotic scarification she sees on so many black people. However, the description is exclusively of Imoinda's body, and is obviously added as an afterthought: "I had forgot to tell you, that those who are nobly born of that Country, are so delicately cut and raised all over the Fore-part of their Bodies, that it looks as if it were japan'd" (45).

32.   Curiously, this willing death is composed by an author who once criticized another (male) writer for making his female speaker obtuse. Behn translated from the French Bernard le Bovierde Fontenelle's *A Conversation on the Plurality of Worlds*. Referring to Behn's translator's preface, Judith Kegan Gardiner says that Behn chose the text because there was a woman in the dialogue, then criticized Fontenelle for making her so stupid (68). Thanks to Ruth Perry for giving me the complete Fontenelle reference.

33.   Thanks to Marianne Novy for making me aware of much of the extensive feminist criticism on *Othello*.

34.   Brown's essay is very thorough here. Citing from accounts by Bryan Edwards' *The History, Civil and Commercial, of the British Colonies in the West Indies*, from John Stedman's *Narrative of a Five Years' Expedition Against the Revolted Negroes of Surinam*, and from an unnamed correspondent to the *London Magazine* in 1767, she offers testimony of the period to indicate how this phenomenon was fairly common punishment meted out to rebellious slaves. The following quotation from Stedman, also referred to by Brown, illustrates the similarity of Oroonoko's gruesome death with that of other rebellious slaves:

> [He] assur'd them, they need not tie him, for he would stand fix'd like a Rock, and endure Death so as should encourage them to die . . . He had learn'd to take Tobacco; and when he was assur'd he should die, he desir'd they should give him a Pipe in his Mouth, ready lighted; which they did: And the executioner came, and first cut off his Members, and threw them into the Fire; after that, with an ill-favor'd Knife, they cut off his Ears and his Nose, and burn'd them; he still smoak'd on, as if nothing had touch'd him; then they hack'd off one of his Arms, and still he bore up, and held his Pipe; but at the cutting off the other Arm, his Head sunk, and his Pipe dropt and he gave up the Ghost, without a Groan, or a Reproach. (77)

Works Cited

Andrade, Susan Z. "The Nigger of the Narcissist." *Callaloo* 16.1 (1993): 213–26.
Armstrong, Nancy. *Desire and Domestic Fiction: A Political History of the Novel*. New York: Oxford UP, 1987.
Barash, Carol Lynn. "Eros, Monarchy and Linguistic Authority: Gender and Myth in Aphra Behn." *English Women Writers and the Body of Monarchy*. Oxford UP, forthcoming.

Behn, Aphra. *Oroonoko: or, the Royal Slave*. 1688. Intro. Lore Metzger. New York: Norton, 1973.

Bernbaum, Ernest. "Mrs. Behn's *Oroonoko*." *Anniversary Papers by Colleagues and Pupils of George Lyman Kittredge*. Boston: Ginn, 1913.

Bhabha, Homi. "Of Mimicry and Man: The Ambivalence of Colonial Discourse." *October* 28 (1984): 125–33.

———. "The Other Question." *Screen* 24.6 (1983): 71–80.

Brown, Laura. "The Romance of Empire: *Oroonoko* and the Trade in Slaves." *The New Eighteenth-Century: Theory, Politics, English Literature*. Ed. Felicity Nussbaum and Laura Brown. New York: Methuen, 1987. 41–61.

Bush, Barbara. *Slave Women in Caribbean Society, 1650–1838*. London: James Currey, 1990.

Campbell, Elaine. "Aphra Behn's Surinam Interlude." *A Double Colonization: Colonial and Post-Colonial Women's Writing*. Ed. Kirsten Holst Petersen and Anna Rutherford. Denmark: Dangaroo, 1986. 25–35.

Carby, Hazel. "'On the Threshold of Woman's Era': Lynching, Empire, and Sexuality in Black Feminist Theory." *Critical Inquiry* 12.1 (1985): 262–77.

Chibka, Robert. "'Oh! Do Not Fear a Woman's Invention': Truth, Falsehood, and Fiction in Aphra Behn's *Oroonoko*." *Tulsa Studies in Literature and Language* 30 (1988): 510–37.

Conde, Maryse. *Heremakhonon*. Trans. Richard Philcox. 1976. *En attendant le bonheur: Heremakhonon*. Paris: Seghers, 1988.

Cowhig, Ruth. "Blacks in English Drama and the Role of Shakespeare's *Othello*." *The Black Presence in English Literature*. Ed. David Dabydeen. Manchester: Manchester UP, 1985. 1–26.

D'Emilio, John, and Estelle Freedman. "Race and Sexuality." *Intimate Matters: A History of Sexuality in America*. New York: Harper, 1988.

Ferguson, Margaret. "Transmuting Othello: Aphra Behn's *Oroonoko*." *Cross-Cultural Perspectives on Shakespeare*. Ed. Marianne Novy. Urbana: U of Illinois P, 1993. 15–49.

Ferguson, Moira. *Subject to Others: British Women Writers and Colonial Slavery, 1670–1834*. London/New York: Routledge, 1992.

Gardiner, Judith Kegan. "Aphra Behn: Sexuality and Self-Respect." *Women's Studies* 17 (1980): 67–78.

Genovese, Eugene D. *Roll, Jordan, Roll: The World the Slaves Made*. 1972. New York: Vintage, 1976.

Gilbert, Sandra M., and Susan Gubar, eds. *The Norton Anthology of Literature by Women: The Tradition in English*. New York: Norton, 1985.

Goreau, Angeline. *Reconstructing Aphra: A Social Biography of Aphra Behn*. New York: Dial, 1980.

Hammond, Dorothy, and Alta Jablow. *The Africa that Never Was: Four Centuries of British Writing About Africa*. New York: Twayne, 1970.

Hayden, Lucy K. "The Black Presence in Eighteenth-Century British Novels." *College Language Association Journal* 24.3 (1981): 400–15.

JanMohamed, Abdul R. "The Economy of the Manichean Allegory: The Function of Racial Difference in Colonialist Literature." *Critical Inquiry* 12.1 (1985): 59–87.

Johnson, Lemuel A. *The Devil, the Gargoyle and the Buffoon: The Negro as Metaphor in Western Literature*. Port Washington: Kennikat, 1971.

Jordan, Winthrop. *White over Black: American Attitudes Toward the Negro, 1550–1812*. Chapel Hill: U of North Carolina P, 1968.

Kramer, Rita. "Aphra Behn: Novelist, Spy, Libertine." *Ms.* Feb. 1973: 16–18.

214 Susan Z. Andrade

214   Susan Z. Andrade

Link, Frederick M. *Aphra Behn*. New York: Twayne, 1968.

Loomba, Ania. *Gender, Race, Renaissance Drama*. Manchester: Manchester UP, 1989.

Newman, Karen. *Fashioning Femininity and English Restoration Drama*. Chicago: U of Chicago P, 1991.

Price, Richard. *The Guiana Maroons: A Historical and Bibliographical Introduction*. Baltimore: Johns Hopkins UP, 1976.

———. *Maroon Societies: Rebel Slave Communities in the Americas*. Garden City: Anchor, 1973.

Rogers, Katherine M. "Fact and Fiction in Aphra Behn's *Oroonoko*." *Studies in the Novel* 20.1 (1988): 1–15.

Sacks, Eva. "Representing Miscegenation Law." *Raritan* 8.2 (1988): 39–69.

Shakespeare, William. *The Complete Signet Classic Shakespeare*. Ed. Sylvan Barnet. New York: Harcourt, 1972.

Spillers, Hortense. "Mama's Baby, Papa's Maybe: An American Grammar Book." *Diacritics* 17.2 (1987): 65–81.

Spivak, Gayatri Chakravorty. "French Feminism in an International Frame." *Yale French Studies* 62 (1981): 154–84. Rpt. in *In Other Worlds: Essays in Cultural Politics*. By Spivak. New York/London: Methuen, 1987.

———. "Three Women's Texts and a Critique of Imperialism." *Critical Inquiry* 12.1 (1985): 243–61.

Stallybrass, Peter. "Patriarchal Territories: The Body Enclosed." *Rewriting the Renaissance*. Ed. M. W. Ferguson, et al. Chicago: U of Chicago P, 1986. 123–42.

Woolf, Virginia. *A Room of One's Own*. San Diego: Harcourt, 1920.

Young, Robert. *White Mythologies: Writing History and the West*. London/New York: Routledge, 1990.

BOOKS RECEIVED

Anderson, Amanda. *Tainted Souls and Painted Faces: The Rhetoric of Fallenness in Victorian Culture*. Ithaca: Cornell UP, 1993.

Barilli, Renato. *A Course on Aesthetics*. Trans. Karen E. Pinkus. Minneapolis: U of Minnesota P, 1993.

Bauman, Zygmunt. *Modernity and the Holocaust*. Ithaca: Cornell UP, 1991.

Beverley, John. *Against Literature*. Minneapolis: U of Minnesota P, 1993.

Bloom, Clive, ed. *Creepers: British Horror and Fantasy in the Twentieth Century*. Boulder: Pluto, 1993.

Bloom, Lisa. *Gender on Ice: American Ideologies of Polar Expeditions*. Minneapolis: U of Minnesota P, 1993.

Boyes, Georgina. *The Imagined Village: Culture, Ideology and the English Folk Revival*. New York: Manchester UP, 1993.

Burke, Peter. *History and Social Theory*. Ithaca: Cornell UP, 1992.

Burkman, Katherine H., and John L. Kundert-Gibbs, eds. *Pinter at Sixty*. Bloomington: Indiana UP, 1993.

Charnes, Linda. *Notorious Identity: Materializing the Subject in Shakespeare*. Cambridge: Harvard UP, 1993.

Cherry, Deborah. *Painting Women: Victorian Women Artists*. New York: Routledge, 1993.

Clark, VèVè A., Ruth-Ellen B. Joeres, and Madelon Sprengnether, eds. *Revising the Word and the World: Essays in Feminist Literary Criticism*. Chicago: U of Chicago P, 1993.

Costlow, Jane T., Stephanie Sandler, and Judith Vowles, eds. *Sexuality and the Body in Russian Culture*. Stanford: Stanford UP, 1993.

Duncan, James, and David Ley, eds. *Place/Culture/Representation*. New York: Routledge, 1993.

During, Simon, ed. *The Cultural Studies Reader*. New York: Routledge, 1993.

Felman, Shoshana. *What Does A Woman Want? Reading and Sexual Difference*. Baltimore: Johns Hopkins UP, 1993.

Ferguson, Moira. *Colonialism and Gender: From Mary Wollstonecraft to Jamaica Kincaid*. New York: Columbia UP, 1993.

Folkenflik, Robert, ed. *The Culture of Autobiography: Constructions of Self-Representation*. Stanford: Stanford UP, 1993.

Fregoso, Rosa Linda. *The Bronze Screen: Chicana and Chicano Film Culture.* Minneapolis: U of Minnesota P, 1993.

Gans, Eric. *Originary Thinking: Elements of Generative Anthropology.* Stanford: Stanford UP, 1993.

Garber, Majorie, Jann Matlock, and Rebecca L. Walkowitz, eds. *Media Spectacles.* New York: Routledge, 1993.

Gilroy, Paul. *The Black Atlantic: Modernity and Double Consciousness.* Cambridge: Harvard UP, 1993.

Giroux, Henry A., and Peter McLaren. *Between Borders: Pedagogy and the Politics of Cultural Studies.* New York: Routledge, 1993.

Goux, Jean-Joseph. *Oedipus, Philosopher.* Trans. Catherine Porter. Stanford: Stanford UP, 1993.

Gross, Larry. *Contested Closets: The Politics and Ethics of Outing.* Minneapolis: U of Minnesota P, 1993.

Harding, Sandra, ed. *The "Racial" Economy of Science: Towards a Democratic Future.* Bloomington: Indiana UP, 1993.

Hein, Hilde, and Carolyn Korsmeyer, eds. *Aesthetics in Feminist Perspective.* Bloomington: Indiana UP, 1993.

Henry, Michel. *The Genealogy of Psychoanalysis.* Trans. Douglas Brick. Stanford: Stanford UP, 1993.

Herwitz, Daniel. *Making Theory/Constructing Art: On the Authority of the Avant-Garde.* Chicago: U of Chicago P, 1993.

Irigaray, Luce. *An Ethics of Sexual Difference.* Trans. Carolyn Burke and Gillian C. Gill. Ithaca: Cornell UP, 1993.

———. *Marine Lover of Friedrich Nietzsche.* Trans. Gillian C. Gill. New York: Columbia UP, 1991.

Kennedy, Duncan. *Sexy Dressing Etc.: Essays on the Power and Politics of Cultural Identity.* Cambridge: Harvard UP, 1993.

Kroker, Arthur, and Marilouise Kroker, eds. *The Last Sex: Feminism and Outlaw Bodies.* New York: St. Martin's, 1993.

Latour, Bruno. *We Have Never Been Modern.* Trans. Catherine Porter. Cambridge: Harvard UP, 1993.

Lemert, Charles, ed. *Social Theory: The Multicultural and Classic Readings.* Boulder: Westview, 1993.

Lohmann, Christoph K., ed. *Discovering Difference: Contemporary Essays in American Culture.* Bloomington: Indiana UP, 1993.

Marshall, Donald G. *Contemporary Critical Theory: A Selective Biography.* New York: The Modern Language Association of America, 1993.

McCarthy, Cameron, and Warren Crichlow, eds. *Race, Identity and Representation in Education.* New York: Routledge, 1993.

McClary, Susan. *Feminine Endings: Music, Gender, and Sexuality.* Minneapolis: U of Minnesota P, 1991.

Miller, Suzanne, and Barbara McCaskill, eds. *Multicultural Literature and Literacies: Making Space for a Difference.* New York: State U of New York P, 1993.

Morgan, W. John, and Peter Preston, eds. *Raymond Williams: Politics, Education, Letters.* New York: St. Martin's, 1993.

Naficy, Hamid. *The Making of Exile Cultures: Iranian Television in Los Angeles.* Minneapolis: U of Minnesota P, 1993.

Nancy, Jean-Luc. *The Birth to Presence.* Trans. Brian Holmes et al. Stanford: Stanford UP, 1993.

Owomoyela, Oyekan, ed. *A History of Twentieth-Century African Literatures.* Lincoln: U of Nebraska P, 1993.

Robertson, James C. *The Casablanca Man: The Cinema of Michael Curtiz.* New York: Routledge, 1993.

Samuels, Andrew. *The Political Psyche.* New York: Routledge, 1993.

Saussy, Haun. *The Problem of a Chinese Aesthetic.* Stanford: Stanford UP, 1993.

Sedgwick, Eve Kosofsky. *Tendencies.* Durham: Duke UP, 1993.

Storey, John. *An Introductory Guide to Cultural Theory and Popular Culture.* Athens: U of Georgia P, 1993.

Thompson, Becky W., and Sangeeta Tyagi, eds. *Beyond a Dream Deferred: Multicultural Education and the Politics of Excellence.* Minneapolis: U of Minnesota P, 1993.

Tylus, Jane. *Writing and Vulnerability in the Late Renaissance.* Stanford: Stanford UP, 1993.

Warner, Michael, ed. *Fear of a Queer Planet: Queer Politics and Social Theory.* Minneapolis: U of Minnesota P, 1993.

Woodhull, Winifred. *Transfigurations of the Maghreb: Feminism, Decolonialism, and Literatures.* Minneapolis: U of Minnesota P, 1993.

CONTRIBUTORS

Susan Z. Andrade teaches African and Caribbean literature and feminist theory in the departments of English and Black Studies at the University of Pittsburgh.

Margot Gayle Backus is an assistant professor of English at St. John Fisher College and has recently completed a study of Gothic depictions of biological and ideological reproduction within the Anglo-Irish settler colonial order. She has published articles on lesbian literary representation in the *Journal of Homosexuality* and in *Signs*.

Michael Bernard-Donals is an assistant professor of English at the University of Missouri at Columbia, where he teaches critical and rhetorical theory. He has written articles on critical theory, contemporary culture, and pedagogy. His book *Mikhail Bakhtin: Between Phenomenology and Marxism* is forthcoming from Cambridge University Press.

Judith Genova teaches philosophy and women's studies at Colorado College. She writes on topics in women and science, philosophy of mind, philosophy and literature, and Wittgenstein studies. She has also recently written a piece, "Turing's Sexual Guessing Game," due to be published by *Social Epistemology*. Her book, *Wittgenstein: A Way of Seeing*, is forthcoming from Routledge.

Laura Grindstaff is a doctoral candidate in sociology and women's studies at the University of California, Santa Barbara, where she teaches courses in the departments of film, sociology, and women's studies. She specializes in popular culture, film, and television and has a master's degree in broadcast journalism.

Ivor Miller is a graduate student in the Department of Performance Studies at Northwestern University. He is currently researching the presence of African-derived religions within the Cuban Revolution.

JoAnn Pavletich is a graduate student and holder of the *Texas Studies in Literature and Language* Fellowship at the University of Texas. Her article "Muscling the Mainstream: Lesbian Murder Mysteries and Fantasies of Justice" was awarded the Popular/American Culture Association's 1993 Jane S. Bakerman Award for the best published article treating popular culture from a feminist perspective. Her dissertation is titled "The

Self in the Wor(l)d: The Reconstruction of Subjectivity in the Twentieth Century."

Janice Peck teaches in the Department of Speech–Communications at the University of Minnesota and has published a book titled *The Gods of Televangelism: The Crisis and Appeal of Religious Television.* Her article in *Cultural Critique* is part of a larger study on television talk shows.

the minnesota review

(a journal of committed writing)

RECENTLY PUBLISHED

"PC Wars"
ns 39, fall/winter 1992/3

"The Politics of AIDS"
ns 40, spring/summer 1993

FORTHCOMING

"The Institution of English"
i. Reconfiguring the Turf: Fields and Theories
ii. Institutional Navigations: Stories and Structures
ns 41-42, fall 1993-spring 1994

iii. The Politics of Publishing
ns 43, fall 1994
(deadline 1 June 1994)
with work by Crystal Bartolovich, Michael Bérubé, Terry Caesar, Ross Chambers, Tom Cohen, Lennard Davis, Ortwin de Graef, Cora Kaplan, Devoney Looser, Eric Lott, Julian Markels, Marc Redfield, Bruce Robbins, Veronica Stewart, Alan Wald, Evan Watkins, Mas'ud Zavarzadeh, and many others

IN PLANNING

"The White Issue"
ns 44, spring 1995

"The Class Story"
ns 45, fall 1995

Subscriptions are $12 a year (two issues), $24 institutions/overseas.
minnesota review is published biannually and originates from East Carolina University.

Please send all queries, comments, suggestions, submissions, and subscriptions to:
Jeffrey Williams, Editor, *minnesota review*, Department of English,
East Carolina University, Greenville, NC 27858-4353